Comparing Defense Innovation Around the World

Gaining a decisive technological edge is a never-ending pursuit for defense establishments and the countries they protect. Intensifying geo-strategic and geo-economic rivalry among major powers, especially the U.S. and China, and the global technology revolution occurring in the civilian and military domains promise to reshape the nature and distribution of global power.

This book examines the state of global defense innovation in a select number of countries chosen because they are representative of the diverse make-up of the global defense innovation community. These include small countries with advanced defense innovation capabilities (Israel and Singapore), closed authoritarian powers (North Korea and Russia), large catch-up states (China and India), and advanced large powers (U.S.).

The chapters in this book were originally published as a special issue of the *Journal of Strategic Studies*.

Tai Ming Cheung is Director of the UC Institute on Global Conflict and Cooperation and Professor in the School of Global Policy and Strategy at the University of California, San Diego, USA. Cheung's research focuses on China's efforts to become a world-class science and technology power, and the relationship between geo-economics, innovation, and national security.

Comparing Defense Innovation Around the World

Edited by
Tai Ming Cheung

LONDON AND NEW YORK

First published 2023
by Routledge
4 Park Square, Milton Park, Abingdon, Oxon, OX14 4RN

and by Routledge
605 Third Avenue, New York, NY 10158

Routledge is an imprint of the Taylor & Francis Group, an informa business

Chapters 2-4 and 6 © 2023 Taylor & Francis
Introduction © 2021 Tai Ming Cheung. Originally published as Open Access.
Chapter 1 © 2021 Eugene Gholz and Harvey M. Sapolsky. Originally published as Open Access.
Chapter 5 © 2021 Stephan Haggard and Tai Ming Cheung. Originally published as Open Access.

With the exception of Introduction, Chapters 1 and 5, no part of this book may be reprinted or reproduced or utilised in any form or by any electronic, mechanical, or other means, now known or hereafter invented, including photocopying and recording, or in any information storage or retrieval system, without permission in writing from the publishers. For details on the rights for Introduction, Chapters 1 and 5, please see the chapters' Open Access footnotes.

Trademark notice: Product or corporate names may be trademarks or registered trademarks, and are used only for identification and explanation without intent to infringe.

British Library Cataloguing-in-Publication Data
A catalogue record for this book is available from the British Library

ISBN13: 978-1-032-35051-6 (hbk)
ISBN13: 978-1-032-35052-3 (pbk)
ISBN13: 978-1-003-32505-5 (ebk)

DOI: 10.4324/9781003325055

Typeset in Myriad Pro
by codeMantra

Publisher's Note
The publisher accepts responsibility for any inconsistencies that may have arisen during the conversion of this book from journal articles to book chapters, namely the inclusion of journal terminology.

Disclaimer
Every effort has been made to contact copyright holders for their permission to reprint material in this book. The publishers would be grateful to hear from any copyright holder who is not here acknowledged and will undertake to rectify any errors or omissions in future editions of this book.

Contents

Citation Information	vi
Notes on Contributors	viii
Introduction: A conceptual framework of defence innovation *Tai Ming Cheung*	1
1 The defense innovation machine: Why the U.S. will remain on the cutting edge *Eugene Gholz and Harvey M. Sapolsky*	28
2 China's quest for quantum advantage—Strategic and defense innovation at a new frontier *Elsa B. Kania*	47
3 Defense innovation in Russia in the 2010s *Vasilii Kashin*	78
4 Examining India's defence innovation performance *Laxman Kumar Behera*	99
5 North Korea's nuclear and missile programs: Foreign absorption and domestic innovation *Stephan Haggard and Tai Ming Cheung*	123
6 Military-technological innovation in small states: The cases of Israel and Singapore *Richard A. Bitzinger*	151
Index	179

Please note that we've retained the variations of US/UK spellings originally published in the *Journal of Strategic Studies* and have not standardized the spellings for the book edition.

Citation Information

The chapters in this book were originally published in the *Journal of Strategic Studies*, volume 44, issue 6 (2021). When citing this material, please use the original page numbering for each article, as follows:

Introduction
A conceptual framework of defence innovation
Tai Ming Cheung
Journal of Strategic Studies, volume 44, issue 6 (2021) pp. 775–801

Chapter 1
The defense innovation machine: Why the U.S. will remain on the cutting edge
Eugene Gholz and Harvey M. Sapolsky
Journal of Strategic Studies, volume 44, issue 6 (2021) pp. 854–872

Chapter 2
China's quest for quantum advantage—Strategic and defense innovation at a new frontier
Elsa B. Kania
Journal of Strategic Studies, volume 44, issue 6 (2021) pp. 922–952

Chapter 3
Defense innovation in Russia in the 2010s
Vasilii Kashin
Journal of Strategic Studies, volume 44, issue 6 (2021) pp. 901–921

Chapter 4
Examining India's defence innovation performance
Laxman Kumar Behera
Journal of Strategic Studies, volume 44, issue 6 (2021) pp. 830–853

Chapter 5
North Korea's nuclear and missile programs: Foreign absorption and domestic innovation
Stephan Haggard and Tai Ming Cheung
Journal of Strategic Studies, volume 44, issue 6 (2021) pp. 802–829

Chapter 6
Military-technological innovation in small states: The cases of Israel and Singapore
Richard A. Bitzinger
Journal of Strategic Studies, volume 44, issue 6 (2021) pp. 873–900

For any permission-related enquiries please visit:
http://www.tandfonline.com/page/help/permissions

Notes on Contributors

Richard A. Bitzinger is Visiting Senior Fellow with the Military Transformations Program at the S. Rajaratnam School of International Studies (RSIS), where his work focuses on a variety of security, defense, and military-technological issues, including military modernization and force transformation in the Asia-Pacific, the global defense industry, armaments production, and the proliferation of armaments and military technologies.

Tai Ming Cheung is Director of the University of California Institute on Global Conflict and Cooperation and Professor at the School of Global Policy and Strategy at the University of California, San Diego, USA.

Eugene Gholz is Associate Professor of Political Science at the University of Notre Dame, USA.

Stephan Haggard is Lawrence and Sallye Krause Professor of Korea-Pacific Studies and serves as Director of the Korea-Pacific Program at the School of Global Policy and Strategy at the University of California, San Diego, USA.

Elsa B. Kania is PhD Candidate in Harvard University's Department of Government, Cambridge, USA, and she is also Adjunct Senior Fellow with the Technology and National Security Program at the Center for a New American Security (CNAS).

Vasilii Kashin graduated from the Moscow State University Institute for Asian and African Studies in 1996 and the State University of Management in 1999. He worked in the Institute of Far Eastern Studies, Russian Academy of Sciences, as well as Reporter for *Vedomosti* business newspaper and Deputy Chief of the RIA Novosti news agency Beijing bureau. Currently, Dr. Kashin works as Senior Research Fellow in the Higher School of Economics in Moscow.

Laxman Kumar Behera is Associate Professor at the Special Centre for National Security Studies (SCNSS) at Jawaharlal Nehru University (JNU), New Delhi. Prior to joining JNU in 2020, Dr Behera was a core member of Defence Economics and Industry Centre of the Institute for Defence Studies and

Analyses (IDSA) where he specialized on issues related to defense procurement, offsets, defense expenditure, arms production, and export control.

Harvey M. Sapolsky is Professor of Public Policy and Organization, Emeritus, at the Massachusetts Institute of Technology (MIT), Cambridge, USA, and the former Director of the MIT Security Studies Program. Sapolsky and Caitlin Talmadge are the co-authors of *US Defense Politics: The Origins of Security Policy*, 4th edition (New York: Routledge, 2021).

INTRODUCTION

🔓 OPEN ACCESS

A conceptual framework of defence innovation

Tai Ming Cheung

ABSTRACT
Gaining a decisive technological edge is a never-ending pursuit for defence establishments. Intensifying geo-strategic and geo-economic rivalry among major powers, especially the U.S and China, and the global technological revolution occurring in the civilian and military domains, promise to reshape the nature and distribution of global power. This article provides a conceptual framework for a series investigating the state of global defence innovation in the twenty-first century. The series examines defence innovation in small countries with advanced defence innovation capabilities (Israel, Singapore), closed authoritarian powers (North Korea, Russia), large catch-up states (China and India) and advanced large powers (U.S.).

Gaining a decisive technological edge is a never-ending pursuit for defence establishments and the states they protect. This long-run competition for superiority has mostly occurred at a steady incremental pace, but has been occasionally punctuated by periods of disruptive upheaval.[1] The world is currently in one of these whirlpools of revolutionary change brought on by the confluence of two transformational developments. First is the intensifying geo-strategic and geo-economic rivalry among major powers, especially between the U.S. and China. Second is a global technological revolution that is occurring in both the civilian and military domains. These dynamics taken together promises to fundamentally reshape the nature and distribution of global power.

This quest for game-changing innovation has become a pressing priority for the world's leading military powers, which has led to the mushrooming of organisations set up to expressly develop advanced military technologies and

---

[1]For technological deterministic perspectives, see Michael C. Horowitz, *The Diffusion of Military Power: Causes and Consequences for International Politics* (Princeton, New Jersey; Princeton University Press, 2010) and Jeremy Black, *War and Technology* (Indiana University Press, 2013). For the political, social, and domestic drivers behind military revolutions, see MacGregor Knox and Williamson Murray (Eds), *The Dynamics of Military Revolution, 1300–2050* (Cambridge: Cambridge University Press 2001); and Geoffrey Parker, *The Military Revolution: Military Innovation and the Rise of the West, 1500–1800* (Cambridge: Cambridge University Press 1996).

This is an Open Access article distributed under the terms of the Creative Commons Attribution-NonCommercial-NoDerivatives License (http://creativecommons.org/licenses/by-nc-nd/4.0/), which permits non-commercial re-use, distribution, and reproduction in any medium, provided the original work is properly cited, and is not altered, transformed, or built upon in any way.

attendant doctrinal and operational strategies in the past decade. The U.S. has been especially prolific, standing up dozens of innovation entities that are part of what is now defined as the national security innovation base. Prominent organisations include the Defense Innovation Unit, Defense Innovation Board, Strategic Capabilities Office, Army Futures Command and NavalX. This augments an already strong innovation bench anchored by storied organisations such as the Defense Advanced Research Projects Agency (DARPA). Other countries have followed suit to differing degrees of urgency and scale, with China second in effort and ambition to the U.S.

The rise of these organisations is a teasing indicator of the importance that defence establishments are attaching to innovation. But this observation by itself offers little explanatory power into how well organised, how effective and how serious these countries are in the pursuit of defence innovation and what types of innovation they are seeking. In order to comprehend the dynamics of the global defence innovation landscape, to identify where countries are in this pursuit for the technological frontier, to determine how fast and effectively they are running, and to assess who is winning now and over the long term, it is imperative to look at the entirety of a country's defence innovation enterprise and how it is connected with the national and global defence technological orders.

This special volume investigates the state of global defence innovation in the twenty-first century through the examination of a select number of states. Seven countries were picked that are representative of the diverse make-up of the global defence innovation community. There are small countries with advanced defence innovation capabilities (Israel and Singapore), closed authoritarian powers (North Korea and Russia), large catch-up states (China and India), and advanced large powers (U.S.). In addition, there is also a case study of emerging technologies focusing on China's efforts in the development of quantum capabilities.

Defining defence innovation

The starting point of our examination into the global state of defence innovation is to have a clear and precise definition of what is and is not meant by defence innovation. This is because defence innovation is sometimes used interchangeably with other terms and concepts that appear similar, if not identical, but have important differences such as military innovation or national security innovation. Tom Mahnken, Andrew Ross and Tai Ming Cheung have defined defence innovation as the *transformation of ideas and knowledge into new or improved products, processes and services for military and dual-use applications.*[2] This refers primarily to organisations and

---

[2] Tai Ming Cheung, Thomas G. Mahnken, and Andrew L. Ross, 'Frameworks for Analyzing Chinese Defense and Military Innovation', in Tai Ming Cheung (Ed), *Forging China's Military Might: A New Framework for Assessing Innovation* (Baltimore: Johns Hopkins University Press, 2014).

activities associated with the defence and dual-use civil–military science, technology and industrial base. They distinguish defence innovation from military innovation, which they say is principally focused on warfighting innovation that encompasses both product innovation and process innovation, technological, operational and organisational innovation and is intended to enhance the military's ability to prepare for, fight and win wars. In other words, defence innovation is broader and encompasses the civilian domain, especially the defence industrial base and related dual-use commercial base, whereas military innovation is more narrowly focused on the military domain.

Mahnken et al. identify three key components for both defence and military innovation: technological, organisational and doctrinal. Technology serves as the source of the hardware dimension of defence and military innovation and its concrete products. Organisational and doctrinal changes, the software of innovation, provide what is characterised in the broader literature as process innovation. While defence and military innovation address the interrelationships between these three dimensions, there are inherent biases in their primary areas of focus. For defence innovation, the technological dimension occupies a more prominent role because of a greater focus on research, development and acquisition processes. Military innovation has tended to place more emphasis on doctrinal and warfighting issues. This volume reflects this bias by paying more attention to the technological domain, but organisational and doctrinal perspectives are still given plenty of consideration.

A conceptual framework of defence innovation

A conceptual framework is offered here to provide a foundation for general comparative inquiry of defence innovation across countries, technologies and products. This framework specifies a comprehensive set of factors, the relationships between them, levels of analysis and examination of other relevant attributes such as soft and hard innovation factors, and a typology of innovation outcomes. This framework, however, is not intended to provide explanations of behaviour or outcomes, which is the purview of theories and models.[3]

This framework is informed by an extensive body of academic research on systems of innovation and public policy processes over the past few decades.[4] The basis of this framework is the concept of a defence innovation

---

[3] See Edella Schlager, 'A Comparison of Frameworks, Theories, and Models of Policy Processes', in Paul A. Sabatier (Ed), *Theories of the Policy Process* (Boulder, Co: Westview 2007).
[4] Charles Edquist and Bjorn Johnson, 'Institutions and Organizations in Systems of Innovation', in Charles Edquist (Ed), *Systems of Innovation: Technologies, Institutions and Organizations* (Oxford: Routledge, 2005); and Charles Edquist, 'Systems of Innovation: Perspectives and Challenges', in Jan Fagerberg, Richard Nelson, and David Mowery, *The Oxford Handbook of Innovation* (Oxford: Oxford University Press, 2004).

system, which derives from the notion of the national innovation system that was put forward in the 1990s.[5] National innovation systems are complex, constantly evolving eco-systems that includes 'all important economic, social, political, organisational, institutional and other factors that influence the development, diffusion and use of innovations'.[6] The different ways that organisations and institutions are set up and operate within countries help to explain the variation in the national style of innovation.

Frameworks and theories from the study of the public policy process have also been useful in the shaping of the defence innovation systems framework. Three in particular stand out. First is the family of institutional rational choice frameworks that focus on how institutional rules shape the behaviour of rational actors.[7] Second is the punctuated equilibrium framework that argues that policy-making usually takes place incrementally over long periods but is punctuated by brief periods of major change.[8] Third is the advocacy coalition framework that examines the interaction of coalitions within policy subsystems.[9] The defence innovation systems framework incorporates a number of concepts put forward in these frameworks such as networks and subsystems and institutional factors.

Defence innovation is defined as the transformation of ideas and knowledge into new or improved products, processes and services for military and dual-use applications. This definition refers primarily to organisations and activities associated with the defence and dual-use civil–military science, technology and industrial base. Included at this level are, for instance, changes in planning, programming, budgeting, research, development, acquisition and other business processes.

A defence innovation system can be broadly defined as a network of organisations and institutions that interactively pursue science, technology and innovation-related activities to further the development of defence interests and capabilities, especially related to strategic, defence and dual-use civil–military activities (See Chart 1). While defence innovation systems have traditionally been bounded by national borders, there has been a growing trend of multi-national defence collaboration, mergers and acquisitions in the post-Cold War era, especially among U.S. and European states, that has eroded this national identity.

---

[5]See Richard Nelson (Ed), *National Innovation Systems* (New York: Oxford University Press, 1993).
[6]Edquist, 'Systems of Innovation: Perspectives and Challenges'.
[7]Elinor Ostrom, 'Institutional Rational Choice: An Assessment of the Institutional Analysis and Development Framework', in Sabatier, *Theories of the Policy Process*.
[8]Frank Baumgartner and Bryan Jones, *Agendas and Instability in American Politics* (Chicago: University of Chicago Press, 1993), and Bryan Jones, Frank Baumgartner, and James True, 'Policy Punctuations: U.S. Budget Authority, 1947–1995', *Journal of Politics*, 60 (February 1998).
[9]Paul Sabatier and Christopher Weible, 'The Advocacy Coalition Framework', in Paul A. Sabatier (Ed), *Theories of the Policy Process* (Boulder, Co: Westview 2007).

Two aspects of this definition of defence innovation systems are worth highlighting. First, organisations refer to entities that are directly or indirectly involved in supporting the innovation process. They would include research institutes, universities, state and party agencies, military units, defence industrial agencies and public and private enterprises at the central and local levels. Second, understanding the nature of interaction between organisations is critical. This is carried out through well-defined institutional arrangements, which are norms, routines, habits, established practices and other rules of the game that exist to guide the workings of the system and the interactions between organisations.[10]

Defence innovation systems come in many shapes, sizes and levels of technological advancement, but only a small number of states, on their own or collectively with partner nations, are willing and able to afford to build and sustain the research, development, engineering and production capabilities required to deliver state-of-the-art armaments and military equipment. These complex systems are comprised of numerous components that relate and interact with each other in varied ways.

Categories of factors

A diverse array of factors are involved in the defence innovation process, and the framework distinguishes seven categories (See Chart 2):

- **Catalytic factors**: Catalysts are the sparks that ignite innovation of a more disruptive nature. These powerful factors are normally external to the defence innovation system and their intervention occurs at the highest and most influential levels of the ecosystem and can produce the conditions for enabling considerable change and disruption. Without these catalytic factors, the defence innovation system would find it very difficult, if not impossible, to engage in higher end innovation and remain tied to routine modes of incremental innovation.
- **Input factors**: These are material, financial, technological and other forms of contributions that flow into the defence innovation system. Most of these inputs are externally sourced but can also come internally. Resource allocations, technology transfers and civil–military integration are important input factors.
- **Institutional factors**: Institutions are rules, norms, routines, established practices, laws and strategies that regulate the relations and interactions between actors (individuals and groups) within and

---

[10]Douglass North, *Institutions, Institutional Change and Economic Performance* (Cambridge: Cambridge University Press 1990), 4–5.

outside of the defence innovation system.[11] Rules can be formal (laws, regulations and standards) or informal (routines, established practice, and common habits). Norms are shared prescriptions guiding conduct between participants within the system. Strategies refer to plans and guidance that are devised by actors within and outside the defence innovation system.

- **Organisations and other factors**: The principal actors within the defence innovation system and main units of analysis of the framework are organisations, which are formal structures with an explicit purpose and they are consciously created. They include firms, state agencies, universities, research institutes and a diverse array of organised units. Other types of actors are also involved, such as individuals, and they are taken into consideration.[12]
- **Networks and subsystems**: Social, professional, virtual and other types of networks allow actors, especially individuals, the means to connect with each other within and beyond defence innovation systems, both domestically and internationally. Networks provide effective channels of sharing information, often more quickly and comprehensively than traditional institutional linkages and they help to overcome barriers to innovation such as rigid compartmentalisation.[13] Subsystems are issue or process-specific networks that link organisations and other actors with each other to produce outputs and outcomes.[14] Numerous subsystems exist within the overall defence innovation system and they can overlap or be nested with each other. The procurement and research and development subsystems are two of the most prominent subsystems.
- **Contextual factors**: This category covers the diverse set of factors that influence and shape the overall defence innovation environment. Contextual determinants that exert strong influence include historical legacy, domestic political environment, development levels and the size of the country and its markets.
- **Output factors**: This category is responsible for determining the nature of the products and processes that come out of the innovation system. They include the production process, commercialisation, the role of market forces such as marketing and sales considerations and the influence of end-user demand.

---

[11] Edquist and Johnson, 'Institutions and Organizations in Systems of Innovation', 46; and Elinor Ostrom, 'Institutional Rational Choice: An Assessment of the Institutional Analysis and Development Framework', in Sabatier, *Theories of the Policy Process*, 26.
[12] Edquist and Johnson, 'Institutions and Organizations in Systems of Innovation', 56.
[13] Mark Zachary Taylor, *The Politics of Innovation* (Oxford: Oxford University Press, 2016), 157–68.
[14] Christopher Weible, Tanya Heikkila, Peter deLeon and Paul Sabatier, 'Understanding and Influencing the Policy Process', *Policy Sciences* 45/1 (March 2012); and Hank C. Jenkins-Smith, Daniel Nohrstedt, Christopher Weible, and Karin Ingold, 'The Advocacy Coalition Framework: An Overview of the Research Program', in Christopher Weible (Ed), *Theories of the Policy Process* (New York: Routledge, 2018).

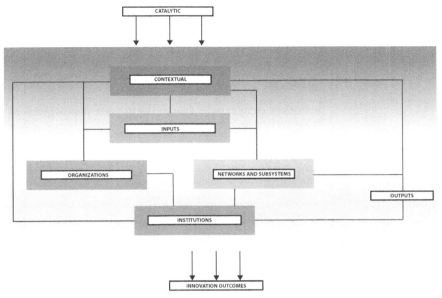

Chart 1. The defence innovation system framework and factor categories.

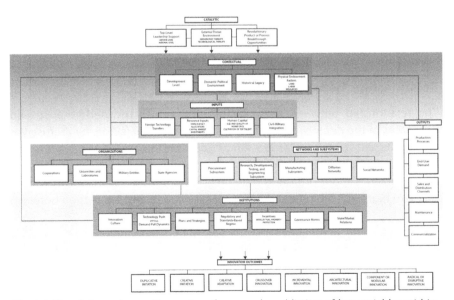

Chart 2. The defence innovation system framework and listing of key variables within the factor categories.

Table 1. List of key categories of factors in the defence innovation system.

Factor Categories	Variables
Catalytic	Top-Level Leadership Support; External Threat Environment; Revolutionary Product or Process Breakthrough Opportunities
Inputs	Foreign Technology Transfers; Resource Inputs (State Budget Allocations, Capital Market Investments); Human Capital (Size and Quality of Workforce, Cultivation of Top Talent), Civil–Military Integration
Institutions	Plans and Strategies; Regulatory and Standards-Based Regime; Incentives (Intellectual Property Protection); Governance Norms; State-Market Relations; Technology Push Vs. Demand Pull Dynamics
Organisations	Defence Corporations, State Agencies, Military Entities; Research and Development System
Networks and Subsystems	Manufacturing Process; Acquisition (Research, Development, and Engineering) system; Social Networks; Diffusion
Contextual	Historical Legacy; Domestic Political Environment; Development Level, Country and Market Size
Outputs	Production Process; Maintenance; Sales and Distribution; End-User Demand; Commercialisation

This extensive list of categories and factors, summarized in Table 1, is by no means exhaustive and is intended as an initial effort to capture the most salient and significant components and drivers of the defence innovation system. It should be pointed out that the boundaries between these categories are porous and there are instances where factors can overlap between classes. For example, the external threat environment can be both a catalytic and contextual factor, especially if security concerns are sufficiently grave that states mobilise their defence innovation systems to respond to these dangers.

Relationships between factors

The relationship between these factors determines the performance and outcomes of the defence innovation system. Individual factors by themselves are insufficient to make a far-reaching impact on the innovation process and it is only when they link and interact with other factors that these clusters are able to exert a more profound influence. A number of observations can be made to highlight prominent patterns of association and interaction between factors.

First, catalytic factors have an outsized influence on innovation, especially on higher and more novel types of innovation. But they are only effective if closely linked to other classes of factors in key parts of the defence innovation system, especially those in the input, organisational, institutional, network and subsystem categories. If top leadership support, for example, is coordinated with resource allocations and the research and development subsystem, this offers the opportunity for engaging in higher more disruptive forms of innovation. If leadership support though is absent or weakly connected with these other categories of factors, then any intervention is unlikely to produce meaningful results.

Second, different cluster patterns of factors can be identified depending on the level of development and strategic goals of the defence innovation system:

- **Incremental catch-up regimes**: In economically and technologically underdeveloped countries and their defence innovation systems, absorption-oriented factors are the most important drivers at work (See Chart 3). They include technology transfers, organisational and institutional factors that emphasise the importance of the role of the state such as government agencies, and subsystems that are primarily engaged in engineering and production. Catalytic factors do not play a prominent role in these regimes, which means their innovation trajectories are incremental in nature. Examples include India and Brazil.

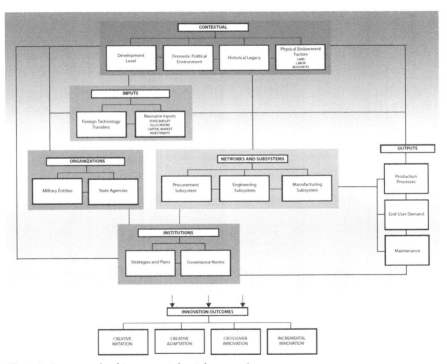

Chart 3. Framework of incremental catch-up regimes.

- **Rapidly catching-up regimes**: Many of the same absorption-oriented factors found in incremental catch-up regimes are present in developing countries seeking rapid advancement, but a critical difference is that catalytic factors, especially leadership support and the threat environment, are prominent and link closely with input factors such as resource allocations along with institutional factors like strategies and plans (See Chart 4). Moreover, many more factors are engaged in the innovation process compared to its incremental catch-up counterpart, such as the research and development subsystem. China is the proto-typical example of this type of regime.
- **Advanced developed regimes**: Factors that promote original innovation are the most important and powerful drivers at play for advanced defence innovation systems (See Chart 5). They include bottom-up institutional factors such as market-based governance regimes and incentives supporting risk-taking and intellectual property protection, organisations that encourage market and research activities such as corporations and universities and research institutes and subsystems focused on the generation of original knowledge and products such as the research and development apparatus. The U.S. is a leading example of an advanced developed regime.
- **Emerging technological domains**: In areas focused on the nurturing of emerging technologies, the most important factors are not organisational, institutional, or subsystem classes of factors that are the pillars of

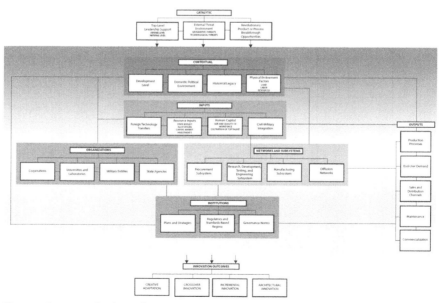

Chart 4. Framework of rapidly catching-up regimes.

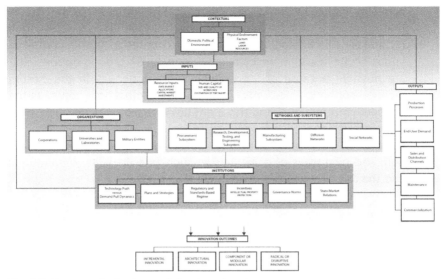

Chart 5. Framework of advanced developed regimes.

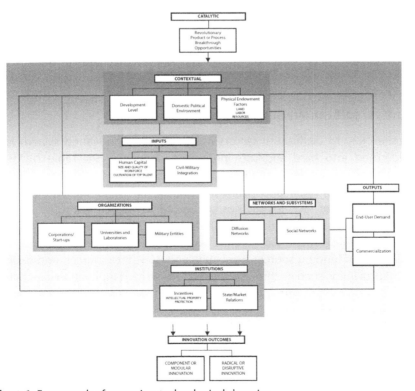

Chart 6. Framework of emerging technological domains.

conventional well-established defence innovation systems, but factors that emphasise new innovation approaches (See Chart 6). This would include (1) a technological environment (counted as both a contextual and catalytic factor) in which revolutionary breakthrough opportunities are possible because of far-reaching shifts underway in the existing techno-economic paradigms; (2) social and professional networks that connect entrepreneurs and those entities focused on early stage, high-risk research; and (3) the embrace of input, market-oriented organisational and institutional factors that encourage risk-taking, experimentation, and new ways of collaboration such as civil–military integration, and the role of start-up and private enterprises.

Levels of analysis

The defence innovation systems framework can be applied to different levels of analysis from the international level to looking at specific projects. In the examination of the country case studies in this volume, the level of analysis is at the national level. But the framework can also be used to look at lower levels such as at the industry sector (e.g. the aviation and shipbuilding industries) or sub-sectoral level (the fighter aviation and surface warship construction sub-industries), at specific technologies (such as artificial intelligence and hypersonics), and also at individual programmes and projects.

Hard vs. soft innovation factors

Another way to distinguish factors in the defence innovation system is to divide them into 'hard' and 'soft' innovation categories (See Table 2).[15] Hard innovation capabilities are input and infrastructure factors intended to advance technological and product development. This includes research and development facilities such as laboratories, research institutes and universities, human capital, firm-level capabilities and participation, manufacturing capabilities, access to foreign technology and knowledge markets, availability of funding sources from state and non-state sources, and geographical proximity, such as through clusters. These hard innovation capabilities attract the most analytical attention because they are tangible and can be measured and quantified.

Soft innovation capabilities are broader in scope than hard factors and cover political, institutional, relational, social, ideational and other factors that shape non-technological and process-related innovative activity. This is what

---

[15]For an expanded discussion, see Tai Ming Cheung, 'The Chinese Defence Economy's Long March from Imitation to Innovation', *Journal of Strategic Studies* 34/3 (June 2011).

Table 2. List of key factors driving the defence innovation system incorporating the hard, soft, and critical factors categories.

Factor Categories	Hard Innovation Factors	Soft Innovation Factors
Catalytic	Revolutionary Product or Process Breakthrough Opportunities	Top-Level Leadership Support; External Threat Environment
Contextual	Historical Legacy; Development Level; Political System	
Input	Foreign Technology Transfers; Resource Inputs (State Budget Allocations, Capital Market Investments); Human Capital (Size and Quality of Workforce, Cultivation of Top Talent)	
Organisational	Corporations; Government Agencies; Research Entities; Individuals; Military Organisations	
Networks and Subsystems	Procurement Subsystem; Research and Development Subsystem	Social Networks; Professional Networks; Technology Push Vs. Demand Pull; Technological Diffusion
Institutional	Plans and Strategies;	Regulatory and Standards-Based Regime; Incentives (Intellectual Property Protection); Governance Norms; Market Forces
Output	Production Process; Maintenance; Sales and Distribution	End-User Demand

innovation scholars define as 'social capability'.[16] These soft capabilities include organisational, marketing and entrepreneurial skills as well as governance factors such as the existence and effectiveness of legal and regulatory regimes, the role of political leadership, promotion of standards, corporate governance mechanisms and the general operating environment that the eco-system is located within.

It should be pointed out that the 'hard–soft' and functional factor frameworks are not dueling approaches but can be integrated to offer an even more nuanced categorisation of the factors at play in the defence innovation system.

Types of innovation outcomes

There are an array of innovation outcomes resulting from the interactions among the various factors of this framework that extend from simple copying at one end to highly sophisticated disruptive innovation at the other:

(1) **Duplicative Imitation**: Products, usually obtained from foreign sources, are closely copied with little or no technological improvements. This is the starting point of industrial and technological

---

[16]Moses Abramovitz, 'Catching Up, Forging Ahead, and Falling Behind', *Journal of Economic History* 46/386 (June,1986).

development for latecomers. The process begins with the acquisition of foreign technology, which then goes directly into production with virtually no technology development or engineering and manufacturing development.

(2) **Creative Imitation**: This represents a more sophisticated form of imitation that generates imitative products with new performance features. Domestic research input is relatively low, but is beginning to find its way into modest improvements in components or non-core areas. The development process becomes more robust with more work done in the technology development and engineering and manufacturing stages. The work here is primarily how to integrate domestic components into the dominant foreign platform.

(3) **Creative Adaptation**: Products are inspired by existing foreign-derived technologies but can differ from them significantly. This can also be called advanced imitation. One of the primary forms of creative adaptation is reverse engineering. There is considerably more research conducted here than in the creative imitation stage, especially in product or concept refinement, and there is also significantly more effort and work to combine higher levels of domestic content onto an existing foreign platform.

(4) **Crossover Innovation**: This refers to products jointly developed by Chinese and foreign partners with significant technology and knowledge transfers to the local side that result in the creation of a R&D base able to conduct independent and original innovation activities. However, there is still considerable reliance on foreign countries for technological and managerial input to ensure that projects come to fruition.

(5) **Incremental Innovation**: This is the limited updating and improvement of existing indigenously developed systems and processes. Incremental innovation can be the gradual upgrading of a system through the introduction of improved subsystems, but it is also often the result of organisational and management inputs aimed at producing different versions of products tailored to different markets and users, rather than significant technological improvements through original research and development.

(6) **Architectural Innovation**: This can be distinguished between product and process variants. Architectural product innovation refers to 'innovations that change the way in which the components of a product are linked together, while leaving the core design concepts (and thus the basic knowledge underlying the components) untouched.'[17] Architectural

---

[17] Rebecca Henderson and Kim Clark, 'Architectural Innovation: The Reconfiguration of Existing Product Technologies and the Failure of Established Firms,' *Administrative Science Quarterly* 35/1 (March 1990) 10.

process innovation refers to the redesign of production systems in an integrated approach (involving management, engineers and workers as well as input from end-users) that significantly improves processes but does not usually result in radical product innovation. The primary enablers are improvements in organisational, marketing, management, systems integration, and doctrinal processes and knowledge that are coupled with a deep understanding of market requirements and close-knit relationships between producers, suppliers and users. As these are also the same factors responsible for driving incremental innovation, distinguishing between these different types of innovation poses a major analytical challenge. While many of these soft capabilities enabling architectural innovation may appear to be modest and unremarkable, they have the potential to cause significant, even discontinuous consequences through the reconfiguration of existing technologies in far more efficient and competitive ways that challenge or overturn the dominance of established leaders.

(7) **Component or modular innovation**: This involves the development of new component technology that can be installed into existing system architecture. Modular innovation emphasises hard innovation capabilities such as advanced R&D facilities, a cadre of experienced scientists and engineers, and large-scale investment outlays.

(8) **Radical or disruptive innovation**: This requires major breakthroughs in both new component technology and architecture and only countries with broad-based, world-class R&D capabilities and personnel along with deep financial resources and a willingness to take risk can engage in this activity.

Case studies

This special issue explores in detail the defence innovation systems of seven countries. Altogether, these case studies provide a rich and varied application of the defence innovation framework that offers insightful comparative perspectives. We will begin by briefly summarizing the major categories of innovation factors shaping each of these defence innovation systems and then discuss the key findings. The cases can be sorted into the four framework variants: incremental catch-up, rapidly catching-up, advanced developed and emerging technological regimes.

Incremental catch-up regimes: India

India is the only state among the case studies that fit the definition of an incremental catch-up regime, although many other countries would fall into this category. Laxman Kumar Behera paints a portrait of a country with a suboptimal performance in defence innovation. This is because of a diverse array of reasons, of which several stand out. First is the absence of catalytic factors in providing leadership, direction, or any outside impetus to a slow-moving and dysfunctional defence innovation system. Behera points out that the role of leadership in defence innovation 'does not often go beyond lip service'. Second, several contextual factors exert an influential role in shaping the fundamental characteristics of India's approach to defence innovation. They include the backward state of the overall science and technology ecosystem and the powerful historical legacy of a state-dominated central planning system.

Third is the throttling of inputs going into the defence innovation system. In the late 2010s, only 6% of the Indian defence budget was annually earmarked for research and development, significantly less than the likes of the U.S. and China. Other input factors are similarly less than sufficient for engaging in moving up the innovation ladder. Behera says that civil–military integration is largely neglected while the nurturing of human capital is underwhelming with only 10% of defence scientists receiving PhDs. One input factor that has had some positive impact is the inflow of foreign technology transfers from the Soviet Union/Russia, Western Europe and more recently the U.S., but the Indian DIS has only been able to partially absorb these foreign capabilities.

Fourth, institutional factors within the Indian DIS hinder more than facilitate innovation. Norms, routines and the governance regime are overly bureaucratic, strictly compartmentalised and risk-adverse. Moreover, Behera argues that there is a lack of strategic planning and guidance and development programmes are often undertaken in ad hoc style. Fifth, organisational factors also contribute to the weak innovation performance of the Indian DIS. The most significant factor is the tight monopoly on the R&D held by the Defence Research and Development Organization (DRDO), whose track record is mixed. Manufacturing is also dominated by a limited number of state-owned entities composed of Defence Public Sector Undertakings and ordnance factories. There are a couple of public firms, Hindustan Aeronautics and Bharat Electronics, but Behera points out that they have only modest intellectual property portfolios.

Sixth, the Indian DIS has a proliferation of subsystems, but there is deep horizontal separation between them, which adds to truncated innovation dynamics. For example, the links between the procurement and production subsystems are limited, and the procurement system itself is characterised by dysfunction caused by strong distrust and competition between end-users and producers and developers. Seventh, output factors reflect the incremental nature of the Indian DIS. The manufacturing base is able to produce third generation conventional platforms, but lacks the technological capabilities to upgrade to more advanced cutting-edge weapons and equipment.

One important caveat though is that the strategic weapons component of the Indian DIS has demonstrated a much better track record for innovation than its conventional counterpart. Innovation in nuclear, ballistic missiles and space capabilities has been a bright spot in an otherwise lackluster Indian innovation landscape.

Rapidly catching-up regimes: North Korea

In contrast to India's weak efforts at defence innovation, North Korea has been far more successful in its efforts to advance up the innovation ladder primarily limited to strategic capabilities. The focus of the essay by Stephan Haggard and Tai Ming Cheung is on North Korea's accomplishments in indigenously building nuclear weapons and long-range ballistic missiles. The North Korean case is particularly fascinating because of this extraordinary development of advanced military capabilities in a severely underdeveloped and isolated country.

Catalytic factors in the form of leadership intervention and a severe external threat environment have been outsized influences in driving the development of North Korea's strategic weapons capabilities. A highly authoritarian and intensely focused leadership has been able to mobilise the entire resources of the country for an extended period to pursue its strategic goal of the indigenous development of a nuclear deterrence capability regardless of the enormous economic and social costs at home and isolation abroad. This is especially the case under Kim Jong Un, who has shown a laser-like focus and dedication to the development of strategic weapons capabilities far greater than his father and grandfather.

This single-minded determination of the Kim dynasty to produce a homegrown nuclear deterrence has been driven by a deep-seated fear that its survival is under threat from the U.S. and its regional allies, especially South Korea and Japan. North Korea has been on a permanent war-footing ever since its founding in the late 1940s. Up until the 1990s, Pyongyang's foremost priority was on building up a conventional military industrial complex. But after losing access to military assistance from the Soviet Union, who had been a long-time patron and strategic ally, North Korea's attention turned to the development of strategic weapons capabilities. North Korea's already profound sense of external threat became even more acute from the 1990s onwards with its protracted nuclear standoff with the international community as well as the spectre of the fall of other pariah regimes such as Libya and Iraq from Western military intervention.

A central focus of Haggard and Cheung's chapter is the close relationship between external technology inputs and domestic innovation capabilities. North Korea has benefited greatly from access to foreign technology and knowledge, especially in the early stages of research and development but also in the later engineering and testing stages. The North Korean state has cultivated a well-connected international network of suppliers and collaborators stretching from Pakistan and India to Libya, Iraq and Syria. The cultivation of human talent is another important input factor accounting for North Korea's progress in developing its strategic weapons capabilities. North Korea has nurtured a cadre of well-trained and experienced scientists and engineers across the full range of scientific, technological and engineering disciplines needed for nuclear weapons and ballistic missiles.

Haggard and Cheung point out that North Korea's ability to effectively marshal its limited resources and push ahead with its nuclear weapons and ballistic missile programmes shows the advantages of its state-socialist system to establish discreet highly functioning and tightly integrated networks and subsystems so long as they enjoy top-level support. The North Korean strategic weapons innovation system has fostered an effective systems integration capability able to manage the complex design, research, development and engineering processes involved in the absorption and reverse engineering of foreign technologies and marrying this with domestically developed technologies.

Another distinctive characteristic and strength of the strategic weapons innovation system is an institutional culture that is willing to take risks, learn from mistakes, be flexible and adaptive, and to learn while doing. Haggard and Cheung say that this attribute stands in sharp contrast with the strict ideological, risk-
adverse and tightly regimented norms of the overall North Korean political system.

In conclusion, Haggard and Cheung argue that the effectiveness of North Korea's strategic weapons innovation system ultimately rests on the relentless buildup of domestic research and heavy industrial capabilities under a highly centralised, state-led and top-down 'big engineering' approach. The North Korean strategic weapons system, along with its conventional weapons counterpart, has become a mainstay of the regime, enjoying privileged status and representation at the highest levels of the state, party and military apparatuses. It has also become the indispensable insurance policy for the Kim dynasty's continued hold on power.

Advanced developed regimes: U.S., Israel, Singapore and Russia

Four of the case studies can be categorised as advanced developed regimes. They are the U.S., Israel, Singapore and Russia. While the defence industrial bases of these states share the common characteristics of being technologically advanced and industrially mature, there are wide variations among them such as size, breadth of technological specialisation and nature of political systems, so it is unsurprising that their defence innovation systems are organised and operate in very different ways.

The U.S. has been the world's unrivalled defence innovation leader since the end of Cold War, and although there is growing debate that its superiority is at serious risk because of fierce external competition and domestic dysfunction, Eugene Gholz and Harvey Sapolsky say they are 'sanguine' that U.S. dominance is intact because the US defence innovation system has a very different and unique set of factors that keeps the country far ahead of any potential rivals. They argue that the combination of hard and soft innovation capabilities that the U.S. excels in will allow the country to 'remain at the cutting edge' and unlikely to be challenged for the foreseeable future. Gholz and Sapolsky highlight a number of factors within the input, organisational and institutional categories that stand out as being central to U.S. defence innovation leadership.

First is the input factor of strong defence R&D spending that extends back over more than seven decades. This mobilisation of resources on such a vast scale and over such a long period means the U.S. 'will not readily fall behind in weapons technology or quality', Gholz and Sapolsky argue. Second is the organisational factor of special public-private hybrid organisations called federally funded research and development centres and university affiliated research centres that provide unbiased technical advice and a mechanism for the accumulation of knowledge. Gholz and Sapolsky say these entities play a vital role in creating and preserving the 'soft' innovation capabilities of the U.S. defence R&D system as a reservoir of institutional memory of past R&D efforts and their independence that prevents capture by the state.

Gholz and Sapolsky also point to three types of institutional factors that act as powerful incentives for innovation. The first is a strong aversion to casualties that is shaped by labour shortages and the democratic nature of the U.S. political system. This has created an institutional culture that favours substituting technology for manpower. Second is the bureaucratic rivalry that exists among different branches of the U.S. defence establishment, especially inter-service competition. Third is a welcoming approach to immigration that has allowed for the importation of new ideas.

While Gholz and Sapolsky also believe that the threat environment plays a highly influential role, they view the threat argument as self-serving, or more precisely self-licking as spelled out in the title of their chapter. They argue that the U.S. is a very secure country surrounded by two big oceans and two unthreatening neighbours. The 'large threat assessment apparatus' that was established during the Cold War is now looking for 'every imaginable threat' to justify the maintenance and upkeep of the huge and very costly U.S. defence innovation system.

Richard Bitzinger contrasts Israel and Singapore and points out that although Israel and Singapore share many similar geo-strategic, national security and defence technological attributes, there is a 'marked gap in achievement' in defence innovation between the two countries. This difference can be teased out when comparing the critical factors at play in the shaping, orchestration and conduct of their defence innovation systems. First, in terms of catalytic factors, the threat environment exerts a profound influence on Israel, which views itself as under permanent siege by hostile neighbours. Singapore also sees itself in a dangerous regional security environment, but its neighbours are far less militant or capable than those in Israel's backyard and so the threat environment is less of a catalytic factor and more of a contextual factor.

Second, Israel and Singapore share a number of similar contextual factors that have played fundamental roles in shaping the foundations of their approaches to defence industrialisation and innovation. They both share a historical legacy of being born in hostile circumstances and needing to arm and defend themselves with overwhelming firepower as quickly as possible. Moreover, they both have similar geographical profiles of a lack of strategic depth and consequently require advanced military capabilities for a strong forward defence. The critical difference though is that Israel has gone to war several times, while Singapore has managed to avoid conflict so far.

Third, there is considerable overlap in the make-up of the input factors of both countries. They both invest heavily in defence S&T. Ten per cent of Singapore's defence budget, for example, is spent on research and development. They both have a very strong and well-educated pool of scientific and technological talent to feed into their defence innovation systems. Both countries are also heavily dependent on foreign acquisitions of military capabilities, especially from the U.S., although Israel is able to modify some of these imports with its own indigenous sub-systems. Civil–military integration is also pursued vigorously by both countries as their industrial economies are too small to compartmentalise between civilian and defence activities.

Fourth, the organisational configuration of the Israeli and Singaporean defence innovation systems is also broadly comparable. State-affiliated actors are the dominant players in the corporate and research and development realms. Three of the four top Israeli defence firms are state-owned, as is Singapore's monopoly defence enterprise. Government agencies exert a powerful grip on the defence S&T apparatus in both countries.

Fifth, one category though where there are significant differences between Israel and Singapore is in institutional factors. Israel has an institutional culture that emphasises improvisation, has limited interest in planning and developing long-range strategies, and embraces continuous ongoing innovation. Singapore by contrast has a far more rigid innovation culture that is risk adverse, strongly embraces planning and strategies, emphasises state control over market forces in picking winners and losers, and has cultivated a conservative governance regime.

Sixth, yet another category that highlights the differences between the Israeli and Singaporean defence innovation systems is networks and subsystems. A central characteristic of Israeli networks is that they are non-hierarchical, informal and adaptive. This allows for excellent access among participants at all levels, strong flows of information and ultimately a highly effective diffusion process. By contrast, Singapore is a more traditional hierarchical regime. One important similarity between these two countries due to their conscription systems is that they both have tight elite networks of politicians, cabinet ministers, corporate chiefs and other well-placed leaders who knew each other while serving in the military. This allows for the leaderships of these defence innovation systems to have access to their counterparts elsewhere within these countries.

Seventh, there are some notable similarities in output factors between Israel and Singapore. The influence of end-user requirements from the warfighters is strong in both the two countries. Another similarity is that they both have specialised niche manufacturing bases as they are both unable to afford or maintain a comprehensive suite of defence production capabilities. Israel though has a more extensive and sophisticated portfolio of products compared to Singapore that has made its companies successful on the international arms market.

In conclusion, while the Israeli and Singaporean defence innovation systems share many common traits, especially in contextual, organisational and output factors, it is the differences that are more significant and explains why the innovation performances and profiles of these two countries are so divergent. These differences are primarily catalytic, institutional and network factors such as the severity of the threat environment, social networks and institutional culture, which are also 'soft' in nature.

Russia has been drawing global attention to its defence innovation developments since the late 2010s. In major policy speeches, President Vladimir Putin has showcased his government's investment in the development of new generations of advanced defence technological capabilities as a cornerstone of his efforts to ensure that Russia remains a leading global military power. Vasily Kashin examines how motivated, capable and ambitious Russia actually is in the pursuit of world class defence innovation.

Kashin points to two events that were catalytic in shaping Russia's strategic and conventional defence innovation efforts in the twenty-first century. The first was the withdrawal of the U.S. from the Anti-Ballistic Missile (ABM) Treaty in 2002, which led Russia to significantly step up the development of strategic capabilities to ensure strategic stability and deterrence. Kashin said Russia focused its efforts on a limited number of highly ambitious but also risky breakthrough projects such as hypersonic glider re-entry vehicles for

ICBMs and new generations of strategic cruise missiles at the expense of the continued upgrading of its existing arsenals.

For the conventional sector, Kashin says the catalytic turning point was Russia's war with Georgia in 2008. Although Russia won the conflict against its much smaller and weaker neighbour, it exposed critical weaknesses in Russia's command and control structure, weak reconnaissance capabilities and inadequate personnel training. Kashin makes an interesting comparison between the May 1999 US bombing of the Chinese Embassy in Belgrade and the Georgia campaign. The embassy bombing sparked Beijing to embark on a major effort to improve its defence innovation system. In the Georgia conflict, Kashin says that there were widespread suspicions among Russian decision-makers that the U.S. was a key instigator behind Georgia's activities against Russia. The conflict led to Russia's reassessment of its relations with the West, which turned from cooperative to more competitive and adversarial.

Kashin offers a detailed layout of the organisational actors and institutional features of the Russian defence innovation system. The principal organisational actors include the Ministry of Defence and the Advanced Research Foundation, which is sometimes compared to DARPA in the U.S., but is very different in set-up and focus. The most important entity though is the Defence Industrial Commission, a government inter-agency body that is directly under the leadership of the Russian President. Vladimir Putin is actively engaged in defence innovation matters and is the supreme arbiter. An important point that Kashin makes is that these organisations are not simply content with focusing their efforts in the defence domain but are keen to broaden their responsibility for promoting innovation across the rest of the Russian national innovation system as well.

But with the limited financial and other resources that the mid-sized Russian economy is able to generate and afford to devote to defence needs compared to the U.S., China and other advanced states, Kashin argues that Russia's only viable option to keep up militarily with the global frontier is to concentrate its efforts in a select few areas such as nuclear-armed long-range intercontinental ballistic missiles, a non-nuclear strategic deterrence such as hypersonic weapons, air defence systems and a limited array of ground-based weapons. Areas not deemed of sufficiently high priority in current Russian military doctrine such as long-range air and naval power projection capabilities are being sacrificed. Kashin points out that Moscow views the long-term international threat environment to be increasingly complex and hostile, which requires continued commitment to the modernisation of its nuclear triad and more attention and resources to be devoted to emerging technologies such as artificial intelligence, directed energy weapons, hypersonic weapons and robotics.

Emerging technological domains: China's efforts in quantum technologies

In addition to the country case studies, there is one emerging technology-focused case study by Elsa Kania on China's development of quantum technologies that have both military and civilian applications. In Kania's examination of China's efforts to develop its quantum capabilities, she sees innovation being driven by some of the same factors that are also prominent in conventional domains, of which top-level leadership support and the threat environment stand out. Kania paints a picture of a rapidly developing Chinese quantum innovation eco-system that enjoys strong high-level support among party, state, military and corporate elites, of which Xi Jinping stands out at the very top. This was highlighted most prominently by a Politburo study session on quantum development that was hosted by Xi in October 2020. Underpinning the leadership's vigorous backing for the development of quantum capabilities are their concerns about the rising threat environment, especially the vulnerability of the country's communications infrastructure through sophisticated technology-based intelligence gathering activities led by the U.S. Kania points to the Edward Snowden incident in 2013 in which the National Security Agency contractor leaked extensive details of U.S. penetration of foreign networks, including within China, as a pivotal event behind the Chinese leadership's embrace of quantum technologies that would provide highly secure communications capabilities such as through unbreakable cryptography.

The development of the Chinese quantum innovation ecosystem offers useful insights into how China more generally is going about in establishing itself as a leading player in a broader array of emerging technology sectors. The general approach is through what can be described as a selective authoritarian mobilisation development model, in which the Chinese authorities mobilize and concentrate resources through a statist top-down allocation process to a highly selective group of sectors.[18] This is done through various mechanisms that Kania points out, such as state-directed plans and policies in the form of Five-Year Science and Technology Development Plans, the Strategic Emerging Industries initiative and the Made in China 2025 industrial plan. But there are also new tools being adopted such as the use of provincial and market-supported funding mechanisms that Kania identifies.

Human talent is another prominent characteristic in driving quantum innovation. While high-end human talent is critical across all defence S&T fields, it is doubly so in the quantum realm. Kania points to a number talent recruitment and educational programmes and activities and argues that China has had considerable success in nurturing a homegrown quantum

---

[18] See Tai Ming Cheung, *Innovate to Dominate: The Making of the Chinese Techno-Security State and Implications for the Global Order* (Forthcoming).

talent pool that makes it less reliant on foreign talent transfers than in other technological domains.

An important distinguishing characteristic of the Chinese quantum innovation system that supports the framework put forward of emerging technological domains is the prominent role played by professional and social networks in promoting knowledge creation and diffusion. Kania points to the forging of domestic and foreign productive partnerships, especially among key quantum hubs such as the Key Laboratory of Quantum Information at the University of Science and Technology of China (USTC) and quantum centres at Tsinghua and Fudan Universities. USTC appears to be the most important node for quantum collaboration with foreign and military entities. This includes a joint research project with the Austrian Academy of Sciences and partnerships with Chinese defence corporations.

Another novel feature of the Chinese quantum innovation system is the role of private sector entities that have been generally absent in China's defense innovation system. The Alibaba Quantum Computing Lab is a rare example of a private entity participating in high-end strategic innovation in China, but whether it is a one-off or represents the start of a new trend of growing private sector involvement in cutting-edge innovation could have a profound impact in shaping China's long-term technology development trajectory.

Key findings

A number of themes emerge from these case studies. First, catalytic factors are critically important. The threat environment and the role of high-level leadership support are highlighted in a number of the cases, especially Israel and North Korea. Catalytic factors are especially critical for the pursuit of disruptive innovation. The oft-noted contemporary intensification of geopolitical competition can be expected to catalyse competition for defence and military prowess generally and for defence and military innovation specifically. Leading and rising catch-up powers perhaps will be the most likely to pursue ambitious, across-the-board innovation programmes. Their defence and military planners and operators will be attracted by new, emerging and over-the-horizon technologies, such as cyber, AI and quantum computing, that are perceived, correctly or incorrectly, as promising either breakthroughs or discontinuous, disruptive innovation (even as those planners and operators struggle with how to effectively employ new cyber, AI, quantum and other tools).

Innovation by mid-size and small states is more likely to be focused on the development of niche rather than across-the-board capabilities; architectural innovation – the reconfiguration of hardware and software, of technology, doctrine and organisation – may prove particularly attractive to this group of states. In the absence of limits on the development, production, acquisition, deployment and employment of new capabilities – the next big, new thing, or game changer, may not be a good thing – the impetus given to defence and military innovation by an intensification of geopolitical conflict may well pose risks to regional and global order and stability.

New, emerging and over-the-horizon technologies – which are as likely as not to be imported by the defence sector from the commercial sector (rather than, as in the past, exported by the defence sector to the commercial sector) and, as a result of the globalisation of R&D, will be broadly disseminated – may be as likely to undermine as to enhance security, even contributing to the onset of, or exacerbation of, arms races and security dilemmas. As, or perhaps if, geopolitically spurred competition for defence and military innovation intensifies, it should not be assumed that a competitive advantage automatically accrues to authoritarian, centrally planned economies that target a select set of emerging technologies. Matthew Evangelista long ago demonstrated that a bottom-up, decentralised approach to defence and military innovation can best a top-down, centralised approach – that the latter can actually inhibit innovation. Gholz and Sapolsky, too, note the advantages of the competitive, decentralised approach to defence and military innovation enjoyed by the U.S.

A third cluster of attributes identified as having considerable impact on innovation are social and strategic culture-related factors, although their influence is more in an indirect context of providing a positive supporting environment rather than playing a direct role. In the case of the U.S., for example, social and political dynamics related to technology substitution for labour and an immigration-friendly social environment are viewed as having had an important role in shaping the U.S. defence innovation culture. The influence of social traits is even more pronounced in Israel with the prevalence of assertive, risk-taking and non-hierarchical norms a key factor behind its free-wheeling disruptive innovation environment. The opposite is true in Singapore where a more risk-adverse and hierarchical social order means that the preference is for more routine incremental innovation.

Fourth, the nature and intensity of innovation will depend on the level of sophistication and development of a state's defence innovation system. Advanced and well-endowed innovation systems such as the U.S. are much more able to pursue higher-end innovation than underdeveloped catch-up countries that will be limited to imitation and lower-end innovation.

Fifth, the linkages between factors, especially different categories of factors, are important. Close working connections between catalytic factors and input, process and institutional-related factors would enable higher levels of innovation outcomes. If top leadership support is closely linked to budgets and acquisition processes, for example, this would identify pathways for innovation to take place. But if leadership support is isolated and affiliated with critical enabling factors elsewhere in the innovation system, then the pathways to progress will be absent.

We conclude with a brief discussion about the state of the defense innovation subfield and the next steps in its development. From the outset, this article was based on the modest goal of offering a conceptual framework of defence innovation that pinpoints and bring together the tacit assumptions that have been made by the articles in this special volume as well as by other scholars toiling in the defence innovation sub-field. The framework offered here represents a summation of the state of the field and is intended to set the stage for more explicit theory building and testing that will help to produce more rigorous and generalisable examinations. These next steps in the research agenda could not be more timely as the world faces the prospects of a more intensive and disruptive phase in the global defence innovation race brought on by the global revolution in technology affairs and the fierce techno-security rivalry between the U.S., China and their allies.

Disclosure statement

No potential conflict of interest was reported by the author(s).

Funding

This work was supported by, or in part by, the U.S. Army Research Laboratory and the U.S. Army Research Office under contract/grant No. W911NF-15-1-0407. Any opinions, findings and conclusions or recommendations expressed in this publication are those of the author(s) and do not necessarily reflect the views of the U.S. Army Research Office.

Bibliography

Abramovitz, Moses, 'Catching Up, Forging Ahead, and Falling Behind', *Journal of Economic History* 46/386 (June 1986), 385–406.

Baumgartner, Frank and Bryan Jones, *Agendas and Instability in American Politics* (Chicago: University of Chicago Press 1993).

Black, Jeremy, *War and Technology* (Bloomington, IN: Indiana University Press 2013).

Cheung, Tai Ming, 'The Chinese Defence Economy's Long March from Imitation to Innovation', *Journal of Strategic Studies* 34/3 (June 2011), 325–354.

Cheung, Tai Ming, *Innovate to Dominate: The Making of the Chinese Techno-Security State and Implications for the Global Order* (Irhaca, NY: Cornell University Press 2022).

Cheung, Tai Ming, Thomas G. Mahnken, and Andrew L. Ross, 'Frameworks for Analyzing Chinese Defense and Military Innovation', in Tai Ming Cheung (ed.), *Forging China's Military Might: A New Framework for Assessing Innovation* (Baltimore: Johns Hopkins University Press 2014, 15–46).

Edquist, Charles, 'Systems of Innovation: Perspectives and Challenges', in Jan Fagerberg, Richard Nelson, and David Mowery (eds.), *The Oxford Handbook of Innovation* (Oxford: Oxford University Press 2004), 181–208.

Edquist, Charles and Bjorn Johnson, 'Institutions and Organizations in Systems of Innovation', in Charles Edquist (ed.), *Systems of Innovation: Technologies, Institutions and Organizations* (Oxford: Routledge 2005), 41–63.

Henderson, Rebecca and Kim Clark, 'Architectural Innovation: The Reconfiguration of Existing Product Technologies and the Failure of Established Firms', *Administrative Science Quarterly* 35/1 (March 1990), 9–30.

Horowitz, Michael C., *The Diffusion of Military Power: Causes and Consequences for International Politics* (Princeton, New Jersey: Princeton University Press 2010).

Jenkins-Smith, Hank C., Daniel Nohrstedt, Christopher Weible, and Karin Ingold, 'The Advocacy Coalition Framework: An Overview of the Research Program', in Christopher Weible (ed.), *Theories of the Policy Process* (New York: Routledge 2018), 135-171.

Jones, Bryan, Frank Baumgartner, and James True, 'Policy Punctuations: U.S. Budget Authority, 1947–1995', *The Journal of Politics* 60/1 (February 1998), 1–33. doi:10.2307/2647999

Knox, MacGregor and Williamson Murray, Eds, *The Dynamics of Military Revolution, 1300-2050* (Cambridge: Cambridge University Press 2001).

Nelson, Richard, Ed, *National Innovation Systems* (New York: Oxford University Press 1993).

North, Douglass, *Institutions, Institutional Change and Economic Performance* (Cambridge: Cambridge University Press 1990).

Ostrom, Elinor, 'Institutional Rational Choice: An Assessment of the Institutional Analysis and Development Framework', in Paul A. Sabatier (ed.), *Theories of the Policy Process*, 2nded. (Boulder, Co: Westview 2007), 21–64.

Parker, Geoffrey, *The Military Revolution: Military Innovation and the Rise of the West, 1500-1800* (Cambridge: Cambridge University Press 1996).

Sabatier, Paul and Christopher Weible, 'The Advocacy Coalition Framework', in Paul A. Sabatier (ed.), *Theories of the Policy Process* (Boulder, Co: Westview 2007), 189–220.

Schlager, Edella, 'A Comparison of Frameworks, Theories, and Models of Policy Processes', in Paul A. Sabatier (ed.), *Theories of the Policy Process* (Boulder, Co: Westview 2007), 293–320.

Taylor, Mark Zachary, *The Politics of Innovation* (Oxford: Oxford University Press 2016).

Weible, Christopher, Tanya Heikkila, Peter deLeon, and Paul Sabatier, 'Understanding and Influencing the Policy Process', *Policy Sciences* 45/1 (March 2012), 1–21.

ⓐ OPEN ACCESS

The defense innovation machine: Why the U.S. will remain on the cutting edge

Eugene Gholz and Harvey M. Sapolsky

ABSTRACT
American security policy discussions commonly warn that the United States is falling behind technologically, especially vis-à-vis China. However, the U.S. military remains at the cutting edge because of its well-developed defense innovation system. No nation (or combination) comes close to U.S. investment in defense R&D. Unmatched political concerns about avoiding casualties, inherent rivalry among participants in the U.S. defense innovation system, and traditional American openness to immigration and new ideas drive the investment. The overly alarmist warnings come from a thriving threat assessment system that continually searches for potential military dangers and technological challenges. The warnings feed the defense innovation system.

The United States is the most powerful nation in the world.[1] It has the most powerful military, the biggest economy, and the most dominating culture. It is the world's leader in science, engineering, and medicine. Its universities are the most admired. Its corporations are the richest and most successful. People eat Big Macs, drink Coca Cola, fly on Boeings, use their iPhones, and watch Hollywood movies around the globe. Everyone knows the name of the American president, what the CIA does, and who you should call if there is trouble on your border.

The United States is also a very secure country. It is surrounded by two big oceans and two unthreatening neighbors. Its surveillance systems scour the globe looking for dangers. It has nuclear weapons, a Navy and Coast Guard on constant patrol, an Air Force on high alert and with a global reach, and an Army and Marine Corps second to none in capability and recent combat experience.

But many Americans believe that this is all slipping away, that America is becoming vulnerable and losing its power and dominance. They cite internal and

---

[1]Michael Beckley, *Unrivaled: Why America Will Remain the World's Sole Superpower* (Ithaca: Cornell University Press, 2018).

This is an Open Access article distributed under the terms of the Creative Commons Attribution-NonCommercial-NoDerivatives License (http://creativecommons.org/licenses/by-nc-nd/4.0/), which permits non-commercial re-use, distribution, and reproduction in any medium, provided the original work is properly cited, and is not altered, transformed, or built upon in any way.

external sources of the vulnerability. American power, they claim, is being frittered away by a dysfunctional Congress, an incompetent president, and a bloated, slow moving, gold-plating acquisition bureaucracy that cannot keep up. Indecision and gridlock have seemingly become the American Way of government. Meanwhile, some fear that agile rival nations, specifically including China, can tap fast moving commercial technology to build modern weapons that will defeat the United States.[2]

Here we examine these concerns that the American military advantage in the Post-Cold War era has dissipated in large part because the Defense Department lags behind in developing advanced technologies. Our judgment is that the American defense research and development system, as honed during the Cold War and expanded since, is fully capable of handling any military challenge. It is a gigantic technology-generating, innovation-producing, war-fighting machine. U.S. 'hard' innovation capabilities – 'input and infrastructure factors' like R&D facilities, human capital, access to foreign technology, and availability of funding – far outstrip those of its potential rivals, even though those factors are the ones often thought of as easier for catch-up countries to obtain.[3] Despite warnings that the United States no longer spends enough on R&D and that Chinese R&D spending is surging, the reality is that the United States dramatically leads in military innovation investment. In functional terms, the United States dominates all other countries, including China, in 'input factors,' starting with resource allocations to defense research and development.

More important, we believe that the American defense technology system is pushed toward innovation by specific contextual factors, the 'soft' categories of attributes and capabilities, that cannot readily transfer to likely rivals.[4] First, the political culture of the United States values technology strongly: technology is assumed to be the solution to most problems, including military ones. American culture also has a strong casualty aversion driven

---

[2]See, for example, Aaron Mehta, 'Pentagon Tech Advisers Want Special Career Track, "Innovation Elevator" for Big Thinkers', *Defense News*, 26 Oct. 2017; Jill Aitoro, 'The Next Sputnik: Here's Why U.S. Stands to Lose Technological Edge to China', *Defense News*, 2 Dec. 2017; Tim Greeff, 'The Pentagon can't develop technology quickly enough to thwart enemies. Here's one way to help', *Defense News*, 1 Aug. 2018; David Ignatius, 'The Chinese threat that an aircraft carrier can't stop', *Washington Post*, 7 Aug. 2018; Joe Gould, 'Reform panel warns Congress to overhaul Pentagon acquisitions, or lose technical edge', *Defense News*, 16 Jan. 2019; Noah Smith, 'U.S. Tech Lead Over China May Not Matter', *Bloomberg Opinion*, 29 Jan. 2020; Christian Brose, *The Kill Chain: Defending America in the Future of High-Tech Warfare* (New York: Hachette, 2020). For extensive discussion of China's possible innovative edge, see the January/February 2019 special issue of *Technology Review*, notably including an article that speculates about China's future military capability: Martin Giles, 'The Father of Quantum', *Technology Review* 122/1 (January/February 2019), 59.
[3]Tai Ming Cheung, 'A Conceptual Framework of Defence Innovation', (2021),12.
[4]For more on the potential barriers that soft innovation factors create for the diffusion of military technology, see Leslie C. Eliason and Emily O. Goldman, 'Introduction: Theoretical and Comparative Perspectives on Innovation and Diffusion', in Emily O. Goldman and Leslie C. Eliason, eds., *The Diffusion of Military Technology and Ideas* (Stanford, CA: Stanford University Press, 2003), 1–30, and other essays in the same volume; Emily O. Goldman, 'Introduction: Military Diffusion and Transformation', in Emily O. Goldman and Thomas G. Mahnken, eds., *The Information Revolution in Military Affairs in Asia* (New York: Palgrave MacMillan, 2004), 1–21.

by an economy traditionally burdened by labor scarcity and by responsive political institutions that encourage the substitution of capital for labor to keep its own people out of harm's way.[5] The All-Volunteer Force reflects this by making military service voluntary and thus making military service expensive for government and service personnel lives ever-more-valuable and in need of husbanding.

Second, competition is deeply engrained in defense, as it is in most of American society, stimulating new ideas and providing a diversity of approaches to any problem, in case one technology trajectory does not work out as hoped. Competition extends among the various military services and agencies, which each seek to propose solutions to the nation's strategic problems, and among firms with different design-team philosophies.

Third, the United States also welcomes foreign ideas much more readily than other countries, given U.S. openness to immigration, especially among the highly skilled and technically expert. Finally, a Cold-War organizational innovation in the United States created special public-private hybrid organizations, Federally-Funded Research and Development Centers (FFRDCs) that offer unbiased technical advice and a mechanism for the accumulation of knowledge – a unique social, relational system for institutional memory and systems integration capability that generally works very well. Other nations, with different divisions between the public and the private and dramatically different governance institutions, cannot easily copy these capabilities.

These soft innovation factors particularly emphasize American advantages in the functional category of institutional factors – norms of seeing technology as a solution, trying hard to minimise casualties, using innovation as a means of competition among organizations, and welcoming foreign ideas. The institutional factors draw from the particular American mix of organizations, notably independent military services with strong identities, competitive firms in the defense industry that readily form networks or teams of suppliers even as each maintains its own core competencies and technical habits, and FFRDCs that help keep systems integration efforts honest and less parochial and that help preserve knowledge of false-start technology trajectories and craft skills that enable high-tech systems to function well.[6]

Because of the robustness of America's input factors and the difficulty of copying its unique institutional factors, we conclude that the American defense innovation system will remain at the cutting edge and will not be surpassed by a potential international rival. In the final section, we explain why American leaders are so nervous anyway.

---

[5] Harvey M. Sapolsky, Eugene Gholz, and Caitlin Talmadge, *U.S. Defense Politics: The Origins of Security Policy* [3rd ed.] (New York: Routledge, 2017), 25–29.

[6] For the distinction between the closely related concepts of 'institutions' and 'organizations,' see Cheung, 'A Conceptual Framework', (2021), 4.

Is the United States losing its military overmatch?

In the early 1990s, with the disintegration of the Soviet Union that marked the end of the Cold War and the rapid defeat of Iraq in the Gulf War, the United States had a dominating military edge against all comers in terms of the capabilities of both its nuclear and conventional forces. Many trace this edge to the so-called Reagan Build-up, which actually began in the last two years of the Carter Administration and then expanded under President Reagan. The buildup involved investments of hundreds of billions of dollars to modernize nearly all parts of the American military. The modernization of nuclear forces, for example, included the acquisition of *Ohio*-class ballistic missile submarines, the highly accurate Trident D-5 and MX Peacekeeper missiles, the B-1B and B-2 bombers, and the acceleration of work on strategic command-and-control, anti-submarine warfare, and anti-ballistic missile systems. Conventional forces improvements included fielding the Abrams tank, Bradley infantry fighting vehicle, Apache attack helicopter, and the Patriot missile system, constructing a nearly 600-ship Navy, and deploying the A-10, F-15, F-16, F/A-18, and JSTARS aircraft, along with important technical improvements in realistic training and investments in troop quality.

The Soviets were especially challenged by the conventional warfare improvements: the battlefield integration of sensors, communication systems, and precision weapons, which they labeled as a 'Military-Technical Revolution' or, in later American terms, a 'Revolution in Military Affairs' (RMA). The combination of new technologies seemingly rendered useless their ability to mass armored forces in a potential drive westward. As the Gulf War demonstrated to the entire world, numerical advantage in heavy metal on the battlefield had been transformed from the source of military power into an easily reduced target set for American forces.

Among the consequences of the Soviet Union's collapse were a one-third reduction in the size of the United States' standing forces and an increased use of the remaining forces in interventions across the globe. Freed from a possible clash with its nuclear-armed rival, the United States could involve itself in various civil wars and, after the 9/11 attacks on the United States homeland, interventions to counter terrorist groups and regimes that might support them. The wars in Afghanistan and Iraq produced persistent insurgencies, where the RMA systems had little relevance and thus no major success.

But it is not the limitations of precision weapons but rather their diffusion that worries many. Both Russia and China, through clever tactics and the fielding of accurate offensive and defensive systems, seem to be on the verge of being able to blunt the global reach of American power.[7] Add in their acquisition of space and cyber weapons, and America's once unquestioned

---

[7] Andrew F. Krepinevich, Jr., 'How to Deter China: The Case for Archipelagic Defense', *Foreign Affairs* 94/2 (March/April 2015), 78–86.

military edge appears in jeopardy. These threats to the previously established American technological advantages seem to require a new round of American innovation.

Strong input factors: Defense R&D spending and the FFRDCs

It is not that the United States cannot lag behind in some fields of militarily relevant technology or be surprised on the battlefield. Technology advances on many fronts and is pioneered in many places. Technological investment by potential adversaries surely can raise the costs to the United States of blithely sticking to operational concepts that previously promised great effectiveness at low cost.[8] However, the United States has been mobilized on such scale, for so long, with a special emphasis on applying its vast science and engineering resources to its defense, that it will not readily fall behind in weapons technology or quality.

The United States invests heavily in defense-related research and development (R&D) activities. Figure 1 shows the past 40 years of history of U.S. inputs to defense research and development. Currently the United States invests more than 75 billion USD each year in defense R&D plus billions more in Department of Energy R&D investment for nuclear weapons. That is about two-thirds of what all other countries in the world, American friend or foe, spend on defense R&D.[9] China is the only great power that spends more on its entire defense effort than the United States spends on just defense R&D. Seventy-five billion dollars is more than Russia, the United Kingdom, France, Germany, or Japan spends on defense.[10]

Moreover, the United States has invested at very high levels for more than 70 years. The United States substantially ramped up its defense R&D investment in the 1950s to levels comparable to today's spending. While it is true that in inflation-adjusted terms, defense R&D totals in the 1950s were lower than today's, that is mainly because of the lower complexity of that era's technological frontier, not because of some subsequent policy shift to greater emphasis on defense R&D investment.[11] The continuing drive to push the military-technological frontier has kept R&D spending high all along, and the overall spending trend has increased in parallel with the increasing

---

[8]Eugene Gholz, 'Why U.S. Strategy Must Adapt to Technological Change', *World Politics Review*, 18 April 2017; Eugene Gholz, Benjamin Friedman, and Enea Gjoza 'Defensive Defense: A Better Way to Protect U.S. Allies in Asia', *The Washington Quarterly* 42/4 (Winter 2019–2020), 171–89.

[9]In 2008 the United States spent more than six times what the entire European Union spent on defense R&D. Finding data on what Russia and China spend on defense R&D is very difficult. See Keith Hartley, 'Defense R&D Spending: A critical review of the economic data', *World Economics* 12/1 (January-March 2011), 103–114.

[10]International Institute for Strategic Studies (IISS), *The Military Balance 2018* (London: Taylor & Francis, 2018).

[11]John A. Alic, 'The Origin and Nature of the US "Military-Industrial Complex"', *Vulcan* 2/1 (June 2014), 63–97, esp. 83.

COMPARING DEFENSE INNOVATION AROUND THE WORLD

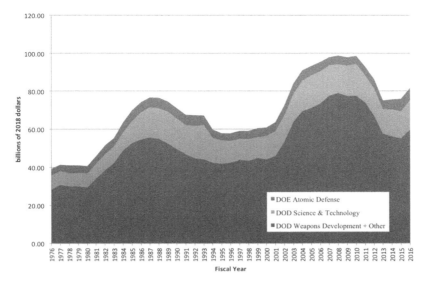

Figure 1. U.S. defense R&D budget authority, 1976–2016 (constant dollars).
Source: AAAS Reports and agency budget data.[12]

complexity rather than lagging behind. While R&D budget increases have not been constant, their cycle (including as shown in Figure 1) has crested and troughed at very high levels. Annual spending has not dropped below 55 billion USD (in 2018 dollars) since 1983, and in several years, it has been very close to 100 billion USD. That high level of spending, year-in and year-out, has a cumulative effect, because it builds a foundation of tacit knowledge, experience in integrating complex systems, and human capital that understands the specialized parameters of military systems, which often differ from those of even high-end civilian systems. For comparison, the much-hyped Chinese *defense* budget (not the Chinese defense R&D budget) did not exceed the level of U.S. defense *R&D* spending until the late-2000s. Cumulative Chinese defense R&D investment is surely quite modest in comparison to cumulative U.S. defense R&D investment.[13]

---

[12]Data available at https://www.aaas.org/programs/r-d-budget-and-policy/historical-trends-federal-rd (accessed 2 February 2019). Data are available for 2017 and 2018 but are not comparable due to a change in accounting rules; in practice, US defense R&D spending has increased in this period. For the DoD FY19 budget request, see Sydney J. Freedberg, Jr., 'DoD R&D Soars 24%, Procurement Up 15%; Army Up Most', *Breaking Defense*, 12 Feb. 2018.

[13]Adam P. Liff and Andrew S. Erickson, 'Demystifying China's Defense Spending: Less Mysterious in the Aggregate', *China Quarterly* 216 (December 2013), 805–30, esp. 820. For arguments about the difficulty of catching up to the cumulative effort to create military-technological capabilities, see Andrea Gilli and Mauro Gilli, 'Why China Has Not Caught Up Yet: Military-Technological Superiority and the Limits of Imitation, Reverse Engineering, and Cyber Espionage', *International Security* 43/3 (Winter 2018/2019), 141–89.

The intensity of U.S. interest in defense research began at the start of the Second World War, with scientists rather than the military. American scientists had been frustrated by the failure of the military to use them effectively in the First World War, when they were confined to military laboratories and subject to military discipline. Led by Vannevar Bush of MIT, they approached President Roosevelt and gained their own organization to manage wartime research, what was eventually called the Office of Scientific Research and Development (OSRD). That organization, not the military, directed the effort to develop the atomic bomb, radar, and many of the other significant technical advances of the war.[14]

In the postwar years scientists remained active in bomb research, though with less independence, in the newly created Atomic Energy Commission (later absorbed in the Department of Energy) and in the expansion of R&D efforts in the newly established Department of Defense (DOD), which sought in particular to exploit the advances in missile, jet propulsion, and submarine technologies of the war, including those made by the Germans. Although OSRD itself was disbanded, at least parts of its work continued in various university- and contractor-managed organizations and laboratories, the Federally Funded Research and Development Centers and University Affiliated Research Centers. Those organizations play a vital role in creating 'soft' innovation capabilities in the United States – preserving the institutional memory about past R&D efforts, cultivating multiple design-team philosophies that enable diverse approaches to technological challenges, and using their independence to prevent the capture of the U.S. R&D effort by rent-seeking activities of government customers and private-sector suppliers.[15]

For example, the Radiation Laboratory at MIT, which worked on radar in the Second World War, was renamed Lincoln Laboratory and continued under MIT management as an FFRDC doing classified work for the Air Force. The University of California manages the nuclear bomb-design laboratories, Los Alamos and Livermore, designated national laboratories for the Atomic Energy Commission. The Navy has its own set of university-managed laboratories, often called Applied Physics Laboratories, at Johns Hopkins University, the University of Hawaii, Pennsylvania State University, the University of Texas, and the University of Washington. The armed services also set up several policy-focused FFRDCs, the best known of which is the RAND Corporation. As new issues came up over the decades, new organizations were created such as the Software Engineering Institute at Carnegie Mellon University and the Institute for Soldier Nanotechnologies at MIT.

FFRDCs and related organizations do more than provide the American military with cutting edge research on important technical and policy

---

[14]Harvey M. Sapolsky, *Science and the Navy: The History of the Office of Naval Research* (Princeton NJ: Princeton University Press, 1990).

[15]Peter J. Dombrowski and Eugene Gholz, *Buying Military Transformation: Technological Innovation and the Defense Industry* (New York: Columbia University Press, 2006), 115–32.

problems. As non-profits dedicated only to serve government agencies, they are a source of valued, unbiased technical advice.[16] In fact, some FFRDCs, specifically MITRE and the Aerospace Corporation but others as well, specialize in advancing systems design and integration skills to help the American military build its biggest systems.[17]

Until the Second World War, contractors hired to produce America's weapons during wars returned to their commercial business at each war's end, as military needs soon faded. But the end of the Second World War was quickly followed by the Cold War and the continuing demand for weapons. Many firms stayed in the weapons business, some focusing exclusively on defense while others formed specialized divisions to serve the military. This was especially true in the aviation industry, where firms like Lockheed, Northrop, Grumman, McDonnell, Douglas, and Boeing grew large developing and building the aircraft and missiles that were central to the Cold War arms competition.

The peak technologies in the arms race changed over time, but the U.S. organizations and level of investment maintained the U.S. lead. The 1950s added space: the shock of the launch of the *Sputnik* satellite spurred dramatic increases in American R&D investments and the commitment to reach the moon before the Soviet Union. The lead the United States already had in ballistic missiles became obvious in the 1960s, as it met milestone after milestone in the quest to deploy strategic nuclear forces and build satellites to support them, all the while fighting a war in Vietnam and reaching the moon. As the Soviet Union sought to catch up, the United States began the investment in sensors and precision weapons that eventually undermined Soviet power and self-confidence. The American emphasis on strategic defenses, sometimes more potential than real, nevertheless threatened to cancel the advantages the Soviets had worked hard to achieve in nuclear missile numbers and warhead size.[18] The conventional warfare revolution took away the Red Army menace that had kept half of Europe in its grip and the other half in its fear for decades.[19] The Soviets lost hope of winning battles that were never fought.

Little of this R&D structure went away at the end of the Cold War. The increase in defense R&D spending that marked the Reagan Build-up was a ratchet. Today, the United States spends more on defense research, in real terms, than it did at the height of the Cold War. Defense industry mergers

---

[16] Harvey M. Sapolsky, Eugene Gholz, and Allen Kaufman, 'Security Lessons from the Cold War', *Foreign Affairs* 78/4 (July/August 1999), 77–89.
[17] Harvey M. Sapolsky, 'Models for Governing Large Systems Projects', in Guy Ben Ari and Pierre A. Chao, eds., *Organizing for a Complex World* (Washington, DC: Center for Strategic and International Studies, 2009).
[18] Frances Fitzgerald, *Way Out There in the Blue* (New York: Simon and Schuster, 2000).
[19] David T. Burbach, Brendan Rittenhouse Green, and Benjamin H. Friedman, 'The Technology of the Revolution in Military Affairs', in Harvey M. Sapolsky, Benjamin H. Friedman, and Brendan Rittenhouse Green, eds., *US Military Innovation since the Cold War* (New York: Routledge, 2009), 14–42.

and base closures reshuffled ownership of some military research facilities but did not shrink many of them. DOD employs nearly 100,000 people in 63 research laboratories and centers.[20] The FFRDCs and similar organizations continued their work supporting the military. The end of the Cold War was a dip, not a cliff.

Soft institutional factors: Incentives for innovation

What also didn't go away with the end of the Cold War were the incentives that drive American military innovation – the institutional factors or 'shared prescriptions guiding conduct [of] participants within the system' that drive the American defense innovation system.[21] There are at least three. One is a concern for avoiding casualties. A second is the rivalry that exists among the various components of the American defense establishment. And the third is the openness of American society to immigrants and their ideas.

The concern for avoiding casualties runs deep in American military operations and stems from both a persistent national labor shortage and the democratic nature of the American polity.[22] There were never enough people to build the country, thus the constant importation of labor, free or not, to tend the fields or run the factories. The earliest defense forces were militias made up of all local men, but it was difficult to assemble significant troops for expeditions or to keep them deployed for long because of the need for their labor back home. Mobilization for wars relied heavily on state forces, which varied in quality and commitment. Later resort to conscription was contentious and often produced evasion and rioting. The United States resisted the maintenance of a large, professional military until the 1950s.[23]

Even when the United States succumbed because of the Cold War, it sought to limit the military's growth through the intense application of technology. The World Wars drew the United States into the age of total war with huge armies, but the combat experience made the United States fully aware of the human costs inherent in modern industrialized warfare. The Army Air Corps became the champion of strategic bombing doctrine that called for fleets of bombers bypassing the carnage of the battlefield to destroy industries that were thought to be central to an opponent's power. Bombers themselves proved vulnerable in World War II, and when they failed

---

[20]'U.S. Military Technological Edge Challenged', *Army* (July 2017), 61.
[21]Cheung, 'A Conceptual Framework', (2021), 4.
[22]Harvey M. Sapolsky and Jeremy Shapiro, 'Casualties, Technology, and America's Future Wars', *Parameters* 26/2 (July 1999), 119–27.
[23]Tensions over manpower are a major theme in American military history. See, for example, Allan R. Millett, Peter Maslowski, and William Feis, *For the Common Defense: A Military History of the United States from 1607 to 2012* [3rd ed.] (New York: The Free Press, 2012); Joseph Glathaar, *The American Military: A Concise History* (New York: Oxford University Press, 2018); Paula G. Thornhill, *Demystifying the American Military: Institutions, Evolution, and Challenges since 1789* (Annapolis, MD: Naval Institute Press, 2019).

to achieve the intended strategic effects, air power advocates repeatedly promised that with just a little more technological progress they would achieve the precision and invulnerability needed to make the operational concept work.[24] The accuracy problem persisted through the Vietnam conflict, where the destruction of specific targets, usually bridges, often required risking the lives or capture of hundreds of pilots in multiple missions involving dozens upon dozens of aircraft each.[25] Given the limited goals at stake in such conflicts, individual losses mattered much politically. Thus, the great and successful effort to improve the accuracy of conventional weapons and the speed and stealth of the platforms that carry them to the point where if a target can be identified and located, it can be destroyed with little or no risk to American personnel.[26] The means depend upon the circumstance, often weather- or platform-determined, and include laser- and GPS-guided weapons. Now drones often take the place of manned aircraft.

The race to develop new weapons and doctrine is spurred on in the American system by inter-service competition.[27] The United States military, unlike those of nearly all big nations, is not dominated by one armed service, the Royal Navy in the United Kingdom or the Red Army in the Soviet Union. The United States does not fear invasions across its borders by foreign armies, nor does it need a navy to link it to distant colonies. Instead, each of its armed services seeks special prominence among the others as being the answer to emerging dangers or the foreign policy desires of the president. There is overlap and duplication in their efforts – and the incentive to innovate.

It was this competition that gave the United States the lead in the race to develop ballistic missiles and satellites of all types.[28] Civilian agencies, particularly the Central Intelligence Agency and the National Aeronautics and Space Administration, sometimes join in. The United States has several intelligence agencies, four air forces, three armies, and a navy or two, and each favors certain technologies and sees a particular threat best. They are rivals for attention, resources, and public acclaim.

The Goldwater-Nichols Act of 1986 and the intelligence reforms that followed the 9/11 terror attacks were intended to foster more cooperation and more central direction among the services and agencies. Certainly, the

---

[24]Eliot Cohen, 'The Mystique of U.S. Air Power', *Foreign Affairs* 73/1 (January/February 1994), 109–24.
[25]Marshall L. Michel, III, *Clashes: Air Combat over North Vietnam 1965–1972* (Annapolis: Naval Institute Press, 1997).
[26]Benjamin S. Lambeth, *The Transformation of American Air Power* (Ithaca, NY: Cornell University Press, 2000).
[27]This logic is extensively discussed, especially under the rubric of the 'enduring question' of the appropriate balance between markets and planning in defense policy, in Sapolsky et al., *U.S. Defense Politics*.
[28]Michael H. Armacost, *The Politics of Weapons Innovation: The Thor-Jupiter Controversy* (New York: Columbia University Press, 1969); Owen R. Coté, Jr., 'The Politics of Innovative Military Doctrine: The U.S. Navy and Fleet Ballistic Missiles' Ph.D. Dissertation (Cambridge, MA: Massachusetts Institute of Technology, 1995).

conflicts among the services are less visible, as all hail (in public) the virtues of Jointness. But it is a soft Jointness, more logrolling than subordination to a common doctrine or an agreed-upon set of priorities. The services still compete for attention and promote their vision of the threat that endangers the nation: witness the reactions of the Army and Marine Corps to the Navy- and Air Force-conceived AirSea Battle doctrine.

The resistance to centralization is protected first and foremost by the military services' strong cultures, with their proud traditions and their situations as 'total organizations' that control their members' entire lives. Even the civilians who work for the services tend to have a relatively strong sense of their organization's mission, compared to other government workers, because of the services' relatively clear definitions of their critical tasks, although the services are also notably complex organizations, and in other circumstances such complexity tends to dilute organizational identity. But in addition to the organizations' natural drive to nurture and protect their professional jurisdiction, Congress, which has often pushed for centralization and planning, also protects inter-service competition by separating out favored causes. At the same time that it passed Goldwater-Nichols, which emphasizes Jointness, Congress created the Special Operations Command, essentially a new service with its own global jurisdiction and budgetary independence. More recently, Congress has elevated cyberwarfare to a separate warfare command and laid the groundwork for the creation of a separate Marine Corps-like Space Corps from within the Air Force.[29] One hand praises centralization and planning while the other advocates decentralization and competition, the stimulants of innovation.

The military power of the United States also benefits from immigration, which is a continuing source of new ideas and great energy. John Ericsson, the much-admired 19th Century American naval engineer who promoted steam propulsion and ironclads, was born in Sweden. John Holland, the pioneer of the modern submarine, was born in Ireland. Igor Sikorsky, the developer of the helicopter, was born in Russia, as was Alexander P. de Seversky, the great promoter of air power. America got to the atomic bomb first, thanks to Albert Einstein and other Jewish refugees from Nazi Germany. In aviation William Boeing was of German origin, the Lockheed brothers were of Scottish descent, and John Knudsen Northrop's family was from Yorkshire. And Abraham Karem, the designer of the Predator drone, immigrated to the United States from Israel.[30]

Immigration may be under scrutiny in the United States these days, but illegal immigration is much more contentious than immigration itself. The United States still admits a million new permanent residents and naturalizes

---

[29]Sandra Erwin, 'Analyst predicts Space Force will fuel infighting among military services', *Space News*, 24 Oct. 2018.
[30]'Immigration and America's National Security', *Defense and Aerospace Report*, 17 Sept. 2018.

another three quarters of million people each year.[31] Immigrants are part of every aspect of American life, but most particularly science and engineering and every field of technology development that is relevant for defense – computer science, aeronautical engineering, nanotechnology, robotics. Just look at American universities or a list of Silicon Valley technology startups.[32] America's main military rivals have no immigrants or asylum seekers. None except desperate North Koreans fleeing an even-more-oppressive regime.

The irrelevance of reform

But doesn't the importance of private organizations (private firms and FFRDCs) for the development of military technology mean that the Department of Defense needs to take special care to connect to the most innovative parts of the United States like Silicon Valley, Cambridge, Massachusetts, and other centers of high technology? Relative labor scarcity and inter-service competition can help the military come up with ideas and wish lists for technology, but if the military intends to tap the technologies of the future, someone else is going to have to actually design and build the systems. Former Defense Secretary Ashton Carter set up initiatives like the DIUx (Defense Innovation Unit – experimental, now no longer experimental and known simply as DIU) during the Obama administration to make these connections, fueled by a concern that the military organizations' style is a poor fit for the modern American culture of innovation.[33] Will a new generation of research scientists relate well to defense's mission of breaking things and accommodate at all to its requirement to apply reams of acquisition rules to its contracts and to take months for reviews in order to make any decisions? Can the private-sector world of stock options and public offerings be a part of the public world of government shutdowns, salary freezes, and debt-ceiling crises?[34]

Because the Defense Department relies heavily upon prime contractors such as Lockheed Martin and Northrop Grumman to design and build its most advanced weapon systems, the technology question really is: can the existing prime contractors effectively use advances in technology to build the best weapon systems? There is no indication that they cannot. With these primes,

---

[31]Zolan Kanno-Youngs, 'As Trump Barricades the Border, Legal Immigration Is Starting to Plunge', *New York Times*, 24 Feb. 2020, A1; Nick Miroff and Josh Dawsey, 'Mulvaney says U.S. is "desperate" for more legal immigrants', *Washington Post*, 20 Feb. 2020.

[32]Remco Zwetsloot and Dahlia Peterson, 'The US-China Tech Wars: China's Immigration Disadvantage', *The Diplomat*, 31 Dec. 2019.

[33]Ashton Carter, 'Remarks Announcing DIUx 2.0,' Mountain View, California, 11 May 2016. Silicon Valley leaders are happy to parrot these arguments, as in Joe Gould, 'How the Pentagon's fear of risk is stifling innovation', *Defense News*, 28 Jan. 2019.

[34]Heather Somerville, 'China Has "Concerning" Leads Over U.S. in Tech, Defense Department Official Says', *Wall Street Journal*, 23 Oct. 2019; Ankit Panda, 'Getting Critical Technologies into U.S. Defense Applications', *National Interest (Online)*, 1 Feb. 2010.

the United States still builds the best weapon systems. The primes already are the integrators of technologies produced by others, including the commercially oriented firms that DIU and the other new agencies are meant to reach.[35] The primes' job is to bring together a network of subcontractors with the appropriate technology and skills and manage them to an exacting schedule and within certain budget limits to build systems that can survive and dominate in the harshest environment of them all, a battlefield, usually after traversing another difficult environment like space or the ocean to get to the fight. The technologies are important, but it is weaponizing them by creating complex systems that can work when stressed that counts the most, and that is what Lockheed, Northrop, and the other primes do for the American military.

The Department of Defense taps into advanced technology by funding some basic research and lots of applied science and engineering at universities through its own research support agencies and its set of service-specific laboratories.[36] For riskier efforts usually involving major prototyping or technology demonstrations, the military uses the Defense Advanced Research Projects Agency (DARPA).[37] The FFRDCs, national laboratories, and dozens of defense-supported specialized institutes are linked in with all of this and have their own ties to academic research. It is this system that gave the United States the lead position in computers, created the internet, pioneered work in oceanography and ocean engineering, and pushed capabilities in remote sensing and satellite imaging.

The Defense Innovation Unit initiative may help a little. So, too, may the Defense Department's Strategic Capabilities Office, the Defense Innovation Board, and the CIA's experimental venture capital unit In-Q-Tel.[38] These initiatives reinforce and complement what defense agencies in the United States have been doing for decades. More important, creating these agencies is also politically smart, as it shows defense agencies dealing directly with what the American public perceives to be the very cutting edge of technology and innovation. Likely unnecessary, but no harm done.

---

[35] For detailed analysis of the subcontractor network supporting U.S. defense acquisition, based on data on hundreds of defense-oriented and commercially oriented facilities as many as five tiers down in the supply chain, see Eugene Gholz, Andrew D. James, and Thomas H. Speller, 'The Second Face of Systems Integration: An Empirical Analysis of Supply Networks to Complex Product Systems', *Research Policy* 47/8 (October 2018), 1478–94.

[36] For extensive explanation of the defense science and technology (S&T) system, encompassing basic research, applied research, and advanced technology development, see Hugh Montgomery, *Bureaucratic Nirvana: Life in the Center of the Box* (Washington: Potomac Institute Press, 2010).

[37] For optimistic discussion of DARPA, see William B. Bonvillian, 'DARPA and its ARPA-E and IARPA Clones: A Unique Innovation Organization Model', *Industrial and Corporate Change*, 27/5 (October 2018), 897–914. For more skeptical discussion, see Sharon Weinberger, *The Imagineers of War* (New York: Knopf, 2017).

[38] 'Defense Innovation Board Chair: Recommendations Making an Impact', *Defense-Aerospace.com*, 25 Oct. 2017, http://www.defense-aerospace.com/articles-view/release/3/187880/pentagon%E2%80%99s-defense-innovation-board-sees-advances.html.

No harm unless the Department of Defense gets so caught up in pursuing the new organizations that it somehow forgets that what it really buys is the expertise in designing and building complex systems specifically for military roles. Systems integration works in any field because the integrators understand their customers' particularities and peculiarities. In defense, that means that the systems integrators that make complex weapons systems need to know a little bit about warfighting, the jargon that the military uses to talk about its unusual missions, and the political deal-making (organizational and electoral) that chooses which projects get funded and survive to eventual deployment with the operational military.[39] The commercial technology companies are already in the mix of weapon systems' supply chains, along with defense-unique suppliers; there is no real lack of technology access. And the commercial technology companies will never specialize in the defense-unique aspects of the weapons or be responsive enough to the military customers' quirks to produce cutting-edge military systems or to keep the demanding military customers happy and to work gracefully with them in the complex political ballet of defense acquisition. DIU and the rest are just a veneer, a new part of that political dance.

Perhaps the perceived decline in American power that worries some is due to failures in the acquisition system, problems with its structure and the inflexibility of its regulations. The Congress obviously thinks so, as it often prescribes changes in both. For example, it recently required that the jurisdiction of the Undersecretary of Defense for Acquisition, Technology and Logistics be divided into separate undersecretaries for research and engineering and for acquisition and sustainment on the argument that technology and innovation needed their own high-level champion within the Defense Department. Of course, it was not too long ago that predecessor offices were combined because, as the argument went, technology development, weapon system acquisition, and the maintenance of complex equipment need to be thought of as one continuous activity and closely coordinated. It is striking that the recent reorganization takes the wiring diagram of the Department of Defense more or less back to what it was in the late-1950s.[40]

There is no more common project in defense than acquisition reform. There have literally been dozens of congressionally mandated and secretarially commanded studies of the weapons acquisition process over the years. Changes in bureaucratic structure and regulatory detail have been constant. Too often unacknowledged in all of this is the difficulty gaining agreement within the fragmented American political system on the value, schedule, and cost of particular weapons. The defense budget is cyclical, with periods of rapid growth and inevitable decline as war fears grow and decline. Advocates

---

[39]Dombrowski and Gholz, *Buying Military Transformation*.
[40]Russell Rumbaugh, 'DoD Plan to Split Acquisition Duties', *CRS Insight*, 18 Aug. 2017.

of particular systems push for quick commitments on the upside, increasing the likelihood of project cost growth and performance failures, while opponents seek delays, hoping to catch the budget downside, when new starts and regular progress are hard to make. Proponents are optimists, and rivals are pessimists. Disappointments beset all complex undertakings, weapon acquisitions included. There are no reform cures for most acquisition problems.[41]

Some believe the problem lies in the Congress itself, its lack of regular order, the reliance on continuing resolutions and the threat of shutdowns. All of this is said to harm defense, disrupting planning, slowing modernization, and hurting force readiness. There certainly have been important changes in Congress in recent years. The growth of party extremes, weakening greatly the opportunity for compromise, is one. Another is the elimination of earmarking, which was a way to gather votes in exchange for funding favorite projects in particular districts. And a third is the weakening of the power of committee chairmen, who used to rule with iron fists.

But the incoherence in Congress on defense matters likely reflects more the disagreement over the nature and saliency of the threats the United States faces than it does the general political cleavages in the society. The partisan divide on defense is in fact weaker than it has been in past.[42] Gone also, though, is the imminent danger posed by the Soviet Union. Instead there is just a long list potential dangers – a resurgent Russia, a rising China, diffusing technologies, cyber hacking, terror threats, climate change – none galvanizing in the way the Soviet Union once was, all hidden off in some distant part of the globe, and many more potential than realized.[43]

The source of discontent

Why the insecurity, when the United States is a very secure country? Although American force structure was cut by about a third (from about 2.1 million to 1.4 million), little else in the security infrastructure created for the Cold War was downsized after the Soviet Union collapsed and the Warsaw Pact disbanded. Some Soviet experts left the field for new occupations, fleeing the unexpected wreckage that was suddenly their careers. But many other defense analysts did well by becoming ethnic-conflict experts or democracy-promotion specialists, the business of the day. Likely the threat assessment meetings were more relaxed sessions than in the past, and fewer serious

---

[41]Sapolsky et al., *U.S. Defense Politics*, 144–46, 148–52.
[42]Stephen M. Walt, *The Hell of Good Intentions: America's Foreign Policy Elite and the Decline of U.S. Primacy* (New York: Farrar, Straus, and Giraux, 2018); Barry R. Posen, *Restraint: A New Foundation for U.S. Grand Strategy* (Ithaca, NY: Cornell University Press, 2014), 4–9.
[43]Benjamin H. Friedman and Harvey M. Sapolsky, 'You Never Know(ism)', *Breakthroughs* (Spring 2006), 1–11.

military exercises were conducted, but nearly all of America's Cold War-focused think tanks, academic research institutes, and contract study groups stayed in place and began searching the globe for other security problems that could possibly replace the East/West one that had served so well as the source of their livelihoods for so long.

Business was good from the start because the American military did not go home, finding missions in Europe, Africa, and Asia trying to prevent ethnic slaughter or staving off famine and political chaos. The National Command Structure expanded rather contracted, adding four-star commands for North America and Africa to complete the globe-spanning regional listing and adding subordinate commands to the functional commands to raise the status of space or to give strategic warfare its due. As new developments occurred, accommodations were made for them: counter-terrorism operations and cyber defense joined the top tier along with nuclear proliferation.

The threat/policy opportunity radars have kept turning.[44] There is reward for identifying new dangers. Terrorism, cyber, and climate change threats have an endless quality to them, ideal to justify continuing planning efforts and making new budget requests.[45] The United States built up a large threat assessment apparatus to ask 'what if' questions for the Cold War. That apparatus, like the defense research and innovation establishment, was not disbanded at war's end. It finds the threats for the others to solve.

The United States pays a lot to avoid being surprised. Part of that price pays for people and organizations that constantly call out dangers, potential gaps, or failures in its multiple layers of defenses. Analysts warn that America is not ready for biological warfare, that its cyber defenses are inadequate, and that it hasn't been paying enough attention to space. Worse, they say, the Defense Department is too slow in fielding this system or that, there is too much red tape, and there is not enough initiative. They call for a defense budget big enough to build the 355-ship Navy, a new strategic bomber, and a new generation of modernized nuclear weapons. These continuing calls for defense investment, especially in new technologies, keep the U.S. defense R&D system on its toes, well supplied with inputs and opportunities to capitalize on the incentives to generate innovations.

The result of such vigilance about strategy and policy maintains a vast network of laboratories, institutes, test ranges, and development centers – public and private, secret and open – that is working on every frontier trying to build better weapons. The network is bigger than everyone else's, and it is better funded. No nation devotes more resources to defense innovation, and

---

[44]David M. Edelstein and Ronald R. Krebs, 'Delusions of Grand Strategy: The Problem with Washington's Planning Obsession', *Foreign Affairs* 94/6 (November/December 2015), 109–16; Michael A. Cohen and Micah Zenko, *Clear and Present Safety: The World Has Never Been Better and Why that Matters to Americans* (New Haven, CT: Yale University Press, 2019).

[45]Alexander Osipovich, 'Pentagon Pits Traders vs. Hackers', *The Wall Street Journal*, 16 Oct. 2017, B1.

no nation has stronger pro-innovation institutions and incentives. The United States spends a lot to make sure that it will continue to be able to respond to every imaginable threat – and to be able to threaten everyone else.

Disclosure statement

No potential conflict of interest was reported by the author(s).

Funding

This work was supported by, or in part by, the U.S. Army Research Laboratory and the U.S. Army Research Office under contract/grant No. W911NF-15-1-0407. Any opinions, findings, and conclusions or recommendations expressed in this publication are those of the author(s) and do not necessarily reflect the views of the U.S. Army Research Office.

Bibliography

Alic, John A., 'The Origin and Nature of the US "Military-industrial Complex"', *Vulcan* 2/1 (June 2014), 63–97. doi:10.1163/22134603-00201003.

Armacost, Michael H., *The Politics of Weapons Innovation: The Thor-Jupiter Controversy* (New York: Columbia University Press 1969).

Beckley, Michael, *Unrivaled: Why America Will Remain the World's Sole Superpower* (Ithaca: Cornell University Press 2018).

Bonvillian, William B., 'DARPA and Its ARPA-E and IARPA Clones: A Unique Innovation Organization Model', *Industrial and Corporate Change* 27/5 (October 2018), 897–914. doi:10.1093/icc/dty026.

Brose, Christian, *The Kill Chain: Defending America in the Future of High-Tech Warfare* (New York: Hachette 2020).

Burbach, David T., Brendan Rittenhouse Green, and Benjamin H. Friedman, 'The Technology of the Revolution in Military Affairs', in Harvey M. Sapolsky, Benjamin H. Friedman, and Brendan Rittenhouse Green (eds.), *US Military Innovation since the Cold War* (New York: Routledge 2009), 14–42.

Cheung, Tai Ming, 'A Conceptual Framework of Defence Innovation', *Journal of Strategic Studies* (2021), doi:10.1080/01402390.2021.1939689.

Cohen, Eliot, 'The Mystique of U.S. Air Power', *Foreign Affairs* 73/1 (January/February 1994), 109–24. doi:10.2307/20045895.

Cohen, Michael A. and Micah Zenko, *Clear and Present Safety: The World Has Never Been Better and Why that Matters to Americans* (New Haven, CT: Yale University Press 2019).

Coté, Owen R., Jr., 'The Politics of Innovative Military Doctrine: The U.S. Navy and Fleet Ballistic Missiles', Ph.D. Dissertation, Massachusetts Institute of Technology, Cambridge, MA, 1995.

Dombrowski, Peter J. and Eugene Gholz, *Buying Military Transformation: Technological Innovation and the Defense Industry* (New York: Columbia University Press 2006).

Edelstein, David M. and Ronald R. Krebs, 'Delusions of Grand Strategy: The Problem with Washington's Planning Obsession', *Foreign Affairs* 94/6 (November/December 2015), 109–16.

Eliason, Leslie C. and Emily O. Goldman, 'Introduction: Theoretical and Comparative Perspectives on Innovation and Diffusion', in Emily O. Goldman and Leslie C. Eliason (eds.), *The Diffusion of Military Technology and Ideas* (Stanford, CA: Stanford University Press 2003), 1–30.

Fitzgerald, Frances, *Way Out There in the Blue* (New York: Simon and Schuster 2000).

Friedman, Benjamin H. and Harvey M. Sapolsky, 'You Never Know(ism)', *'Breakthroughs* (Spring 2006), 15/1, 1–11.

Gholz, Eugene, Benjamin Friedman, and Enea Gjoza, 'Defensive Defense: A Better Way to Protect U.S. Allies in Asia', *The Washington Quarterly* 42/4 (Winter 2019-2020), 171–89. doi:10.1080/0163660X.2019.1693103.

Gholz, Eugene, Andrew D. James, and Thomas H. Speller, 'The Second Face of Systems Integration: An Empirical Analysis of Supply Networks to Complex Product Systems', *Research Policy* 47/8 (October 2018), 1478–94. doi:10.1016/j.respol.2018.05.001.

Giles, Martin, 'The Father of Quantum', *Technology Review* 122/1 (January/February 2019), 56–59.

Gilli, Andrea and Mauro Gilli, 'Why China Has Not Caught up Yet: Military-Technological Superiority and the Limits of Imitation, Reverse Engineering, and Cyber Espionage', *International Security* 43/3 (Winter 2018/2019), 141–89. doi:10.1162/isec_a_00337.

Glathaar, Joseph, *The American Military: A Concise History* (New York: Oxford University Press 2018).

Goldman, Emily O., 'Introduction: Military Diffusion and Transformation', in Emily O. Goldman and Thomas G. Mahnken (eds.), *The Information Revolution in Military Affairs in Asia* (New York: Palgrave MacMillan 2004), 1–21.

Hartley, Keith, 'Defense R&D Spending: A Critical Review of the Economic Data', *World Economics* 12/1 (January-March 2011), 103–14.

International Institute for Strategic Studies (IISS), *The Military Balance 2018* (London: Taylor & Francis 2018).

Krepinevich, Andrew F., Jr., 'How to Deter China: The Case for Archipelagic Defense', *Foreign Affairs* 94/2 (March/April 2015), 78–86.

Lambeth, Benjamin S., *The Transformation of American Air Power* (Ithaca, NY: Cornell University Press 2000).

Liff, Adam P. and Andrew S. Erickson, 'Demystifying China's Defense Spending: Less Mysterious in the Aggregate', *The China Quarterly* 216 (December 2013), 805–30. doi:10.1017/S0305741013000295.

Michel, Marshall L., III, *Clashes: Air Combat over North Vietnam 1965-1972* (Annapolis: Naval Institute Press 1997).

Millett, Allan R., Peter Maslowski, and William Feis, *For the Common Defense: A Military History of the United States from 1607 to 2012* 3rd ed. (New York: The Free Press 2012).

Montgomery, Hugh, *Bureaucratic Nirvana: Life in the Center of the Box* (Washington: Potomac Institute Press 2010).

Posen, Barry R., *Restraint: A New Foundation for U.S. Grand Strategy* (Ithaca, NY: Cornell University Press 2014).

Sapolsky, Harvey M., *Science and the Navy: The History of the Office of Naval Research* (Princeton NJ: Princeton University Press 1990).

Sapolsky, Harvey M., 'Models for Governing Large Systems Projects', in Guy Ben Ari and Pierre A. Chao (eds.), *Organizing for a Complex World,* 24–30. (Washington, DC: Center for Strategic and International Studies 2009).

Sapolsky, Harvey M., Eugene Gholz, and Allen Kaufman, 'Security Lessons from the Cold War', *Foreign Affairs* 78/4 (July/August 1999), 77–89. doi:10.2307/20049366.

Sapolsky, Harvey M., Eugene Gholz, and Caitlin Talmadge, *U.S. Defense Politics: The Origins of Security Policy* 3rd ed. (New York: Routledge 2017).

Sapolsky, Harvey M. and Jeremy Shapiro, 'Casualties, Technology, and America's Future Wars', *Parameters* 26/2 (July 1999), 119–27.

Thornhill, Paula G., *Demystifying the American Military: Institutions, Evolution, and Challenges since 1789* (Annapolis, MD: Naval Institute Press 2019).

Walt, Stephen M., *The Hell of Good Intentions: America's Foreign Policy Elite and the Decline of U.S. Primacy* (New York: Farrar, Straus, and Giraux 2018).

Weinberger, Sharon, *The Imagineers of War* (New York: Knopf 2017).

China's quest for quantum advantage—Strategic and defense innovation at a new frontier

Elsa B. Kania

ABSTRACT
China has prioritized quantum science and technology as a critical frontier for its national security and development. To date, Chinese research has already reached a leading position within the discipline, enabled by state support and funding, as well as the recruitment and cultivation of talent. The rapid advances on this front can provide a valuable illustration of the dynamics of China's evolving innovation ecosystem, including the increased prominence of leading technology companies, and even start-ups, as serious contenders. China's strategy of military–civil fusion, which aims to create a more integrated ecosystem in science and technology, can contribute to enabling progress in dual-use developments. This case study draws upon the shared framework for this special issue, which provides a method by which to consider the factors that enable defense innovation. Looking forward, these advances could prove consequential for the future strategic balance between China and the United States.

Introduction

The future trajectory of U.S.–China strategic competition will be influenced by advances in emerging technologies that could contribute to growth in new industries and enable future military capabilities. U.S.–China rivalry has been intensifying at a moment when rapid advances in science and technology are poised to catalyze a new industrial revolution. In the view of China's leaders, this is a time of 'profound changes unseen in a century', including those catalyzed by such technological transformation, that may accelerate the potential for power transition.[1] In

---

[1]'In the 24th collective study session of the Political Bureau of the Central Committee, Xi Jinping a the profound understanding of the significance of advancing the development of quantum science and technology' [习近平在中央政治局第二十四次集体学习时强调 深刻认识推进量子科技发展重大意义], Xinhua, 17 October 2020, http://www.xinhuanet.com/politics/2020-10/17/c_1126623288.htm.

particular, quantum technology is recognized to possess great importance to China's national security and economic development.[2] Such developments also could change the character of conflict, perhaps disrupting the future military and strategic balance between great powers.

As a latecomer, China has strived to catch up by all means available.[3] In the past, China was relegated to a position of relative backwardness, only able to be a fast follower in looking to keep pace with the technologies of the time. Traditionally, China's efforts in indigenous innovation have leveraged the absorption of foreign technologies, including through licit technology transfer and industrial espionage.[4] There have been ongoing initiatives directed to the 'going out' and 'bringing in' of overseas talent and foreign advanced technologies.[5] While calling for open science and looking to promote research cooperation, China's policies have still looked to leverage 'international innovation resources' through targeted investments and acquisitions, as well as joint ventures and overseas research centers.[6]

At present, China's ambitions in innovation are evolving toward a new paradigm with the aim to undertake original, disruptive innovation. China's leaders regard this moment as one of historic opportunity. Xi Jinping has positioned 'innovation-driven' development at the center of his strategy, even ideology.[7] In China's pursuit of national rejuvenation, strengthening the nation through science and technology (科技强国) and thereby becoming a powerful country in science and technology in turn are regarded as important elements of this agenda.[8] 'The second quantum revolution is the first technological revolution in which our country has the ability and

---

[2]There are a range of commentaries and perspectives from experts and scientists. See, for instance: 'How important is quantum technology to China? Experts: Quantum technology is a strategic domain related to national security and high-quality social and economic development' [量子科技对中国有多重要? 专家:量子科技是事关国家安全和社会经济高质量发展的战略性领域], *Global Times*, 20 October 2020, https://world.huanqiu.com/article/40MwRNUcSEw.

[3]For an academic assessment of the challenges of catching up, particularly in contemporary technologies of greater complexity, see: Andrea Gilli and Mauro Gilli, 'Why China Has Not Caught Up Yet: Military-Technological Superiority and the Limits of Imitation, Reverse Engineering, and Cyber Espionage', International Security 43/3 (2019), 141–189.

[4]Hannas, William C., James Mulvenon, and Anna B. Puglisi. *Chinese industrial espionage: Technology acquisition and military modernization*. Routledge, 2019.

[5]Miao Lü [苗绿], Wang Huiyao [王辉耀], Zheng Jinlian [郑金连], 'Science and Technology Talent Policy Boots Construction of World Science and Technology Power – – Take International Science and Technology Talent Introduction Policy as An Example' [科技人才政策助推世界科技强国建设 – – 以国际科技人才引进政策突破为例], Bulletin of Chinese Academy of Sciences [中国科学院院刊], 2017.

[6]Ibid.

[7]See the official strategy released on innovation-driven development, "The CCP Central Commission and State Council Release the 'National Innovation-Driven Development Strategy Outline' [中共中央 国务院印发《国家创新驱动发展战略纲要》], Xinhua, 19 May 2016, http://news.xinhuanet.com/politics/2016-05/19/c_1118898033.htm.

[8]'Xi Jinping: More than any other period in history, we need to build a world powerhouse in science and technology' [习近平:我们比历史上任何时期都更需要建设世界科技强国], Learning China [学习中国], 5 June 2018, https://china.huanqiu.com/article/9CaKrnK97ka.

foundation to fully get involved and participate in hundreds of years' according to Xue Qikun, director of the Beijing Academy of Quantum Information Sciences at Tsinghua University.[9]

The Chinese government has continued to mobilize state support to advance a series of national megaprojects to which sizable amounts of funding have been dedicated, while undertaking active efforts to recruit and educate top talent. For the period of the 14th Five-Year Plan and beyond,[10]

China's initiatives in quantum science and technology may only accelerate.[11] As Pan Jianwei, often described as the 'father of quantum' in China, has argued, advent of the 'second quantum revolution' gives China a 'historic opportunity to transform from a follower and imitator in the era of classical information technology to a leader in information technology in the future'.[12] He has urged that his country must, 'Take the lead in the world to master disruptive technologies that can form first-mover advantages', thereby 'leading future development of disruptive technologies'.

At the same time, China's national strategy of military–civil fusion (军民融合) seeks to create a more integrated ecosystem for technological development, including through partnerships in scientific research. The capacity to leverage commercial developments, including advances from China's nascent quantum industry, could provide important contributions to future military capabilities.[13] In particular, the Chinese People's Liberation Army (PLA) is pursuing defense innovation with the objective to become a 'world-class' military.[14] The PLA seeks to capitalize upon opportunities presented by the operationalization of technologies and emerging capabilities that are believed to contribute to an ongoing Revolution in Military Affairs (RMA).[15]

---

[9]'The quantum technology revolution is a major historical opportunity' [量子科技革命是重大历史机遇], Global Times, 16 January 2021, https://tech.huanqiu.com/article/41Y8oTNbqKs.
[10]'Zhao Yong: The "14th Five-Year Plan" is a critical period for rapid breakthroughs in quantum information' [赵勇:'十四五'是量子信息快速突破关键时期], 11 March 2021, http://news.sciencenet.cn/htmlnews/2021/3/454421.shtm.
[11]'Seize the commanding heights of quantum technology: Interview with Pan Jianwei, member of the National Committee of the Chinese People's Political Consultative Conference and academician of the Chinese Academy of Sciences' [抢占量子科技制高点：访全国政协委员、中国科学院院士潘建伟], Central Commission for Discipline Inspection and State Supervision Commission website, 10 March 2021, http://www.ccdi.gov.cn/yaowen/202103/t20210310_237524.html.
[12]Pan Jianwei [潘建伟], 'Better promote the development of my country's quantum technology' [更好推进我国量子科技发展], Red Flag Manuscript [红旗文稿], 8 December 2020.
[13]For a more detailed assessment, see also: Elsa B. Kania and John K. Costello, 'Quantum Hegemony? – China's Ambitions and the Challenge to U.S. Innovation Leadership', Center for a New American Security, September 2018, https://www.cnas.org/publications/reports/quantum-hegemony.
[14]'Xi Jinping: strive to achieve the party's goal of strengthening the army in the new era and building the people's Army into a world-class army in an all-round way' [习近平:为实现党在新时代的强军目标把人民军队全面建成世界一流军队而奋斗], Xinhua, 26 October 2017, http://www.xinhuanet.com/politics/19cpcnc/2017-10/26/c_1121862632.htm.
[15]'China's National Defense in the New Era' [新时代的中国国防], State Council Information Office [国务院新闻办公室], 24 July 2019, http://www.xinhuanet.com/politics/2019-07/24/c_1124792450.htm.

Analytical approach

China's quantum science, industry, and technologies present a case study for a new paradigm of innovation. The analytic approach draws upon the framework developed by Dr Cheung, which created a typology for and identified factors that enable defense innovation: catalyts, input and resources, organizations, and networks, as well as contextual influences, that create the conditions for outputs.[16] Since quantum science and technology as a domain remain at a nascent stage in development, this case study provides, at best, an initial analysis of these factors. Instead, this assessment seeks to establish a foundation for continued research by examining several factors that will be important to evaluate recent advances and anticipate future progress in these domains. To evaluate the state of play and future potential of complex technologies that are so rapidly evolving is inherently challenging, yet a systematic consideration of the salient factors can provide a useful baseline from which to track future trends.

The state of play in China's quantum science and technology suggests the start of a far-reaching transformation of its national capabilities in innovation, especially in dual-use and defense technologies. Whereas its past model was primarily absorptive in nature, today's research in quantum science and advances in quantum technology involves more original innovation and cutting-edge discoveries at new frontiers. Chinese research is already leading in implementation and applications of quantum communications, contesting the forefront of efforts in quantum computing, and pursuing robust developments in quantum precision measurement. So too, the PLA has been seeking not merely to catch up but also to establish potential advantages in its own right, even seeking to design future warfare through pursuing emerging technologies and capabilities. Looking forward, China's prospects for success in innovation remain contingent upon its capacity to overcome certain critical chokepoints and various bottlenecks, such as in semiconductors. Regardless, the progress in quantum science and technology to date has already illustrated a story of striking successes that appear on track to continue in the years ahead.

China's innovation imperative

Innovation has become a prime imperative within China's agenda for national rejuvenation. Although science and technology have long been recognized as critical drivers of national development, the importance of innovation has been further heightened during Xi Jinping's tenure. In

---

[16]For the initial articulation of this framework, see: Tai Ming Cheung, Thomas Mahnken, and Andrew Ross, 'Frameworks for Analyzing Chinese Defense and Military Innovation', Study of Innovation and Technology in China, 2011, https://escholarship.org/uc/item/5cr8j76s.

particular, the Outline of the National Strategy for Innovation-Driven Development, released in 2016 by the Politburo and State Council, has elevated its centrality as a parading for China's growth and trajectory toward rejuvenation.[17] This strategy highlights that technology has been critical throughout history to the rise and fall of great powers.[18] In the past, when China was unable to keep pace with the technologies of the era, its relative weakness enabled predation by foreign powers. Resultingly, the Chinese government has looked to increase capacity in indigenous innovation, whether based on the transfer and leveraging of foreign technologies and knowledge, or through ongoing initiatives intended to bolster China's innovation ecosystem. Unlike in its history, China is today poised with the potential to be a major contender, even potential leader, within these latest frontiers.

Today, China's leaders believe the nation's prospects to rise as a great power will depend upon increasing its capability in innovation. In particular, the rapid advances in emerging technologies, which are believed to be catalyzing a new industrial revolution, present particular challenges and opportunities. Consequently, China has been pursuing an array of policies intended to capitalize upon this potential of disruptive technologies and mitigate the threat of technological disadvantage. Among the salient trends in PRC policy have been gradual increases in spending on basic research and new guidance funds that target investment to emerging industries. The Chinese government has also undertaken plans and initiatives aimed at the cultivation and recruitment of top talent. In parallel, the continued operationalization of military–civil fusion as national strategy has been intended to coordinate and leverage critical synergies in domains that are recognized as essential to China's economic and military transformation, including quantum science and technology.[19]

---

[17] See the official strategy released on innovation-driven development, 'The CCP Central Commission and State Council Release the 'National Innovation-Driven Development Strategy Outline' [中共中央 国务院印发《国家创新驱动发展战略纲要》], Xinhua, 19 May 2016, http://news.xinhuanet.com/politics/2016-05/19/c_1118898033.htm. See also Xi Jinping's remarks on this approach in the context of military modernization: 'Xi Jinping: Comprehensively Advance an Innovation-Driven Development Strategy, Promote New Leaps in National Defence and Military Construction' [习近平:全面实施创新驱动发展战略 推动国防和军队建设实现新跨越], Xinhua, 13 March 2016, http://news.xinhuanet.com/politics/2016lh/2016-03/13/c_1118316426.htm.

[18] 'Xi Jinping: Accurately Grasp the New Trend in Global Military Developments and Keep Pace with the Times, Strongly Advancing Military Innovation' [习近平:准确把握世界军事发展新趋势 与时俱进大力推进军事创新], Xinhua, 30 August 2014, http://news.xinhuanet.com/politics/2014-08/30/c_1112294869.htm.

[19] 'Military-Civil Fusion Development Committee Established' [军民融合发展委成立], Xinhua, 23 January 2017, http://news.xinhuanet.com/finance/2017-01/23/c_129458492.htm. '13th Five-Year Science and Technology Military-Civil Fusion Development Special Plan' (Full Text) ['十三五'科技军民融合发展专项规划》全文].

Indeed, quantum science and technology has been a consistent direction of development under the 13th Five-Year Plan (2016–2020) and is reaffirmed as a major project for the 14th Five-Year Plan (2021–2025) and beyond.[20] These efforts have started to yield notable dividends. According to Pan Jianwei, as a generalized assessment, China is now 'in global leading status in the research and application of quantum communications, at the same level line as developed countries in quantum computing, and rapidly developing in quantum precision measurement'.[21] These trends and this trajectory will continue to merit analytic and academic attention.

The advent of quantum science and technology

While American research had initially pioneered progress within the discipline, China today aspires to lead the 'second quantum revolution', by which continued advances in quantum science have been enabling advances in new and potentially disruptive technologies.[22] While the first quantum revolution had enabled novel discoveries about the nature of reality, this second revolution introduces the potential to realize new capabilities based on these advances. The principles of quantum physics, often paradoxical, can be leveraged as a means of developing hitherto unprecedented technologies. With advances in quantum cryptography comes the possibility of advances in security that may allow for 'provable security' for information and communications. The creation of a 'quantum bit' (qubit) that can be in a superposition of 0 and 1 could increase computing capabilities dramatically. Meanwhile, advances in quantum precision measurement promise greater accuracy and sensitivity than would be possible through classical techniques. However, in each case, the technology in question and its applications remain nascent and uncertain, yet there is often hype that can generate exuberant expectations that outpace technical realities and difficulties that remain.

The advent of quantum technology may have significant implications for cybersecurity, military affairs, and economic competitiveness. When used to secure sensitive communications, such as that of military, government, or

---

[20] 'Xi Jinping: Explanation of the "Proposals of the CCP Central Committee on Formulating the 14th Five-Year Plan for National Economic and Social Development and Long-Term Goals for 2035" [习近平:关于《中共中央关于制定国民经济和社会发展第十四个五年规划和二〇三五年远景目标的建议》的说明], Xinhua, 3 November 2020, https://web.archive.org/web/20201212142251/http://www.xinhuanet.com/politics/leaders/2020-11/03/c_1126693341.htm.

[21] 'Quantum Science and Technology: It is necessary to sit firmly on the top of the pyramid, but also promote to the general public' [量子科技: 既要稳坐金字塔尖,也要走向普罗大众], S&T Daily, 4 March 2021, http://www.stdaily.com/zhuanti/lhssw/2021-03/04/content_1085408.shtml.

[22] See: Manjit Kumar, Quantum: Einstein, Bohr, and the Great Debate about the Nature of Reality, W. W. Norton & Company, 2011. Jonathan P. Dowling and Gerard J. Milburne, 'Quantum Technology: the Second Quantum Revolution', Philosophical Transactions of the Royal Society of London A: Mathematical, Physical and Engineering Sciences 361/1809 (2003), 1655–1674, https://arxiv.org/pdf/quant-ph/0206091.pdf.

financial institutions, quantum cryptography can allow for unique security, perhaps defending against intrusion or espionage, or so intended at the very least. By contrast, the eventual realization of quantum computing could allow for immense capabilities that will be applicable for a range of general and specialized applications.[23] Infamously and troublingly, a potential application of quantum computing is anticipated to occur based on Shor's algorithm, which can be used to factor large numbers. This technique can be employed to break the public-key cryptography upon which so much of the modern Internet depends. Beyond that, even early variants of quantum computing are starting to be used in machine learning or for research in biology and chemistry.[24] And quantum precision measurement could enable new options for detection or navigation with salient military and commercial applications.[25]

Although the future trajectory of quantum technologies remains difficult to predict, recognition of their potential and possible strategic importance has started to intensify the international competition that is underway to advance their development and applications. China has been undertaking major plays to accelerate progress in quantum science, technology, and industries that will likely be leveraged for impactful commercial and important military applications. As a national priority, this major project is advancing, including through the construction of a new national laboratory. In parallel, and to some degree in response, the United States has also launched the National Quantum Initiative as a federal program to accelerate quantum research at scale, yet the scale of this effort has been critiqued as inadequate relative to the potential opportunities.[26] Such national initiatives in quantum science, as well as new entrants among leading technology companies and start-up enterprises, may spur progress but also create challenges to the open character of research in this domain, which has remained collaborative and relatively international throughout much of its history. Rivalry may spur progress but may also undercut the global research cooperation that had been critical to early stages of development.

This article provides an initial overview of factors that have created conditions for China's efforts to become a leading player in quantum science and technology. This analysis will look in turn at the catalytic factors, input

---

[23]Li, Rongji, Juan Xu, Jiabin Yuan, and Dan Li, 'An Introduction to Quantum Machine Learning Algorithms', In *Proceedings of the 9th International Conference on Computer Engineering and Networks*, pp. 519–532. Springer, Singapore, 2021. Huang, Y., Hang Lei, and Xiao-Yu Li, 'A survey on quantum machine learning', *Chinese Journal of Computers* 41/1 (2018), 145–163.

[24]Liu, Hua-Ying, Xiao-Hui Tian, Changsheng Gu, Pengfei Fan, Xin Ni, Ran Yang, Ji-Ning Zhang et al. 'Optical-relayed entanglement distribution using drones as mobile nodes', *Physical Review Letters* 126/2 (2021), 020503.

[25]For instance, the University of Science and Technology of China set up a group specializing in quantum precision measurement in 2010. See: 'Quantum Precision Measurement Group', http://staff.ustc.edu.cn/~gyxiang/en/.

[26]See: 'quantum.gov', https://www.quantum.gov/.

resources, organizations, and networks that have shaped progress in this discipline, while also examining initial outputs in this discipline, in accordance with the shared framework used for this special issue. While neither complete nor comprehensive, this assessment thereby attempts to contribute to an understanding of the influences and determinants of China's innovation in emerging technologies.

Factors for China's quantum innovation.

Catalysts	Inputs or resources	Organizations	Networks	Outputs
Cyber insecurity (e.g., Snowden incident)	Funding for basic research	S&T plans and policies	Research partnerships among academia, industry, defense	Quantum satellite (Micius) and experimental advancements
Leadership attentions and National quantum	prioritization	Support from local governments	Major projects and 'flagship program' communications infrastructure	National quantum laboratory and research network
National prestige and	prominence	Recruitment and cultivation of top talent	Leading academic institutions (e.g., CAS, USTC)	Military–civil fusion initiatives and partnerships
Initial progress in quantum computing (e.g., Jiuzhang, Zu Chongzhi)				
Foundation from prior successes	Initial			commercialization
Major commercial enterprises	Exchange with global research community	Prototypes for precision measurement		

This table is not necessarily comprehensive nor is every factor included discussed at length.

Catalytic factors

Cybersecurity concerns

Within the past decade, the discipline of quantum science and technology has become a core priority in China's agenda for innovation. Among the initial impetuses for support to research and development at this scientific frontier came from cybersecurity threats. In particular, leaks by NSA contractor Edward Snowden in May 2013 had heightened the anxieties of Chinese leaders about the country's information insecurity. This incident had revealed the extent of U.S. intelligence capabilities and activities within China – and thereby heightened awareness about its susceptibility to foreign cyber espionage. Chinese scientists, especially Pan Jianwei, advocated in response for quantum communications as a means of providing notionally 'unconditional' security.[27] Notably, the documents that Snowden leaked also revealed at the time the NSA was investing in the development of quantum computing through a program called 'Penetrating Hard Targets' with the aim of achieving the capability to break encryption.[28]

This incident thus reinforced the perceived importance of quantum science and technology to national security, while intensifying concerns in China about falling behind relative to U.S. capabilities.[29] Consequently, the use of quantum cryptography to allow for more secure communications emerged as a potential solution that has been said to allow for 'absolute security'.[30] Indeed, Xi Jinping, along with other Politburo members, had visited a company specialized this technique and observed a demonstration of quantum communications not long afterward, in September 2013.[31] Due to the apparent impacts of the leaks, Snowden has even been characterized in PRC state media as one of two individuals with primary involvement in the drama of China's quantum agenda, along with Pan Jianwei himself.[32]

Since, Chinese scientists have been provided seemingly extensive resources on this front.[33] However, any promises of perfect security are very likely to be illusory in actuality. Moreover, according to recent statements from the National Security Agency, the added utility of quantum cryptography relative to classical techniques is limited at most and when compared to the best classical

---

[27]'Demystifying the world's first quantum satellite – – Toward the door to "unconditional secure communication"' [揭秘全球首颗量子卫星 – – 迈向'无条件安全通信'的大门], China Youth Daily, August 117, 2016, https://www.cas.cn/zt/kjzt/lzwx/jzjd/201608/t20160817_4571527.shtml.

[28]'Snowden revealed that the U.S. Security Agency is developing a quantum computer that can decipher any code' [斯诺登曝美国安局正研发量子计算机 可破译任何密码], People's Daily International,6 January 2014, http://world.people.com.cn/n/2014/0106/c157278-24034339.html. Steven Rich and Barton Gellman, 'NSA seeks to build quantum computer that could crack most types of encryption', The Washington Post, 2 January 2014, https://www.washingtonpost.com/world/national-security/nsa-seeks-to-build-quantum-computer-that-could-crack-most-types-of-encryption/2014/01/02/8fff297e-7195-11e3-8def-a33011492df2_story.html.

[29]'China Will Establish a Global Quantum Communications Network By 2030' [中国将力争在2030年前后建成全球量子通信网], Xinhua, 16 August 2016, http://news.sina.com.cn/c/sd/2016-08-16/doc-ifxuxnpy9658879.shtml.

[30]Xu, Feihu, Xiongfeng Ma, Qiang Zhang, Hoi-Kwong Lo, and Jian-Wei Pan. 'Secure quantum key distribution with realistic devices', Reviews of Modern Physics 92/2 (2020), 025002.

[31]'Anhui Quantum Communications Innovation Successfully Featured in Politburo Collective Learning Activities' [安徽量子通信创新成果 亮相中央政治局集体学习活动], Quantum CTek, 30 September 2013, http://www.quantum-sh.com/news/146.html.

[32]'China Will Establish a Global Quantum Communications Network By 2030' [中国将力争在2030年前后建成全球量子通信网], Xinhua, 16 August 2016, http://news.sina.com.cn/c/sd/2016-08-16/doc-ifxuxnpy9658879.shtml.

[33]This is said to be the case based on conversations with Chinese academics.

alternatives, including options for new types of 'quantum-resistant' cryptography.[34] The discrepancy between the significant developments in quantum encryption and communications in China relative to more skeptical regard for the benefits of such capabilities within the United States highlights an interesting divergence in outlook and prioritization. At present, debate remains whether the leveraging of quantum cryptography and communications at scale may yield dividends that exceed American expectations, or whether this program in China should be regarded as a suboptimal investment given the current expectation of perhaps modest increases in security and continued technical limitations.

Prestige and leadership prioritization

Given the dual impetus of insecurity and opportunity, quantum science has attracted the attention of China's leadership at the highest levels. Xi Jinping has personally emphasized the strategic importance of quantum science and technology in China's national security, especially in cybersecurity. While one among multiple priorities, quantum technology has been consistently emphasized in a new round of PRC S&T policies and planning. Notably, quantum computing and communications were included in the list of major science and technology projects prioritized for major breakthroughs by 2030 as of November 2015.[35] In April 2016, Xi visited the University of Science and Technology of China, a trip during which he praised Pan's progress.[36]

China's agenda in quantum science first captured the world's attention in earnest with its launch of the world's first quantum satellite, Micius (墨子) in August 2016. This milestone was featured prominently in state media, lauded as a signifier of China's prowess in science and technology, and also captured headlines around the world. While a quantum satellite was not itself a dramatic breakthrough, the launch of Mozi created a platform and provided a unique capability that set the stage for future experimental advancements, including new records that commanded more news coverage. Thereafter, Xi Jinping again emphasized the importance of advancing indigenous

---

[34] 'NSA Cybersecurity Perspectives on Quantum Key Distribution and Quantum Cryptography', 26October 2020. https://www.nsa.gov/News-Features/Feature-Stories/Article-View/Article/2394053/nsa-cybersecurity-perspectives-on-quantum-key-distribution-and-quantum-cryptogr/.

[35] 'Xi Jinping: Explanations Regarding the 'CCP Central Committee Suggestions Regarding the Formation of the National Economic and Social Development Thirteenth Five-Year Plan' [习近平:关于《中共中央关于制定国民经济和社会发展第十三个五年规划的建议》的说明], *Xinhua*, 3 November 2015, http://news.xinhuanet.com/politics/2015-11/03/c_1117029621_3.htm.

[36] 'Xi Jinping Inspected USTC: Must Advance Independent Innovation in the Process of Opening' [习近平考察中科大:要在开放中推进自主创新], *Xinhua*, 27 April 2016, http://news.xinhuanet.com/politics/2016-04/27/c_1118744858.htm.

innovation in quantum communications, among other critical cyber and information technologies, during a Politburo study session on cybersecurity in October 2016.[37]

As global concern and international competition in quantum technology has intensified, China's leaders have continued to prioritize this domain and recognized the unique position in which China is situated as a first mover. Xi Jinping also convened a Politburo study session on the topic of quantum development in October 2020. His remarks at the time emphasized that China should 'grasp the general trend and play good first moves'.[38] With these advances, China had a chance to 'seize the commanding heights of international competition in quantum technology, and build new development advantages' within this domain. By his account, future advances would require the pursuit of long-term major projects, interdisciplinary integration, a 'systematic capability' for future development, and collaborative developments internationally in quantum science and technology, enabled by favorable policies, investments in scientific research, and the cultivation of a team of 'high-level talents'. Such factors can be examined as impactful in China's trajectory to date and contributing to progress going forward.

Input factors

Plans and policies

China's progression to become a leading nation in quantum information science has been enabled by strong state support. During the 1990s and 2000s, support for basic and applied research in quantum information science was initially provided through National High-Technology Research and Development Plan ('863 Plan') and the National Key Basic Research and Development Plan ('973 Plan').[39] As of May 2015, Made in China 2025 initiative had included advances in quantum computing among its priorities, in the category of the 'next-generation information technology industry'.[40] The

---

[37]'Xi Jinping: Accelerate the Advancement Independent Innovation in Cyber and Information Technology, Unrelentingly Strive towards the Objective of Constructing a Cyber Power' [习近平:加快推进网络信息技术自主创新 朝着建设网络强国目标不懈努力], *Xinhua*, 9 October 2016, http://news.xinhuanet.com/politics/2016-10/09/c_1119682204.htm.
[38]'Xi Focus: Xi stresses advancing development of quantum science and technology', Xinhua, 17 October 2020, http://www.xinhuanet.com/english/2020-10/17/c_139447976.htm. In the 24th collective study session of the Political Bureau of the Central Committee, Xi Jinping a the profound understanding of the significance of advancing the development of quantum science and technology" [习近平在中央政治局第二十四次集体学习时强调 深刻认识推进量子科技发展重大意义], Xinhua, 17 October 2020, http://www.xinhuanet.com/politics/2020-10/17/c_1126623288.htm.
[39]'Our Nation Launched Four Major Science Research Programs' [我国启动四项重大科学研究计划], *Science and Technology Daily*, 16 November 2006.
[40]"The State Council's Notice on the Printing and Distribution of 'Made in China 2025' [国务院关于印发《中国制造2025》的通知], Ministry of Industry and Information Technology, 19 May 2015, http://www.miit.gov.cn/n11293472/n11293877/n16553775/n16553792/16594486.html.

Timeline of certain milestones in China's quantum information science (2000–2021).

Year	Events
2001	The University of Science and Technology of China established the State Key Laboratory of Quantum Information, the first major quantum laboratory in China.
2006	The Ministry of Science and Technology announced a major national project on 'quantum control'. The Chinese Academy of Sciences launched several research projects, including on long-distance quantum communication.
2011	The project Quantum Experiments at Space Scale (QUESS) was officially launched through the Chinese Academy of Sciences. The National Natural Science Foundation of China announced a new project in quantum metrology.
2013	In June, Edward Snowden, a former contractor with the NSA, leaked allegations about U.S. intelligence activities, including within China. In August, Xi Jinping and Politburo members visited company specialized in quantum cryptography. The project to create the Beijing-Shanghai 'quantum secure' backbone network was initiated.
2015	'Made in China 2025' included quantum science among the priorities of strategic emerging industries. The Alibaba Quantum Computing Laboratory was established as a partnership between the company and the Chinese Academy of Science.
2016	As of March, the 13th Five-Year Plan included quantum computing and communications among major projects. The Ministry of Science and Technology also started a key project in 'quantum control and quantum information'. In August, China launched Mozi, the world's first quantum satellite.
2017	Ongoing experiments using Micius were reported to achieve successful outcomes, and the satellite was used to secure intercontinental communication between Beijing and Vienna. The Beijing-Shanghai backbone network was officially launched for use by government and commercial stakeholders.
2018	In February, Alibaba released a quantum computing cloud platform with 11 qubits. In March, Baidu officially initiated its Institute for Quantum Computing.
2019	In August, a team of Chinese scientists achieved a 20-qubit entanglement, exceeding the previous record of 12 qubits. In October, Google claimed to have achieved quantum supremacy, but that claim was challenged by Alibaba researchers.
2020	In May, Baidu released Paddle Quantum, an open source toolkit for quantum machine learning. In October, the Politburo Standing Committee organized a study session on quantum science and technology. In December, Chinese researchers achieved quantum supremacy (or quantum advantage) through a photonic quantum computer known as Jiuzhang.
2021	The 14th Five-Year Plan reaffirmed quantum computing and communications among priority projects. In May, Chinese scientists achieved quantum advantage and demonstrated 'quantum walks' through a new superconducting quantum computer prototype known as Zu Chongzhi.

National Key Research and Development Plan (国家重点研发计划), which replaced the 863 and 973 Plans as of February 2016, has since provided funding for research in quantum information science.[41]

For China, quantum computing and communications have been introduced as a major 'flagship' project and prioritized for advances in five-year plans looking to 2030.[42] The lines of effort pursuant to the initiative has been targeted to include metropolitan and inter-city free space quantum communications technology, the development and manufacture of common-use quantum computing prototypes, and the development and manufacture of actual-use quantum simulators.[43] Notably, the 13th Five-Year Plan (2016–2020) featured quantum information science in the category of basic research related to national strategic requirements, and the National Science and Technology Innovation Plan for that timeframe included quantum control and quantum information as priorities, calling for China to achieve breakthroughs in quantum communication and the quantum anomalous Hall effect.[44] Moreover, the 13th Five-Year National Strategic Emerging Industries Development Plan included a call to develop quantum chips, programming, software, and related key technology to promote applications of quantum computing and simulations in December 2016.[45] With the focus on looking to new 'growth points' and advancing new-type infrastructure, especially in the wake of the pandemic, the development of a quantum communications infrastructure will likely continue to expand.[46] With its initial release, the 14th Five-Year Plan (2021–2025) has reaffirmed quantum computing and communications as strategic priorities among major strategic projects.[47]

---

[41] 973、863 plans canceled; the National Key Research and Development Plan to start" [973、863计划取消 国家重点研发计划启动], Xinhua, 17 February 2016, http://news.sciencenet.cn/htmlnews/2016/2/338353.shtm.

[42] "Xi Jinping: Explanations of the 'CCP Central Committee Suggestions Regarding the Formation of the National Economic and Social Development Thirteenth Five-Year Plan' [习近平:关于《中共中央关于制定国民经济和社会发展第十三个五年规划的建议》的说明], Xinhua, 3 November 2015, http://news.xinhuanet.com/politics/2015-11/03/c_1117029621_3.htm.

[43] "China's 'Science and Technology Innovation 2030 Megaprojects Will Newly Add "Artificial Intelligence 2.0"' [中国'科技创新2030 – 重大项目'将新增'人工智能2.0'], Ministry of Science and Technology of the People's Republic of China, 16 February 2017.

[44] 'Notice of the State Council on the Printing and Distribution of the Thirteenth Five-Year National Science and Technology Innovation Plan' [国务院关于印发'十三五'国家科技创新规划的通知], State Council, 8 August 2016, http://www.gov.cn/zhengce/content/2016-08/08/content_5098072.htm.

[45] 'State Council Notice Regarding the Issuance of the Thirteenth Five-Year National Strategic Emerging Industries Development Plan' [国务院关于印发'十三五'国家战略性新兴产业发展规划的通知],19 December 2016, http://www.gov.cn/zhengce/content/2016-12/19/content_5150090.htm.

[46] 'Guiding Opinions on Expanding Investment in Strategic Emerging Industries and Cultivating Strengthened New Growth Points and Growth Poles' [关于扩大战略性新兴产业投资 培育壮大新增长点增长极的指导意见], NDRC High Technology (2020) Document No. 1409.号.

[47] 'Proposal of the Central Committee of the Communist Party of China on Formulating the Fourteenth Five-Year Plan for National Economic and Social Development and the Long-term Goals for 2035' [中共中央关于制定国民经济和社会发展第十四个五年规划和二〇三五年远景目标的建议],
Xinhua, 3 November 2020, http://www.gov.cn/zhengce/2020-11/03/content_5556991.htm. '"14th Five-Year Plan" is coming, how will it be released?' ['十四五'规划要来了,它将如何出炉?], Xinhua, 27 November 2019, http://www.gov.cn/xinwen/2019-11/27/content_5456153.htm.

Funding and investment

While levels of funding for research and development in quantum science and technology remain difficult to estimate, and the return on such investments also remains to be seen, it is evident that the resources available within this discipline in China have been considerable and will likely continue increasing. The past decade of research funding for quantum information research, which came primarily from the central and several local governments, is reported to have totaled approximately $987 million as of 2019 according to an estimate from Chinese scientists involved in these programs.[48] China also dedicated about 1.9 billion RMB (approximately $300 million) in quantum science between 2013 and 2015 alone, according to official media.[49]

Given the increased concentration on basic research, funding will likely continue to increase in the years to come. The first phase of investment to a new national laboratory that had been under construction since 2017 was reported to be 7 billion RMB (over $1 billion) and further phases are expected to dedicate additional billions to this national initiative, up to 100 billion RMB (over $15 billion) in its first 5 years.[50] There has also been also funding provided to varied projects through China's National Natural Sciences Foundation,[51] and the Ministry of Science and Technology has supported the 'quantum control and quantum information', which, for instance, supported projects with 125 million RMB ($19 million) and 160 million RMB ($24 million) in 2020 and 2019.[52]

Beyond national programs and funding, there are also a growing number of local and provincial initiatives. For instance, the new Anhui Quantum Science Industry Development Fund, created in December 2017, had announced plans to devote ten billion RMB (nearly $1.6 billion) in funding to quantum computing, communications, and measurement.[53] Shandong Province, which also announced a 2018–2025 plan for quantum technology innovation, created the Jinan

---

[48] Zhang, Qiang, Feihu Xu, Li Li, Nai-Le Liu, and Jian-Wei Pan, 'Quantum information research in China', *Quantum Science and Technology* 4, no. 4 (2019): 040503.
[49] 'State Council's Several Opinions Regarding Comprehensively Strengthening Basic Research' [国务院关于全面加强基础科学研究的若干意见], State Council, 31 January 2018, http://www.gov.cn/zhengce/content/2018-01/31/content_5262539.htm.
[50] 'China's quantum science and technology out of the laboratory: communication has advantages, computing needs to catch up' [中国量子科技走出实验室:通信有优势 计算需追赶], Sina, 18 October 2020, https://finance.sina.com.cn/stock/hyyj/2020-10-18/doc-iiznezxr6702397.shtml.
[51] 'National Natural Sciences Fund 2016 Supported All Kinds of Projects' [国家自然科学基金2016年资助各类项目], Xinhua, 29 March 2017, http://webcache.googleusercontent.com/search?q=cache:a99L0k3rzoMJ:www.nsfc.gov.cn/publish/portal0/tab351/info68370.htm+&cd=1&hl=en&ct=clnk&gl=us.
[52] "Key Special Project of 'Quantum Control and Quantum Information: 2020 Annual Project Application Guidelines' ['量子调控与量子信息'重点专项 2020 年度项目申报指南], http://www.hf.cas.cn/lmjx/glbm/kyghc/kyc_kyghc/kyc_tzggz/202003/P020200331372775273093.pdf .
[53] 'Hundred Yuan Anhui Quantum Science Industry Development Fund Starts Operations' [百亿元安徽量子科学产业发展基金启动运营], China News Network, 12 December 2017, http://webcache.googleusercontent.com/search?q=cache:Yu9KlnNMrE0J:news.sina.com.cn/o/2017-12-12/doc-ifypnyqi4346545.shtml+&cd=4&hl=en&ct=clnk&gl=us.

Quantum Institute and established a new fund to promote progress in this discipline and emerging industry.[54] Shenzhen announced as of 2021 plans to invest upward of $108 billion in R&D in emerging technologies, including quantum technology over the next 5 years.[55] There have also been efforts underway to promote quantum industry and infrastructure in Chongqing, Zhejiang Province, Guangdong Province, among other locales.[56] However, the actual allocation and efficacy of this funding remains to be seen.

There is also funding allocated to dual-use research and development through military funding and new military–civil funding initiatives. Of note, the PLA's Equipment Development Department is also supporting research in quantum technologies, including through the National Defence Key Laboratories Fund, which provided funding for several relevant projects during the 13th Five-Year Plan.[57] In military–civil fusion initiatives, emerging technologies, including quantum technology, have been a clear priority and recognized by strategists as a particularly promising direction for development, often highlighted as of strategic importance.[58] Meanwhile, there is direct support and research underway through several of the PLA's leading universities, including the Academy of Military Science, which contributes to the Beijing Academy for Quantum Information Sciences, and the National University of Defense Technology, which established its Quantum Information Interdisciplinary Center in April 2015 with its special funding and support from the central government.[59]

Human capital resources

The education and recruitment of world-class talent in quantum science will be a critical determinant of China's potential future trajectory in this domain. The Chinese government has undertaken dedicated initiatives to recruit top talent through a wide range state plans. These include the Changjiang

---

[54]'Technology leads innovation and breakthroughs; Shandong is unswervingly building an innovative province' [科技引领创新突破 山东坚定不移建设创新大省], 15 May 2021, http://sd.people.com.cn/n2/2021/0515/c166192-34726892.html.

[55]Guo Rui, 'China's tech hub Shenzhen to invest US$108 billion in R&D over 5 years', 7 May 2021, https://www.scmp.com/news/china/science/article/3132651/chinas-tech-hub-shenzhen-invest-us108-billion-rd-over-5-years.

[56]China quantum technology accelerates the realization of space-earth integration" [中国量子科技加快实现天地一体化], People's Daily [人民日报], 10 November 2020, http://www.xinhuanet.com/tech/2020-11/10/c_1126719068.htm.

[57]The sources and additional information are available upon request.

[58]'13th Five-Year Science and Technology Military-Civil Fusion Development Special Plan' (Full Text) ['十三五'科技军民融合发展专项规划》全文].

[59]'National University of Defense Technology's Quantum Information Interdisciplinary Center recruits postdoctoral fellows and experimental technical engineers'[国防科学技术大学量子信息学科交叉中心招聘博士后以及实验技术工程师], National University of Defense Technology, 10 June 2016, https://www.nudt.edu.cn/rczp/6745154b0a7344d795a05e3f2465ffb2.htm.

Scholars program and Thousand Talents Plan, which do appear to be a major factor in incentivizing returns of students from overseas. Of course, Pan Jianwei himself had started out in the field under the tutelage of Anton Zeilinger at the University of Vienna.

Since the early 2000s, under Pan Jianwei's leadership, a number of Chinese students were sent abroad to leading research programs to learn important technologies. Ultimately, those at the center of indigenous developments today returned to China with the commitment to contribute to building up an indigenous research program.[60] A significant proportion leading Chinese quantum physicists have returned to become key figures in Chinese quantum innovation after receiving PhDs from top U.S. and international institutions. For example, Wang Haohua, who has contributed to notable advances in quantum computing, was a postdoc at the University of California, Santa Barbara, where he collaborated with John Martinis' team, which was later recruited to Google, on quantum computing, including the use of superconducting qubits.[61] While such flows of talent and exchange of are hardly surprising and not problematic necessarily, there have been cases where more targeted recruitment, including with a link to military initiatives, has raised concerns.[62] Chinese companies entering this space have recruited foreign researchers as well.[63]

Looking forward, the education and recruitment of talent to expand the team on these issues will remain a major priority. According to Xue Qikun, 'the talent pool for quantum technology is insufficient ... Talent training takes time'.[64] As U.S.–China technological competition has intensified, Chinese academics have been concerned about the restrictions on their capacity to leverage the 'blood transfusion' of 'introducing high-level talents from abroad', as Guo Guangcan, a leading academician in quantum science, has discussed, highlighting the importance to train talents, especially the high technology of quantum information, which is blocked by foreign countries.[65]

---

[60]Jeanne Whalen, 'The quantum revolution is coming, and Chinese scientists are at the forefront', The Washington Post, 18 August 2019, https://www.washingtonpost.com/business/2019/08/18/quantum-revolution-is-coming-chinese-scientists-are-forefront/.
[61]'Martinis Group: Josephson Junction Quantum Computing at UCSB', https://web.physics.ucsb.edu/~martinisgroup/alumni.shtml.
[62]For a detailed assessment of talent recruitment, see also: Alex Joske, 'Hunting the Phoenix', Australian Strategic Policy Institue, https://www.aspi.org.au/report/hunting-phoenix.
[63]For Alibaba's recruitment, see, for instance: Alizila Staff, 'Alibaba Hires Chief Quantum Scientist in Continued Cloud Push', 13 October 2017, https://www.alizila.com/alibaba-hires-chief-quantum-scientist-in-contineud-cloud-push/.
[64].
[65]'Dialogue with Academician Guo Guangcan: The basic knowledge in the field of quantum information should be cultivated from the university' [对话郭光灿院士:应该从大学开始培养量子信息领域基础知识], Beijing News, 26 October 2020, http://www.sohu.com/a/427435468_114988.

However, the consistent successes achieved by teams at USTC and other top research institutes does reflect that Chinese advances in quantum science are considerably less reliant upon tech and talent transfer than other domains.

Institutional factors

Research collaborations

Chinese research in quantum science has demonstrated the strength of an evolving ecosystem of leading universities that have been at the center of a series of productive partnerships.[66] An initial centers for Chinese quantum information science was the Key Laboratory of Quantum Information, established in 2001 under the aegis of the Chinese Academy of Sciences, located at the University of Science and Technology of China (USTC). At the same time, Pan Jianwei (潘建伟), returned to China after receiving a PhD from the University of Vienna.[67] His research at USTC would progress to pioneer advances in quantum communications, in competition with his mentor and onetime professor Dr. Anton Zeilinger.

At first glance, China's leadership in quantum cryptography and communications, as well as initial advances in quantum computing, might appear to reflect fully independent innovation, but the impact of international collaborations and state plans to attract top talent, have also been a factor. The Quantum Experiments at Space Scale (QUESS) project, initiated in 2011, which has involved collaboration between a team led by leading Chinese quantum scientist Pan Jianwei from the University of Science and Technology of China, the Chinese Academy of Sciences (CAS), and the Austrian Academy of Sciences.[68] Although the Austrian and Chinese teams had initially competed, reportedly, this collaboration arose after the European Union was unwilling to fund a comparable project.[69]

---

[66] Beyond USTC, several Chinese universities, have also developed research programs, including Tsinghua University's Center for Quantum Information, established in 2011, and National Key Laboratory of Low-Dimensional Quantum Physics, and Fudan University's Center for Quantum ControlBeyond USTC, several Chinese universities, have also developed research programs, including Tsinghua University's Center for Quantum Information, established in 2011, and National Key Laboratory of Low-Dimensional Quantum Physics, and Fudan University's Center for Quantum Control.
[67] See: *Xinhua*, http://news.sina.com.cn/c/sd/2016-08-16/doc-ifxuxnpy9658879.shtml.
[68] Lee Billings, 'China Shatters "Spooky Action at a Distance" Record, Preps for Quantum Internet', Scientific American, 15 June 2017, https://www.scientificamerican.com/article/china-shatters-ldquo-spooky-action-at-a-distance-rdquo-record-preps-for-quantum-internet/.
[69] Ibid.

New institutions and partnerships

China's efforts to redouble research in quantum science have leveraged the creation of new institutions that are intended to advance cutting-edge research. Notably, the Chinese government has been building the National Laboratory for Quantum Information Science (量子信息科学国家实验室) in Anhui Province starting from September 2017, which is intended to become the world's largest quantum research facility.[70] This new national laboratory will pursue advances in quantum computing and could engage in research 'of immediate use' to China's armed forces, according to initial reports.[71] This centralization of resources and researchers is intended to enable synergies among the expertise and experience of talent across multiple disciplines in order to overcome current technical and engineering obstacles.

Beyond the reported billions of funding it will receive for research and development, while there has been only limited information available about its initial progress, such new initiatives may allow for important consolidation of research.[72] For instance, Beijing is a critical center of gravity for quantum research and development in China. The Beijing Quantum Institute has looked to open up 'walls' that previously inhibited progress, including between research units, between research and industry, and between disciplines, recognizing the importance of integration to a model of innovation within this discipline, according to its dean Xue Qikun.[73]

As quantum technology has progressed toward promising applications, Chinese companies have joined the fray in earnest. The Chinese Academy of Sciences first joined forces with Alibaba's cloud computing arm, Aliyun, to create the Alibaba Quantum Computing Lab in 2015, which was intended undertake 'frontier' research to realize the practical applications of quantum computing.[74] Their pursuit of quantum computing looked to leverage 'the technical advantages of Aliyun in classical calculation algorithms, structures and cloud computing with those of CAS in quantum computing, quantum analogue computing and quantum artificial intelligence'.[75] The Alibaba Quantum Computing Lab was quick to articulate ambitious goals, including

---

[70] Stephen Chen, 'China building world's biggest quantum research facility,' *South China Morning Post*, 11 September 2017, http://www.scmp.com/news/china/society/article/2110563/china-building-worlds-biggest-quantum-research-facility. "Hefei's Construction of a National Science Center from 'Design' to 'Construction Map' [合肥建设国家科学中心 从'设计图'转为"施工图], China News Network, 13 September 2017, http://www.chinanews.com/gn/2017/09-13/8330201.shtml.
[71] Ibid.
[72] 'Anhui Reports on the Construction of the National Laboratory of Quantum Information Science, Total Investment 7 Billion Yuan' [安徽拟申报建设量子信息科学国家实验室,总投资约70亿元], 11 July 2017, http://news.163.com/17/0711/15/CP2TJ9V7000187VE.html.
[73] 'Forge ahead in the "ongoing" of quantum technology development' [在量子科技发展'进行时'中奋进], China Science News [中国科学报], 19 October 2020, http://wap.sciencenet.cn/mobile.php?type=detail&cat=news&id=447084&mobile=1.
[74] 'Aliyun and Chinese Academy of Sciences Sign MoU for Quantum Computing Laboratory', Alibaba, 3 July 2015, http://www.alibabagroup.com/en/news/article?news=p150730.
[75] Ibid.

the development of quantum simulation by 2025 and of a quantum computer prototype with 50–100 qubits by 2030.[76] Alibaba was among the first to create and has since opened up access to its cloud platform for quantum computing, which can allow for experiments and upgrades.[77]

Chinese state-owned defense conglomerates have also started to engage in research and development regarding the military applications of quantum technology. In addition, in November 2017, the China Shipbuilding Industry Corporation and USTC signed an agreement to establish three joint laboratories focusing on the development of quantum navigation, quantum communications, and quantum detection.[78] Within CETC, several research institutes may be involved in research and development on quantum radars.[79] Despite the relative opacity of research within the Chinese defense industry, there have been some public reports of advances in technologies that could have very direct military applications.

Output factors

China has emerged at the forefront of applications of quantum communications, started to advance in quantum computing, despite still lagging behind the top teams, and also achieved at least experimental demonstration of prototypes in quantum sensing and technologies. Such progress and the intense interest is evidenced by the fact that China already surpassed the U.S. in terms of patents as early as 2017, filing twice as many patents at the time, though the magnitude of its contributions reflected primarily its unique positioning in quantum key distribution, despite lesser efforts at that time in quantum computing, according to analysis from Patinformatics.[80] The scope and scale of Chinese efforts in quantum information science, along with the rapid progression of advances in basic and applied research, suggest that China will remain a serious contender within this domain.

---

[76] Chinese Academy of Sciences, Hand in Hand with Alibaba Will Establish a 'Quantum Computing Laboratory' in Shanghai" [中国科学院携手阿里巴巴在沪建立'量子计算实验室'], *Xinhua*, 31 July 2015, http://news.xinhuanet.com/2015-07/31/c_1116104188.htm. 'Chinese Academy of Sciences – Alibaba Quantum Computing Lab' [中国科学院 – 阿里巴巴量子计算实验室挂牌], Chinese Academy of Sciences, 2 September 2015, http://www.bsc.cas.cn/gzdt/201509/t20150902_4419884.html.
[77] 'Chinese research institute updates Quantum Computing Cloud Platform, grants access to public', Global Times, 21 April 2021, https://www.globaltimes.cn/page/202104/1221651.shtml.
[78] 'China Shipbuilding Industry Corporation and the University of Science and Technology of China Establish Quantum Joint Laboratories' [中船重工与中国科大成立量子联合实验室], Sina, 28 November 2017, http://news.sina.com.cn/o/2017-11-28/doc-ifypacti8966967.shtml; Jon Grevatt, 'China looks to quantum technologies to boost naval programmes', 29 November 2017, http://www.janes.com/article/76021/china-looks-to-quantum-technologies-to-boost-naval-programmes.
[79] 'CETC First Single Photon Quantum Radar System Successfully Researched and Developed' [中国电科首部单光子量子雷达系统研制成功], CETC 14th Research Institute, September 7, http://wmdw.jswmw.com/home/content/?1174-3887947.html.
[80] 'Quantum Computing Applications: A Patent Landscape Report', https://patinformatics.com/wp-content/uploads/2018/01/Quantum-Applications-Patent-Landscape-Report-Opt.pdf.

Quantum cryptography and communications

China is rapidly progressing to actualize quantum communications to secure sensitive national, military, and industry communications. In parallel, Chinese researchers have continued achieving consistent experimental advances that enhance its utility. According to Pan Jianwei,

> It is precisely because of the early stage when the practical value of quantum information has not yet been fully demonstrated, we took the lead in seizing the opportunity internationally, which pushed us to finally achieve the international leading position in quantum communication.[81]

Indeed, his team has pioneered a range of experimental advancements, from enhanced security to notably resolving the so-called 'nocturnal problem' that had once limited free space quantum communication to nighttime, through adjusting the wavelength to enhance signal clarity.[82] Despite claims that the eventual outcome of these advances may be dramatic improvements in security, there are reasons to take a sanguine attitude about the possible technical limitations that may allow for improvements to remain relatively incremental.[83]

Building upon prior progress in quantum entanglement and teleportation, the quantum satellite Micius has enabled numerous milestones through a series of tests performed under the Quantum Experiments at Space Scale program.[84] Through Micius, Chinese scientists achieved ground-to-satellite quantum teleportation at a distance of 1400 kilometers, considered a critical step toward a future 'quantum Internet' at a global scale.[85] Micius was also utilized for the first realization of space-to-ground quantum entanglement, as well as key distribution.[86] In one such experiment, quantum keys were sent

---

[81]'Seize the commanding heights of quantum technology: Interview with Pan Jianwei, member of the National Committee of the Chinese People's Political Consultative Conference and academician of the Chinese Academy of Sciences' [抢占量子科技制高点：访全国政协委员、中国科学院士潘建伟], *Central Commission for Discipline Inspection and State Supervision Commission website*, 10 March 2021, http://www.ccdi.gov.cn/yaowen/202103/t20210310_237524.html.

[82]Stephen Chen, 'Chinese scientists solve quantum communication's "nocturnal curse", paving way for sending of secure messages 24/7', *South China Morning Post*, 3 January 2017, http://www.scmp.com/news/china/article/2054219/chinese-scientists-solve-quantum-communications-nocturnal-curse-allowing.

[83]See, for instance: Lindsay, Jon R. 'Surviving the Quantum Cryptopocalypse', Strategic Studies Quarterly 14/2 (2020), 49–73.

[84]Yin, Juan, Ji-Gang Ren, Sheng-Kai Liao, Yuan Cao, Wen-Qi Cai, Cheng-Zhi Peng, and Jian-Wei Pan. 'Quantum Science Experiments with Micius Satellite', In *CLEO: Applications and Technology*, pp. JTu3G-4. Optical Society of America, 2019.

[85]Ji-Gang Ren et al., 'Ground-to-satellite quantum teleportation', *Nature*, 9 August 2017, http://www.nature.com/nature/journal/v549/n7670/full/nature23675.html.

[86]Han, Xuan, Hai-Lin Yong, Ping Xu, Kui-Xing Yang, Shuang-Lin Li, Wei-Yang Wang, Hua-Jian Xue et al. 'Polarization design for ground-to-satellite quantum entanglement distribution', *Optics Express* 28/1 (2020), 369–378.

from Micius to ground stations at distances ranging from 645 to 12,000 kilometers, achieving a gain in efficiency an estimated 20 orders of magnitude greater than the use of optical fiber.[87]

Leveraging previous research and ongoing experimentation, China's national quantum communications infrastructure has continued to progress. As of September 2017, the Jing-Hu (Beijing-Shanghai) backbone network, a 2000-kilometer quantum communications link that connects Beijing, Jinan, Hefei, and Shanghai with optical fiber through 32 nodes and integrated with Mozi through satellite ground stations, entered official operations.[88] This network has been capable of providing bandwidth of 100 G, and its bandwidth and capability are expected to increase.[89] The utility of this system was initially demonstrated when Micius was used for a video call between the presidents of the Austrian and Chinese Academies of Sciences.[90] At an early stage, there are were already over 150 users, and the security dividends from this initiative are expected to be significant, according to one professor involved in the project: 'The changes will take place unnoticed; people will enjoy absolute information security without even realizing it'.[91] This architecture will continue to be expanded with China's drive for new-type infrastructure as a priority for stimulus, especially in the wake of the pandemic as China's leaders have turned to digital industries to spur and sustain development.

This project has targeted the objective of creating a quantum communications network between Asia and Europe by 2020 and ultimately a global network by 2030. This architecture will leverage both terrestrial networks and multiple quantum satellites linked with ground stations, which are expanding nationwide.[92] Chinese scientists advanced a step closer to that objective when, as of January 2021, the USTC team achieved satellite-to-earth quantum key distribution spanning 4600

---

[87]Sheng-Kai Liao et al., 'Satellite-to-ground quantum key distribution', Nature, 9 August 2017, http://www.nature.com/nature/journal/v549/n7670/full/nature23655.html.
[88]'China builds the world's first satellite-to-earth quantum communication network' [我国构建全球首个星地量子通信网], Guangming Daily, 8 January 2021, http://www.gov.cn/xinwen/2021-01/08/content_5577894.htm. l.
[89]'Beijing-Shanghai Quantum Communication Network Put into Use', Chinese Academy of Sciences, 1 September 2017, http://english.cas.cn/newsroom/archive/news_archive/nu2017/201703/t20170324_175288.shtml.
[90]'China Demonstrates Quantum Encryption By Hosting a Video Call', IEEE Spectrum, 3 October 2017, https://spectrum.ieee.org/tech-talk/telecom/security/china-successfully-demonstrates-quantum-encryption-by-hosting-a-video-call.
[91]'Beijing-Shanghai Quantum Communication Network Put into Use,' Chinese Academy of Sciences, 1 September 2017, http://english.cas.cn/newsroom/archive/news_archive/nu2017/201703/t20170324_175288.shtml.
[92]'China to build global quantum communication network in 2030', Xinhua, 2 November 2014, http://news.xinhuanet.com/english/china/2014-11/02/c_127169705.htm.

kilometers.⁹³ The scaling up of this network so far through integrating fiber networks and 'free space' linkages to satellites, of which Mozi is only the first of what will become a future constellation, hints at the promise of a truly global quantum network or future 'quantum network', such as Pan Jianwei and his team have discussed their aspiration to develop.⁹⁴

The large-scale adoption of quantum communications has been facilitated and accelerated by commercial implementation, including the efforts of important enterprises. According to industry predictions, by 2023, the market size of quantum communications as an industry nationwide will reach 80.5 billion RMB (nearly $12.5 billion).⁹⁵ Several Chinese companies, including Qasky, QuantumCTek, and Shenzhou Quantum, have already developed sizable patent portfolios and contributed to local and national projects.⁹⁶ For instance, Quantum CTek has launched the QSS-ME, an open platform product supporting the development of mobile application products and also a new 'quantum mobile phone' with ZTE.⁹⁷ National Shield Quantum Technology Co. Ltd. (or Guodun Quantum, 国盾量子) was founded to commercialize quantum communications, especially concentrating on quantum network infrastructure for national projects and commercial applications, actively promoted by state and local governments.⁹⁸ There are robust industry clusters emerging across several locales Within Jinan's 'Quantum Valley', a growing number of companies have been involved in quantum industry, which is targeted to reach ten billion RMB ($1.6 billion) by 2025.⁹⁹

As China's quantum communication lines continue to expand, these networks are likely to be leveraged for dual-use applications. 'China is completely capable of making full use of quantum communications in a local war. The

---

⁹³Li, Zheng-Da, Rui Zhang, Xu-Fei Yin, Li-Zheng Liu, Yi Hu, Yu-Qiang Fang, Yue-Yang Fei et al. 'Experimental quantum repeater without quantum memory.' *Nature Photonics* 13, no. 9 (2019): 644–648.

⁹⁴Chen, Yu-Ao, Qiang Zhang, Teng-Yun Chen, Wen-Qi Cai, Sheng-Kai Liao, Jun Zhang, Kai Chen et al., 'An integrated space-to-ground quantum communication network over 4,600 kilometres', *Nature* 589/7841 (2021), 214–219.

⁹⁵'China builds the world's first satellite-to-earth quantum communication network' [中国构建全球首个星地量子通信网], *Central Commission for Discipline Inspection and State Supervision Commission*, http://www.ccdi.gov.cn/zghjf/202101/t20210108_233496.html.

⁹⁶Quantum Information Technology (QIT): A Patent Landscape Report, https://patinformatics.com/wp-content/uploads/2018/01/Quantum-Information-Technology-Patent-Landscape-Report-Opt.pdf.

⁹⁷'The world's first commercial "quantum mobile phone" came out of the quantum communication laboratory' [球首款商用'量子手机'问世 量子通信走出实验室], Anhui Business Daily, 7 February 2018, http://ah.sina.com.cn/news/2018-02-07/detail-ifyrhcqz3796393.shtml.

⁹⁸'S&T innovation is the urban temperament integrated into his bones' [科技创新是融入骨子裡的城市氣質], Chenfei Development and Reform [郜肥發改], 10 August 2020, https://www.xptshanghai.com/keji/detail/483045fbfb.html.

⁹⁹Jinan will become a 10 billion-class quantum industrial cluster center by 2025'[济南到2025年将成全省百亿级量子产业集群中心], *Jinan Times*, 6 March 2018, http://webcache.googleusercontent.com/search?q=cache:kUJ9TXOzYx4J:news.e23.cn/jnnews/2018-03-06/2018030600030.html+&cd=4&hl=en&ct=clnk&gl=au.

direction of development in the future calls for using relay satellites to realize quantum communications and control that covers the entire army', Pan Jianwei had claimed as early as 2016.[100] Considering experimental demonstrations of the feasibility of underwater quantum communications,[101] Chinese quantum networks might also extend to include submarines to facilitate command and control of PLA SSBNs as a means of assured communications with China's nuclear deterrent, though water quality could be a - limitation.[102] Yet considering the potential vulnerabilities of these networks to interference, the practicality of their use in a contested environment remains to be seen.

Quantum computing

While China has appeared to be lagged behind in quantum computing, Chinese scientists are also emerging as avid contenders in the global competition actualize it. As leading quantum scientist Guo Guangcan has emphasized, 'Chinese scientists have been going all out to win the worldwide race to develop a quantum computer', which will continue for decades to come.[103] For instance, in August 2016, USTC scientists announced their development of a semiconductor quantum chip, which could enable quantum operations and information processing,[104] and also achieved a breakthrough in the preparation and measurement of 600 pairs of entangled quantum particles.[105] In March 2017, USTC scientists succeeded in entangling ten superconducting qubits, an important step toward future quantum computing.[106] A team of Chinese scientists achieved a 20 qubit entanglement that lasted for 187 nanoseconds, exceeding the previous record of 12 qubits, in August 2019.[107]

---

[100]Yu Dawei, 'In China, Quantum Communications Comes of Age', *Caixin*, 6 February 2015.
[101]Ling Ji et al., 'Towards quantum communications in free-space seawater', Optics Express, Volume 25, Issue 17, 2017, https://www.osapublishing.org/oe/abstract.cfm?uri=oe-25-17-19795.
[102]Raymond Wang, 'Quantum Communications and Chinese SSBN Strategy', The Diplomat, 4 November 2017, https://thediplomat.com/2017/11/quantum-communications-and-chinese-ssbn-strategy/.
[103]Zhu Lixin, 'Progress made in development of quantum memory', *China Daily*, 20 August 2016, http://usa.chinadaily.com.cn/epaper/2016-08/20/content_26559829.htm.
[104]'China Successfully Develops Semiconductor Quantum Chip,' Chinese Academy of Sciences, 12 August 2016, http://english.cas.cn/newsroom/news/201608/t20160812_166433.shtml.
[105]'China Makes New Breakthrough in Quantum Computation', Chinese Academy of Sciences, 26 August 2016, http://english.cas.cn/newsroom/mutimedia_news/201608/t20160826_166818.shtml.
[106]'Ten superconducting qubits entangled by physicists in China', Physics World, April 2017, http://physicsworld.com/cws/article/news/2017/apr/13/ten-superconducting-qubits-entangled-by-physicists-in-china.
[107]'Scientists Create 20-qubit Schrödinger Cat States with Superconducting Quantum Processor', 12 August 2019, http://english.cas.cn/newsroom/research_news/phys/201908/t20190812_214026.shtml. However, foreign media accounts of the event reported that a German team that first reached 20 qubits, and the Chinese team then replicated the work with 18. '187 Nanoseconds, Witness the Miracle of 20 Qubit Entangled States' [187纳秒,见证20量子比特纠缠态奇迹], Xinhua Net [新华网], 15 August 2019, http://www.xinhuanet.com/tech/2019-08/15/c_1124877158.htm.

While Google proved the first to the symbolic milestone of 'quantum supremacy', the point at which a quantum computer surpasses a classical computer, in October 2019, its results, based on the use of superconducting qubits in a device known as Sycamore, initially provoked controversy.[108] In particular, researchers from rival Alibaba claimed the error rates for Google's qubits remained too high for their claim to be credible.[109] Thereafter, Chinese researchers had achieved quantum supremacy in their own right, using a different technique with a quantum computer, known as 'Jiuzhang' in December 2020.[110] Jiuzhang was reported to be capable of processing at a rate reported to be ten *billion* times faster than Google's quantum computer, as its developers hastened to point out, in a questionable comparison.[111] At the time, Pan Jianwei declared, 'We have shown that we can use photons, the fundamental unit of light, to demonstrate quantum computational power well beyond the classical counterpart'.[112] This was the first demonstration of 'quantum advantage' using this technique and as applied to a calculation known as boson sampling.[113]

While these quantum computers remain perhaps decades from general-purpose applications, the prestige and symbolism of this advance was evident.[114] Nonetheless, Jiuzhang was only a 'champion in one single area' for now, though researchers anticipate its potential applications that may include graph theory, machine learning, and quantum chemistry going forward.[115] However, this advance in photonic computing was quickly followed by a new step toward quantum advantage with a quantum computer that, like Google's Sycamore, was designed based on superconducting qubits, and exceeded Sycamore in number to set a new world record. This 62-qubit programmable superconducting quantum processor initially demonstrated its capability through 'two-dimensional programmable quantum walks on

---

[108]Sundar Pichai, 'What our quantum computing milestone means', Google, 23 October 2019, https://www.blog.google/perspectives/sundar-pichai/what-our-quantum-computing-milestone-means/.
[109]'New Analysis: Has Humanity Realized "Quantum Hegemony" for the First Time?' [新闻分析:人类首次实现'量子霸权'了吗], *Xinhua Net* [新华网], 24 October 2019, http://www.xinhuanet.com/tech/2019-10/24/c_1125147396.htm.
[110]'My country's scientists build 76-photon quantum computing prototype "Jiuzhang"' [我科学家构建76个光子量子计算原型机'九章'], *Science and Technology Daily [科技日报]*, 4 December 2020.
[111]Qiang, Xiaogang, Yizhi Wang, Shichuan Xue, Renyou Ge, Lifeng Chen, Yingwen Liu, Anqi Huang et al. 'Implementing graph-theoretic quantum algorithms on a silicon photonic quantum walk processor.' *Science Advances* 7, no. 9 (2021): eabb8375.
[112]Philip Ball, 'Physicists in China challenge Google's "quantum advantage"', *Nature*, 3 December 2020, https://www.nature.com/articles/d41586-020-03434-7.
[113]Zhong, Han-Sen, Hui Wang, Yu-Hao Deng, Ming-Cheng Chen, Li-Chao Peng, Yi-Han Luo, Jian Qin et al. 'Quantum computational advantage using photons', *Science* (2020).
[114]'Pan Jianwei Reveals the Three Stages of Quantum Computing Development' [潘建伟揭示量子计算发展三阶段], People's Net [人民网], 15 January 2020, http://scitech.people.cn/n1/2020/0115/c1007-31549405.html.
[115]'China Focus: Chinese scientists achieve quantum computational advantage', *Xinhua*, 4 December 2020, http://www.xinhuanet.com/english/2020-12/04/c_139561941.htm.

the system'.[116] While that test illustrated the proof of concept, its developers have claimed that *Zu Chongzhi* processor will possess potential to do 'everything' in the years to come.[117]

While Chinese scientists remain concerned that their efforts continue to lag behind those of American contenders, such successes pointed to China's progress in a race that may prove to be more of a marathon in the years, even decades, to come. The achievement of quantum computational advantage in surpassing existing supercomputers should be regarded as a 'threshold', as Lu Chaoyang, a leading scientist and protégé of Pan Jianwei, noted at the time, providing a proof of concept for possible future breakthroughs. The superiority of both of these approaches to existing supercomputers does not mean another type of qubit may not yet prove superior to both.[118] For instance, while no team has yet publicly reported achieving quantum supremacy or advantaged based on the use of trapped ions as qubits, this technique appears to be among the most promising.[119]

While academia was at the forefront of Chinese quantum science, industry may enter a leading position as quantum technology continues to progress. Baidu has also launched its own program and investments in quantum computing, the Institute for Quantum Computing, as of 2018.[120] Tencent was quick to follow with its own quantum laboratory set up that same year, which intended 'to connect fundamental theory with practical applications in the fast-growing sector of quantum information technology', according to its website.[121] Notably, in 2020, Baidu released Paddle Quantum, a quantum machine learning development toolkit, claiming 'From now on, researchers in the quantum field can use Paddle Quantum to develop quantum artificial intelligence, and our deep learning enthusiasts have a shortcut to learning quantum computing'.[122] Huawei, too, looked to pursue quantum simulation through its cloud platform and leverage quantum algorithms that might contribute to advances in AI through the capacity to transcend the previous limitation of Moore's Law.[123]

---

[116]Wan Lin, 'Chinese team designs 62-qubit quantum processor with world's largest number of superconducting qubits', Global Times, 9 May 2021, https://www.globaltimes.cn/page/202105/1222944.shtml.
[117]Ibid.
[118]Ibid.
[119]Jeremy Hsu, 'Photonic Quantum Computer Displays "Supremacy" Over Supercomputers', IEEE Spectrum, 9 December 2020, https://spectrum.ieee.org/tech-talk/computing/hardware/photonic-quantum-computer-shows-advantage-over-supercomputer.
[120]'Baidu Establishes Institute for Quantum Computing', 36Kr, 9 March 2018, https://pandaily.com/baidu-establishes-institute-for-quantum-computing-starting-quantum-rivalry-with-alibaba-and-tencent/.
[121]'Tencent Quantum Lab: About Us', https://quantum.tencent.com/en-us/about/.
[122]'Introducing Paddle Quantum: How Baidu's Deep Learning Platform PaddlePaddle Empowers Quantum Computing', 27 May 2020, http://research.baidu.com/Blog/index-view?id=137.
[123]Man-Hong Yung 'Going beyond Moore's Law with quantum computing', Huawei, 28 December 2018, https://www.huawei.com/us/publications/communicate/86/quantum-computing-ai.

Beyond the tech giants, new start-ups are also starting to make their mark in quantum computing. Origin (*Benyuan*) Quantum (本源量子) Computing Technology Company was the first start-up in China to develop a quantum computer based on supercomputing qubits. The company emerged from the CAS Key Laboratory of Quantum Information, demonstrating initial successes in translating basic research into applications.[124] 'Quantum computing is a battleground for cutting-edge technology. We are running on this track with all our strength. At present, 70% of the components have been independently and controllable', according to Zhang Hui (张辉), its vice president.[125]

Going forward, among the major priorities for development will be quantum chips that are specialized to quantum computing applications. Across the board in information technology developments, China's advances in semiconductors continue to be a major challenge and bottleneck, yet the massive resources dedicated to this problematic bottleneck are starting to yield dividends, and early efforts to develop specialized semiconductors for quantum chips may allow supply chains to keep pace with scientific prowess. Notably, Origin Quantum Computing Co and Nexchip Semiconductor Corp agreed to establish a new joint laboratory for 'quantum chips' as of 2021 in order to develop low-temperature integrated circuit technology.[126] Their concern was to develop a "complete production chain for the crucial high-tech component of the future that is currently dominated by foreign industry leaders, according to foreign at the time.[127]

While progress may be slow, efforts to catch up are regarded as having a relatively positive prognosis looking a decade out. According to its director Zhang Xiaorong,

> China has to start R&D on quantum chips and quantum computing. Otherwise, it may face the pain of a lack of core technology in chips again, as it does today. Therefore, even if the period for R&D is very long, maybe with no economic benefit in the short term, China can't fall behind.[128]

The lessons learned from previous failures and challenges may inform China's attempts to establish genuine self-reliance in its quantum science, technology, and nascent industries.

---

[124]"Seize new highs and accelerate the transformation of 'flower of science and technology' into 'fruit of industry' [抢占创新高点 加快'科技之花'转化为'产业之果'], Anhui News Net [安徽新闻网], 11 May 2020.
[125]Ibid.
[126]'Essence Quantum and Jinghe Integration to Build a Joint Laboratory of Quantum Computing Chips' [本源量子与晶合集成共建量子计算芯片联合实验室], Anhui Daily [安徽日报], 3 April 2021.
[127]'Chinese firms to set up quantum chip R&D lab to catch up with global leaders', Global Times, 11 April 2021, https://www.globaltimes.cn/page/202104/1220767.shtml.
[128]'Chinese firms to set up quantum chip R&D lab to catch up with global leaders', Global Times, 11 April 2021, https://www.globaltimes.cn/page/202104/1220767.shtml.

Quantum precision measurement

Chinese advances within the discipline of quantum precision measurement could have industry and direct military applications. By the reckoning of Pan Jianwei, while there is still a 'certain gap' between China's efforts in this particular discipline relative to those of the United States, this gap has been rapidly narrowing in recent years, and in some directions, it has reached the highest level of publicly reported internationally".[129] Ongoing initiatives to create quantum navigation capabilities (i.e., a 'quantum compass') may have direct utility for naval and maritime operations, as could techniques that may be applicable to the detection of submarines.[130] Despite limitations, advances in quantum sensing and detection also promise a degree of precision and sensitivity in detection that is hitherto unprecedented. This frontier of progress will merit ongoing analysis China's efforts on this front progress.

The reports of progress and reasons for skepticism about reports of a Chinese prototype of quantum radar illustrate the excitement and consternation that can accompany reported advances. A team of Chinese scientists from CETC had publicized their progress in toward creating a single-photon quantum radar that is capable of detecting targets up to 100 kilometers away with improved accuracy in 2016.[131] The range of this quantum radar, which utilizes advantage of entanglement between photon pairs, was reported to be five times that of a laboratory prototype jointly created last year by an international team of researchers, resulting in doubts on the veracity of this report, which cannot be verified and about which no detailed technical information was required.[132] The prospects for quantum radar have provoked enthusiasm in military circles because of the notional potential to defeat stealth, as well as the expectation of relevant impacts in electronic warfare as well.[133]

---

[129]'Quantum computing is changing from a "toy" to a "tool"-Interview with Pan Jianwei, an academician of the Chinese Academy of Sciences and a professor at the University of Science and Technology of China' [量子计算正从'玩具'变成'工具' －－ 访中国科学院院士、中国科学技术大学教授潘建伟], Science and Technology Daily, 4 January 2021, http://www.hfnl.ustc.edu.cn/detail?id=17687.

[130]Stephen Chen, 'Has China developed the world's most powerful submarine detector?', The South China Morning Post, 24 June 2017, http://www.scmp.com/news/china/society/article/2099640/has-china-developed-worlds-most-powerful-submarine-detector.

[131]China Electronics Technology Group Corporation's (CETC) 14th Research Institute's Intelligent Sensing Technology Key Laboratory (智能感知技术重点实验室) 'The Coming of the Quantum Radar That Makes Stealth Fighter in Profile' [让隐形战机显形的量子雷达来了], Science and Technology Daily, 13 September 2016. 'China's First Single-Photon Quantum Radar Successfully Developed', [中国首部单光子量子雷达系统研制成功], CETC, 18 September 2016, http://www.cetc.com.cn/zgdzkj/_300931/_300939/445284/index.html.

[132]'New research signals big future for quantum radar', Phys.org, 26 February 2015, http://phys.org/news/2015-02-big-future-quantum-radar.html.

[133]Wang Shilong [王士龙], 'The application prospects of quantum radar in future electronic warfare' [量子雷达在未来电子战中的应用前景], Information and Communication [信息通信] 3 (2019).

However, the initial research on quantum radar or 'illumination' had started at MIT in 2008,[134] and American scientists familiar with the progress and technical limitations, especially of range, are skeptical of its utility under actual operational conditions.[135] Unless solutions to likely limitations have been discovered completely in secret and unbeknownst to the entire global scientific establishment, which appears a more distant possibility, there are reasons to regard with initial doubts the claim, as when raised in PRC media, that China's quantum radar will be the future 'nemesis' of American stealth fighters.[136] Nonetheless, despite and beyond the hype, quantum precision measurement as a discipline does convey unique potential.

Changing paradigms in Chinese defense innovation

The quest for quantum innovation in China may augur the emergence of a new paradigm for innovation in frontier technologies. As the second quantum revolution continues to take shape, China's Party-state and military are poised to leverage the potential of quantum technologies to the fullest to enhance economic dynamism, national security, and future capabilities. While these advances are dual-use or general-purpose in character, and the discipline of quantum science and technology remains at a nascent moment in its development, the promise and perceived potentials of these advances are already provoking increased concerns about military applications and national security implications.

In the years and perhaps decades to come, China's national strategy of military–civil fusion could become a defining feature and critical advantage in its defense innovation. In particular, the capacity already demonstrated within quantum science and technology to start to break down barriers and facilitate partnerships between the military, academia, and industry indicates that this will be a notable feature of this field in the future, likely provoking continued controversy about the implications of that military potential and defense involvement for the international engagement and collaboration that has characterized the discipline to date. The development of prototypes in quantum navigation and potential employment of quantum communications in a maritime environment highlights the reality of advances once dismissed as spooky or science fictional.

---

[134]Cho, Adrian. 'Quantum Flashlight Pierces the Darkness With a Few Percent as Many Photons.' (2008): 1433–1443.
[135]Shapiro, Jeffrey H. 'The quantum illumination story', *IEEE Aerospace and Electronic Systems Magazine* 35/4 (2020), 8–20.
[136]'The Coming of the Quantum Radar That Makes Stealth Fighter in Profile' [让隐形战机显形的量子雷达来了], *Science and Technology Daily*, 13 September 2016. 'China's First Single-Photon Quantum Radar Successfully Developed' [中国首部单光子量子雷达系统研制成功], CETC, 18 September 2016, http://www.cetc.com.cn/zgdzkj/_300931/_300939/445284/index.html.

At this point, strategists are starting to speculate about the impact of quantum technology on the future battlefield.[137] For instance, quantum cryptography is believed to be a critical emerging technology that could 'infuse information operations with new vitality', according to Ye Zheng, an influential theorist of information warfare theorist.[138] A number of PLA academics have highlighted the potential offensive employment of the immense potential of quantum computing, including to crack cryptography.[139] Despite the technical challenges that remain, military scientists have pointed to the seemingly 'infinite' potential of quantum computing in the long term.[140] Going forward, quantum technology is also expected variously to increase not only security through 'uncrackable' cryptography and advances in computing capabilities,[141] but also allow high-precision navigation and anti-jamming imaging.[142] The use of quantum communications is anticipated to enhance battlefield information processing capabilities, enabling the construction of a more robust combat system.[143]

As quantum technology continues to advance, Chinese military strategists will be watching closely. As the information age undergoes a 'leap' toward the 'quantum information age', these technologies are considered a 'forward position' for a great power's comprehensive national power, scientific level, and strategic contests of military power, according to another Chinese military officer.[144] The PLA has been acutely aware of the criticality of adapting to and capitalizing upon progress in these domains, given its fears of the emergence of another 'generational gap' between its capabilities and those of the U.S. military. Although the PLA will confront considerable challenges in its efforts to progress from experimentation to implementation in these emerging technologies, these initial results could prelude greater progress.

Indeed, China is prioritizing defense and military innovation in quantum technology, domains in which the United States has not realized and may not be able to achieve a decisive advantage. Since the U.S. is perceived as

---

[137]Chen Jian [陈健], and Ban Feihu [班飞虎], 'The main impact of quantum information technology on the military field' [量子信息技术对军事领域的主要影响], *Military Digest* [军事文摘] (2020).
[138]Ye Zheng [叶征], *Lectures on the Science of Information Operations* [信息作战学习教程], Military Science Press [军事科学出版社], 2013, p. 79.
[139]Tu Chenxin [屠晨昕], 'Quantum Technology: Remodeling Humankind's Military Affairs Forces' [量子技术:重塑人类军事力量], *Qianjiang Evening News* [黔江晚报], 4 June 2014.
[140]'Researcher Qiang Xiaogang tells you: "Quantum Computing" with Infinite Potential' [强晓刚研究员为你讲述:潜力无穷的'量子计算'], China Military Network, 16 April 2021, http://www.81.cn/ss/2021-04/16/content_10023644.htm.
[141]Yuan Yi [袁艺], Quantum Cryptography: The 'Magic Weapon' in Future Warfare [量子密码:未来战争'神器'], *Guangming Daily* [光明日报], 28 May 2014.
[142]Gao Dongguang [高东广], 'Quantum: "Dark Horse" was born beyond the ordinary' [量子:'黑马'出世超凡脱俗], China Military Online, 15 February 2019, http://www.81.cn/jfjbmap/content/2019-02/15/content_227391.htm.
[143]An Weiping [安卫平], 'Quantum Communications Sparks Off Transformation in the Military Domain [量子通信引发军事领域变革]', *PLA Daily*, 27 September 2016, http://jz.chinamil.com.cn/n2014/tp/content_7278464.htm.
[144]Ibid.

a powerful adversary (强敌) – and the key metric for comparison – U.S.–China strategic competition will remain a primary driver of Chinese technological development, as well as military modernization, against the backdrop of a worsening security dilemma. Such an impetus of insecurity has historically been and will remain a major driver for innovation in China.[145] However, given its strengths in quantum science and technology, the opportunity for China to contest a competitive advantage through seeking to turn sharply to surpass (弯道超车) in quantum innovation cannot be dismissed or overlooked.[146]

Disclosure statement

No potential conflict of interest was reported by the author(s).

Bibliography

Cheung, Tai Ming, Thomas Mahnken, and Andrew Ross, 'Frameworks for Analyzing Chinese Defence and Military Innovation', Study of Innovation and Technology in China, 2011. https://escholarship.org/uc/item/5cr8j76s

Dowling, Jonathan P. and Gerard J. Milburne, 'Quantum Technology: The Second Quantum Revolution', *Philosophical Transactions of the Royal Society of London A: Mathematical, Physical and Engineering Sciences* 361/1809 (2003), 1655–74. https://arxiv.org/pdf/quant-ph/0206091.pdf

Gilli, Andrea and Mauro Gilli, 'Why China Has Not Caught up Yet: Military-Technological Superiority and the Limits of Imitation, Reverse Engineering, and Cyber Espionage', *International Security* 43/3 (2019), 141–89. doi:10.1162/isec_a_00337.

Han, Xuan, Hai-Lin Yong, Ping Xu, Kui-Xing Yang, Li Shuang-Lin, Wei-Yang Wang, Hua-Jian Xue, et al., 'Polarization Design for Ground-to-satellite Quantum Entanglement Distribution', *Optics Express* 28/1 (2020), 369–78. doi:10.1364/OE.28.000369.

Ji, Ling, et al., 'Towards Quantum Communications in Free-space Seawater', *Optics Express* 25/17 (2017), 19795. doi:10.1364/OE.25.019795.

---

[145] This is consistent with the theory of 'creative insecurity' that Taylor proposed. Mark Zachary Taylor, *The Politics of Innovation: Why Some Countries Are Better Than Others at Science and Technology*, Oxford University Press, 2016.

[146] 'How To Achieve Paradigm Changes in the Domain of National Defence Science and Technology' [国防科技领域如何实现弯道超车], *PLA Daily*, 30 June 2016, http://jz.chinamil.com.cn/n2014/tp/content_7126648.htm.

Jianwei, P. A. N., 'Progress of the Quantum Experiment Science Satellite (QUESS) Micius Project', 空间科学学报 40/5 (2020), 643–47.

Kania, Elsa B. and John K. Costello, 'Quantum Hegemony? – China's Ambitions and the Challenge to U.S. Innovation Leadership', Center for a New American Security, Sept. 2018.

Lee, Min Soo, Min Ki Woo, Yong-Su Kim, Young-Wook Cho, Sang-Wook Han, and Sung Moon, 'Quantum Hacking on a Free-space Quantum Key Distribution System without Measuring Quantum Signals', *JOSA B* 36/3 (2019), B77–B82. doi:10.1364/JOSAB.36.000B77.

Lindsay, Jon R., 'Surviving the Quantum Cryptopocalypse', *Strategic Studies Quarterly* 14/2 (2020), 49–73.

Lü, Miao, [苗绿], Wang Huiyao [王辉耀], and Zheng Jinlian [郑金连], 'Science and Technology Talent Policy Boots Construction of World Science and Technology Power——Take International Science and Technology Talent Introduction Policy as an Example' [科技人才政策助推世界科技强国建设——以国际科技人才引进政策突破为例], *Bulletin of Chinese Academy of Sciences* [中国科学院院刊] (2017).

Ren, Ji-Gang, et al., 'Ground-to-satellite Quantum Teleportation', *Nature*, 9 Aug. 2017.

Renema, Jelmer J., Hui Wang, Jian Qin, Xiang You, Chaoyang Lu, and Jianwei Pan, 'Sample-efficient Benchmarking of Multi-photon Interference on a Boson Sampler in the Sparse Regime', *arXiv preprint arXiv:2008.09077* (2020).

Ruihong, Qiao and Meng Ying, 'Research Progress of Quantum Repeaters', *Journal of Physics. Conference Series* 1237/5 (2019), 052032. IOP Publishing.

Smith, Frank L, III, 'Quantum Technology Hype and National Security', *Security Dialogue* 51/5 (2020), 499–516. doi:10.1177/0967010620904922.

Taylor, Mark Zachary, *The Politics of Innovation: Why Some Countries are Better than Others at Science and Technology* (Oxford University Press 2016).

Xu, Feihu, Xiongfeng Ma, Qiang Zhang, Hoi-Kwong Lo, and Jian-Wei Pan, 'Secure Quantum Key Distribution with Realistic Devices', *Reviews of Modern Physics* 92/2 (2020), 025002. Chen, Yu-Ao, Z. Q., et al. (2020), Submitted. doi:10.1103/RevModPhys.92.025002.

Yin, Juan, Ji-Gang Ren, Sheng-Kai Liao, Yuan Cao, Wen-Qi Cai, Cheng-Zhi Peng, and Jian-Wei Pan, 'Quantum Science Experiments with Micius Satellite', in *CLEO: Applications and Technology* (Optical Society of America 2019), JTu3G–4.

Zhang, Qiang, Feihu Xu, Li Li, Nai-Le Liu, and Jian-Wei Pan, 'Quantum Information Research in China', *Quantum Science and Technology* 4/4 (2019), 040503. doi:10.1088/2058-9565/ab4bea.

Zheng, Ye, [叶征], *Lectures on the Science of Information Operations* [信息作战学习教程] (Military Science Press [军事科学出版社] 2013).

Defense innovation in Russia in the 2010s

Vasilii Kashin

ABSTRACT
The chapter examines the driving forces and the institutions behind the Russian military buildup in the period between 2010 and 2020. The beginning of the rapid Russian military modernization in late 2000s was the result of the shifting threat assesments by the Russian political leadership and the painful lessons of the war with Georgia in 2008. Russia had to conduct an throughout and painful restructuring of the military institutions and the defense industrial complex in order to be able to meet the ambitious goals of its' rearmament program. The result was significant growth in the Russian military capabilities by the middle of the decade.

In a relatively short period between 2008 and 2014 the Russian defense industry and the Russian military underwent deep transformation which had a deep impact on the Russian behavior on the international arena. Military conflict with Georgia in August 2008 although small scale and successful for Russia has shown huge gap in the Russian military and defense industrial capabilities. They included poor C4ISR systems, lack of precision strike capabilities, low interoperability between services and branches of the military, general poor state of much of the defense equipment. Using such a military in conflict with a more potent opponent would inevitably end in disaster. In such a state the Russian military could hardly be used as an effective foreign policy tool while the Russian foreign policy has been growing more and more assertive.

Less than six years later the same military was capable to bloodlessly take the strategically important Crimean peninsula where more that 20 thousand Ukrainian troops were stationed. In September 2015 Russia started a military operation in Syria and succeded in changing the course of war, saving the Assad regime and taking much of the country under its' control. The Syrian operation was conducted while being almost constantly on the brink of direct military confrontation with a number of the regional militaries and in some moments with the US. Simultaneously Russia managed to significantly upgrade the national strategic nuclear deterrent force and obtain a number of other strategic capabilities, strengthening its' position globally.

The evolution of post-Soviet Russian policies dealing with the armed forces, the defense industry, and defense innovation in general can be broadly divided into two large periods. The first period started after the Soviet Union's collapse and lasted until 2008. The second period started after the military conflict with Georgia which led to the introduction of sweeping Russian military reforms, which also affected relations between the military and the defense industry. In the strategic weapons sector, however, the rise of innovation activity started years earlier. This was triggered by the U.S. decision to leave the 1972 Anti Ballistic Missile Treaty Treaty, which the Russian leadership feared could lead to a serious erosion in the credibility of the Russian nuclear force.

This chapter attempts to evaluate the Russian system of defense innovation as it emerged out of the reforms, which mainly took place in the early 2010s. These reforms led to major progress in the technological modernization of the Russian military, which was most recently reflected in Russian military performance during the Ukrainian crisis after 2014 and its intervention in Syria starting in 2015.

Catalytic factors for military reform and defense innovation: Reevaluation of threats in 2002 and 2008

The Russian government is quite clear about the technological aspects of the military threats addressed by Russian defense policies. The Military Doctrine of the Russian Federation adopted in 2014 identifies the following key areas of concern[1]:

- The development of strategic missile defense systems, which undermines strategic stability and destroys the balance of forces in the field of strategic weapons. The list of highly destabilizing systems developed abroad includes the Prompt Global Strike program as well as the plans to deploy strategic non-nuclear weapon systems and to develop space-based weapons.
- Proliferation of weapons of mass destruction and missile technologies.
- The use of information and mass communication technologies to influence public opinion, undermining both the sovereignty of foreign countries and global stability.

---

[1] Russian Federation Military Doctrine [Военная доктрина Российской Федерации], https://rg.ru/2014/12/30/doktrina-dok.html.

During future conflicts, adversaries are expected to attempt to disrupt the Russian civilian and military command and control systems and undermine the strategic nuclear forces command and control chain and ballistic missile early warning systems. Nuclear weapons storage systems, nuclear power plants, and environmentally hazardous industries are expected to come under attack.[2]

Russian military planners expect that hypersonic weapons, new types of electronic warfare systems, ground, air, and naval robotic systems, as well as 'weapons on the new physical principles'[3] will be widely used in future military conflicts.

The Russian National Security Strategy of 2015 also takes note of the dangers associated with the rapid development of biotechnology. According to the document, there was uncertainty concerning the real capabilities of some foreign states in developing biological weapons and over how the U.S. military network of biological laboratories was growing near Russia's borders.[4]

The Russian Information Security Doctrine notes that a number of foreign countries are boosting their capabilities to influence Russian information networks in pursuit of military goals. The growing assertiveness of foreign technical intelligence organizations against the Russian government and defense industry is also observed. Certain foreign states are accused of conducting a propaganda war against Russia by using technology to influence internal Russian politics and disrupt Russian media activities abroad.[5]

Russia also considers itself to be subject to an increasing number of complex, coordinated, and large-scale cyber-attacks on the key chokepoints of Russian infrastructure aimed at undermining Russia's sovereignty and internal stability. Russia recognizes its weaknesses in information technology. These include the low competitiveness of Russian technology in this field and a lack of domestic advanced electronic components production. As a result, Russia is heavily dependent on foreign software and computer equipment to satisfy the needs of the economy.[6]

In recent years, another major policy change has created stronger incentives for Russian defense innovation. In the current environment, the Russian ability to cooperate with the West on science and technology has been severely limited. This has weakened groups within the Russian establishment that previously relied on exchanges with the West. It also meant that Russian

---

[2]Ibid.
[3]In practice, Russia uses this term most often to refer to electromagnetic pulse weapons.
[4]Russian Federation National Security strategy, 2015 [Стратегия национальной безопасности России, 2015] https://rg.ru/2015/12/31/nac-bezopasnost-site-dok.html.
[5]Russian Federation Information Security Doctrine[Доктрина информационной безопасности Российской Федерации, 6 декабря 2016 г] https://rg.ru/2016/12/06/doktrina-infobezobasnost-site-dok.html.
[6]Ibid.

strategies for boosting innovation development for the general economy had to rely more on domestic resources, which are still concentrated in the defense sector.

From the time of the USSR's collapse at the beginning of the 1990s to around 2008, the Russian government conducted limited incremental reforms of its military establishment. The reforms addressed some of the major shortcomings of the old military order that had become evident during the two wars in the Northern Caucasus and other local conflicts in the former USSR during the 1990s and first decade of the twenty-first century. However, except for gradual downsizing, the reforms did little to adapt the Russian military for the new realities it faced. Russia cut its 1992 troop level of 2.5–2.8 million personnel to less than 1.6 million in 1996, then to less than 1.2 million in 1999.[7] In 2001, Russian President Vladimir Putin signed a decree that set the optimal number of Russian military personnel at one million. Although that number has been periodically increased or decreased slightly in subsequent presidential decrees,[8] the actual number of military personnel has not exceeded roughly 800,000 since at least the late 2000s.[9]

The military retained many of its Soviet Cold-War era institutions, structures, and procedures, including an antiquated procurement system not suitable for a market economy. Additionally, many defense industry assets were subject to relatively chaotic privatization in the 1990s. The procurement system in particular was a major obstacle to defense innovation.

Defense industry restructuring policies implemented by the Russian government starting in 2002 led to the creation of major defense industry corporations such as Rostech, United Aircraft Corporation, United Shipbuilding Corporation, Tactical Missiles Corporation, Almaz-Antei, among others. However, lack of financial resources and the relatively low priority given to defense issues during President Boris Yeltsin's rule as well as during the first two terms of Vladimir Putin's presidency made proactive defense innovation difficult, with the exception of some highly prioritized sectors (such as nuclear weapons and strategic delivery systems).

The catalyst for the revival of the Russian strategic weapons sector was the declaration by George W. Bush in December 2001 that the United States would leave the 1972 ABM Treaty.[10] Russian leadership never fully believed U.S. assertions about its need to defend against 'rogue states' such as Iran and

---

[7]'The Changes in Russian Military Manpower', TASS, http://tass.ru/info/4135532.
[8]For example, Presidential Decree No. 1878сс [Указ Президента РФ от 29.12.2008 N 1878сс (ред. от 08.07.2016) 'О некоторых вопросах Вооруженных Сил Российской Федерации'], Presidential Decree No.1, 2008 [Указ Президента РФ от 01.01.2008 N 1 'О штатной численности Вооруженных Сил Российской Федерации'], Presidential Decree No 1372s [Указ Президента Российской Федерации от 28.11.2005 г. № 1372с], among others. The decrees are renewed on a yearly basis.
[9]'Contractors will be hired at the recruiting stations', Komsomolskaya Pravda, 05.10.2011 [Контрактников будут набирать на вербовочных станциях], https://www.kp.ru/daily/25765/2750335/.
[10]The withdrawal took effect in mid-2002.

North Korea, and immediately became concerned about the possible loss of the credibility of the Russian strategic deterrent. According to Vladimir Putin's 2018 address to the Russian Parliament, immediately after the U.S. withdrawal the Russian government authorized a number of new R&D projects to ensure the viability of Russian strategic delivery systems in the new strategic environment. These included the development of hypersonic glider reentry vehicles for ICBMs, new generations of strategic cruise missiles, and other systems.

Although it enjoyed better financing and greater attention from leadership throughout the 1990s and 2000s, the strategic weapons sector was still affected by the general decline of the Russian defense sector. The industry slightly increased the production of the Topol-M (SS-27 Mod 1) ICBMs in mobile and silo versions and put the newer RS-24 Yars (SS-27 Mod 2) MIRV capable ICBM into production. However, more complicated projects, such as the construction of the Project 995 SSBNs and development of the SS-N-30 (Bulava) SLBMs and Kh-101/102 air launched cruise missiles, were severely, almost chronically, delayed.[11] Russia could embark on large-scale modernization of its strategic forces only after the general defense industry overhaul began in 2009.

Procurement of conventional weapon systems by the Russian government was very limited until 2009, thus arms exports were the key source of revenue for Russian producers of conventional arms. Export deals were also key innovation drivers in some areas. Some of the major Russian weapon systems now in production were originally developed for foreign customers. For example, development of the 'Tigr' (Tiger) armored vehicle and the Pantsir-S1 SAM (SS-22 Greyhound) was financed by the United Arab Emirates. The Project 1135.6 frigates currently being built for the Russian Navy are based on projects of the early 2000s for the Indian and Chinese navies.

The Russian government understood the limitations of its existing armed forces structure and started to prepare for a new round of more radical reform as early as 2006–2007. Some reforms were developed under the guidance of General Yury Baluyevsky, chief of the General Staff of the Russian Armed Forces during that period.[12] Reforms were planned to proceed gradually, to avoid discontent within the ranks and to limit the burden on the economy.

The military conflict against Georgia in August 2008, although won by the Russian forces with relative ease, exposed critical weaknesses in the Russian command and control structure, its weak reconnaissance capabilities, and inadequate training of personnel, especially in the Air Force.

---

[11] V. Litovkin. Solomonov's Gold Star. How Bulava was Made to Fly. [В. Литовкин. Золотая звезда Соломонова. Как заставили полететь Булаву], https://tass.ru/opinions/9896349.

[12] Army During War and Peace. General Baluevsky about Reforms and Reformers. [Армия на войне и мире. Генерал Балуеувский о реформах и реформаторах] AIF.RU, 23.02.2020, https://aif.ru/society/army/armiya_na_voyne_i_v_mire_general_baluevskiy_o_reformah_i_reformatorah.

The role of the 2008 Georgian war in the development of the Russian military and defense innovation system is generally comparable to the role of the May 1999 Belgrade Embassy bombing in Chinese defense efforts. Russian military officials initially suspected that the United States,[13] which had a significant number of civilian and military personnel posted in Georgia and attached to various Georgian government agencies, not only knew about the coming attack against South Ossetia and the Russian forces there, but also approved of it unofficially. Although later the dominant point of view was that the attack was caused by miscommunication between U.S. officials and Georgians, suspicions remained, and the threat assessment changed significantly on the Russian side. The conflict led to a deep reassessment of relations with the West. Going forward, the Russian government expected the United States and its allies to intervene in the affairs of the ex-Soviet satellites, with the ultimate goal of undermining the Russian political system.

On 14 October 2008, Russian Defense Minister Anatoly Serdyukov declared the start of the reforms, which were supposed to continue until 2020. Although reforms had long been part of the Russian government's plans, the conflict with Georgia seems to have forced Moscow to pursue reforms more vigorously.

More than two years later, on 31 December 2010, President Dmitry Medvedev signed the State Armament Program (GPV) 2020, which was supposed to increase the share of advanced weapons in the Russian military's inventory to 70% by 2020. In 2011, however, the Ministry of Defense (MoD) assessed the share of advanced weapon systems to be about 20% for the strategic nuclear forces and 10% for conventional forces.[14]

The implementation of this massive program (with a declared cost of 19 trillion rubles or about US $633 billion at 2010 exchange rates) has transformed the Russian defense industry as well as the Russian Ministry of Defense departments responsible for innovation and science and technology planning.

The reforms included the following elements[15]:

(1) Maintenance of troop levels at under 1 million personnel.

---

[13]Russian General Staff. US Participated in War on Georgian Side. [Генштаб ВС РФ. США участвовали в войне на стороне Грузии]. RBC.RU, 09.09.2008 https://www.rbc.ru/politics/09/09/2008/5703ced29a79473dc8148cc4.

[14]'New state armaments program prioritizes high tech equipment'. National Defense, 14.03.2011 [В новой государственной программе вооружения приоритет отдан высокотехнологичным образцам. Национальная оборона, 14.03.2011] 'http://oborona.ru/includes/periodics/maintheme/2011/0314/21345724/detail.shtml.

[15]See M. Barabanov. Russia's New Army. Center For Analysis of Strategies and Technologies 2010. [М. Барабанов. Новая армия России. Центр Анализа Стратегий и Технологий, 2010], http://cast.ru/books/novaya-armiya-rossii.html; Mikhail Barabanov, Konstantin Makienko, Ruslan Pukhov. Military Regorm. On the Path Toward the New Layout of the Russian Army. Valdai Discussions Club 2012.[М. Барабанов, К.Макиенко, Р.Пухов. Военная реформа. На пути к новому облику российской армии. Дискуссионный клуб Валдай, 2012].

(2) Restructuring of the officer corps, reducing it from 355,000 to 150,000 personnel.
(3) Centralization of military education, with 65 institutions slated to be reorganized into 10 systemic institutions. This decision was considered too extreme and later partly reversed.
(4) Reorganization of the central military commands. This included the Ministry of Defense and General Staff. The number of personnel was also cut.
(5) Creation of four new Joint Strategic Commands to replace the seven military districts. The Joint Strategic Commands control all forces in their areas of responsibility.
(6) Outsourcing of maintenance, catering, and similar services to commercial providers.
(7) Elimination of cadre units of the Ground Forces. All units were transformed into permanent readiness forces.
(8) Reorganization of the reservist training system.
(9) Transition to a mixed system of recruiting for the Armed Forces to gradually increase the share of professional soldiers and decrease the share of conscripts.
(10) Reduction in the number of military units, garrisons, and military bases. Transfer of land forces to the brigade base and abolition of divisional and regimental units, with the subsequent transfer of brigades to a fundamentally new structure.
(11) Reorganization of the Air Force and air defense with the abolition of armies, corps, divisions, and aviation regiments and transition to a system of air bases and brigades for aerospace defense.
(12) Reorganization of the Navy.

The reforms started with an assessment of the global political and military situation. It was decided that the Russian military had to be able to fight in local conflicts in Russia, the former Soviet bloc states, and neighboring countries. Simplifying the command structure of the military forces was also a priority. The previously existing structure of divisions and regiments was changed. The new structure, which consists of the General Staff, theater commands, armies, and brigades, was considered more suitable for success in local wars. A goal of reducing mobilization time from one day to one hour was also set.

Russian strategy in defense innovation

Political relations between Russia and the US have been steadily deteriorating since the first half of the 2000s. Russian political leadership has been increasingly viewing the NATO expansion and growing competition with the US and EU for influence in the former Soviet Union republics as key challenges for the country's foreign policy. US decision to leave the Anti Ballistic Missile Defense treaty in 2002, 'colored revolutions' in a number of post-Soviet countries and military conflict with Georgia has fueled the Russian fears. After the beginning of the Ukrainina crisis in 2014 and especially Russian intervention in Syria in 2015 Russia and the US have occasionally found themselves on the brink of direct military conflict.

Based on such threat assessments by the Russian military/political leaderhip, priorities in the Russian rearmament program include: the development of new types of precision guided munitions and methods to counter such munitions; new air, space, and missile defense systems; new C4ISR (command, control, communications, computers, intelligence, surveillance and reconnaissance) systems; robotic weapon systems; a new generation of the air transports; and protective equipment for military personnel.[16]

Russian planning is based on the assumption of successful development of an upgraded missile defense system by the United States. China is expected to be able to deploy 'the core elements' of a strategic missile defense system in the coming years. At the same time, the United States is expected to field the first hypersonic missile systems by 2025. Russian experts also note that NATO countries are actively working on kinetic weapons, laser weapon systems, new types of guidance systems and space-based weapons, electronic warfare, and reconnaissance satellites. Robotic systems are gradually expected to replace traditional combat platforms.[17]

The long-term goals of the Russian defense innovation programs are focused on the development of the disruptive technologies that are expected to define the battlefield of the future. These include directed energy and hypersonic weapon systems, kinetic weapons, robotic systems, and cyber weapons.[18]

Russia will also develop measures to protect its domestic information infrastructure and command and control systems from attacks and attempts to establish control from abroad. Russia is developing policies to eliminate dependence on foreign software and equipment. This is to be achieved through support for domestic software and equipment production and domestic electronic components production.[19]

---

[16] Russian Federation Military Doctrine [Военная доктрина Российской Федерации], https://rg.ru/2014/12/30/doktrina-dok.html.

[17] O.B. Achasov, S.S. Smirnov, A.Y. Pronin, 'Main directions of the technological development of the Russian Armed Forces Weapons Systems', *Armaments and Economics* 1/34 (2016). [О.Б.Ачасов, С.С. Смирнов, А.Ю.Пронин. Основные направления технологического развития системы вооружений Вооруженных Сил Российской Федерации. Вооружение и Экономика. 1 (34), 2016,] http://viek.ru/34/9-19.pdf.

[18] S.E. Pankov, I.I. Borisenkov, S.S. Smirnov, R.V. Reulov. Planning of basic and applied research in the defense and security areas in the current conditions. Armaments and Economics 2(39), 2017. [С.Е. Панков, И.И. Борисенков, С.С.Смирнов, Р.В.Реулов. Планирование фундаментальных и прикладных исследований в области обороны и безопасности государства в современных условиях. Вооружение и Экономика. 2 (39), 2017], http://www.viek.ru/39/43-54.pdf.

[19] Russian Federation Information Security Doctrine [Доктрина информационной безопасности Российской Федерации, 6 декабря 2016 г], https://rg.ru/2016/12/06/doktrina-infobezobasnost-site-dok.html.

More broadly, Russia plans to pursue a general reindustrialization policy that includes strengthening positions in industries that are already internationally competitive (nuclear, space, defense) and rebuilding a number of older industries that declined after the USSR collapsed (heavy machines, civilian aircraft, electronics, and industrial tools production, among others). The defense industry is supposed to drive this industrial modernization through government investment in modernization of defense enterprises.[20] The Russian government hopes that the defense industry concerns established in the 2000s will eventually repeat the success of their Chinese counterparts and become diversified international industrial companies. The share of the civilian goods and services in defense industry revenues is projected to rise from 16% in 2016 to 30% in 2025 and then to 50% in 2030–35. The defense industry is supposed to expand the production of medical equipment, energy equipment, civilian ships, and aircraft production.[21]

President Putin's March 2018 address shed some light on the Russian top leadership's approach to defense innovation. In his speech, he clearly stated that after the U.S. decision to withdraw unilaterally from the ABM Treaty in 2002 the Russian government decided to launch a number of extremely ambitious and technologically risky projects to ensure strategic stability.[22] These included new generations of ICBM, hypersonic weapons, and non-ballistic nuclear delivery platforms, as well as laser weapons and new types of ICBMs.

Putin's statement helps to clarify one of the known peculiarities of the Russian defense budget of the mid-2000s—a high level of R&D expenditure relative to weapons procurement. For example, in 2003 13.3% of the defense budget was spent on R&D and 18.7% on procurement. In 2005, 11.4% was spent on R&D and 15.6% on procurement. This changed after the reforms began: the share of R&D remained more or less the same and procurement expenditures grew rapidly.[23] At present R&D expenditures account for roughly one-sixth of the procurement budget.

Before the reforms, among the limited resources available for the force development (procurement and R&D), the government was ready to spend more than 40% on R&D, mostly on expensive and risky future projects,

---

[20] Russia National Security Strategy, 2015. [Стратегия национальной безопасности России, 2015], https://rg.ru/2015/12/31/nac-bezopasnost-site-dok.html.

[21] Putin ordered to increase the share of the civilian production on the defense sector factories to 50% by 2035 [«Путин поручил увеличить долю гражданской продукции на заводах ОПК до 50% к 2035 году»], https://rns.online/military/Putin-poruchil-uelichit-dolyu-grazhdanskoi-produktsii-na-zavodah-OPK-k-2035-godu-dolzhna-do-50-2016-12-01/.

[22] www.interfax.ru/business/598,085.

[23] A.E. Varshavsky, Y.A. Makarova. 'The analisys of the defense industrial complex R&D financing during the growth and contraction of the military expenditure', *National Interests: Priorities and Security* 18/255 (2014), 2–16. [А. Е. Варшавский and Ю. А. Макарова, Анализ особенностей финансирования сферы НИОКР оборонно-промышленного комплекса на этапах роста и сокращения военных расходов. Национальные интересы: Приоритеты и безопасность. 18(255) 2014, стр. 2–16].

sacrificing the needs of its military, which was still involved in the war in the Northern Caucasus at that time. R&D investment at the expense of current procurement also adversely affected Russian military performance during the military conflict with Georgia in 2008, which was fought using old equipment such as T-62 tanks and BMD-1 airborne armored vehicles. However, this heavy investment brought significant results by the mid-2010s when the Russian military increasingly used new equipment and weapons not based on Soviet prototypes.

The technology areas favored for this kind of high-risk investment are those where a certain level of technological capability has existed since Soviet times. For example, the Soviets had conducted experiments with laser weapons and hypersonic vehicles. If Putin's statements are accurate, Russia has already become one of the leaders in laser weapon technology and the first country to field a hypersonic cruise missile. Other known priorities are land-based SAM and missile defense systems and electronic warfare systems.

Attempts to create technological capabilities in the areas where the USSR did not have significant expertise are sometimes mired in difficulties. Modern UAVs are one such example. Although Russia has managed to satisfy domestic demand for tactical reconnaissance UAVs, Russian industry has managed to start the mass production of the Russian medium altitude long endurance (MALE) combat UAV as late as 2020, lagging behind not just the United States and China, but also Turkey and Iran.

In its defense modernization drive Russia has certain advantages and some major challenges. The advantages include a historically well established R&D and industrial capabilities in the defense sector and some adjacent industries such as nuclear energy and space. The key weakness is the generally unbalanced and backward structure of the Russian economy which is still dominated by the extraction industries providing for the majority of the export revenues. Another major problem are the general failure of the Russian government efforts to effectively reform the civilian research and development infrastructure. As result the Russian plans for technological and industrial modernization are increasingly being taken over by the military and the defense industry.

Institutional factors: Russian threat assessments and views on the role of modern technology

The Ministry of Defense seeks to take the lead in managing major innovation programs not just for the military, but also for the economy in general. Since the early years of the Ukrainian crisis, the MoD has played up the role the national defense industry could play as a main driver of general industrial development. For example, in 2015 Deputy Defense Minister Tatyana Shevtsova stated that the growth of defense procurement would help to modernize the Russian general industrial base.[24] Efforts led by the MoD and the defense industry were expected to speed up import substitution in critically important areas where Russia was dependent on the West. In 2017, the Ministry of Defense began development of the Era Innovation Center in southern Russia (near Anapa). The center is often described as the military equivalent of the Skolkovo Innovation Center, which was started in 2009 during the presidency of Dmitriy Medvedev.[25] According to Deputy Defense Minister Pavel Popov, MoD innovation activities are supposed to boost rearmament and also benefit the wider economy.[26]

An early issue during the implementation of the GPV 2020 was how to determine pricing. The government sets certain maximum levels of profitability for the enterprises involved in the defense production chain, depending on their role. In accordance with the decision of the President of the Russian Federation No. Пр-3443 from 25 November 2010, the Ministry of Defense implemented an approach to pricing that excludes 'winding up' the profits of the lead executors from the costs of third-party organizations. This can lead to a cost savings of 15–20%.[27] This arrangement led to numerous complaints from the defense industry about the low profitability of defense contracts. In the reform's early stages, the profit margin on state armament contracts for some of the final assembly enterprises was as low as 3–5%. In May 2011, Vladimir Putin personally intervened and stated that the profitability of such contracts for the defense industry should be no lower than 15%.[28]

The profitability of defense contracts is defined currently by the Russian Cabinet of Ministers Act N 1465 of 2 December 2017. The Act states maximum profit margins of 20% on direct costs and 1% on indirect (outsourced) costs.[29]

---

[24]Shevtsova: the growth of the State Armaments Order will make the defense industry a driver for the Russian Economy. RIA Novosti, 23.01.2015 [Шевцова: Рост гособоронзаказа сделает ВПК драйвером экономики РФ. РИА Новости, 23.01.2015,] https://ria.ru/economy/20150123/1043959462.html.

[25]Military Skolkovo. Why Shoigu builds a high tech city near Anapa. RBC. 13.03.2018 [Военное Сколково. Зачем Шойгу строит технополис в Анапе. РБК, 13.03.2018] https://www.rbc.ru/politics/13/03/2018/5a9e82869a7947860d0516ca.

[26]Pavel Popov. Time for innovations for the State and the Army. Independent military observer. 12.03.2018 [Павел Попов. Эра инноваций для государства и армии. Независимое военное обозрение, 12.03.2018.] https://nvo.ng.ru/armament/2018-03-09/1_987_tehnopolys.html.

[27]The work on the MoD suggestions for the State Armament order are on the finishing phase. The National Defense 11.07.2011 [«Формирование предложений Минобороны в проект гособоронзаказа на 2012–2014 годы находится в завершающей стадии». Национальная оборона. 11.0.2011] http://www.nationaldefense.ru/includes/periodics/maintheme/2011/1107/18327630/print.shtml.

[28]Putin: Defense Industry Profitability Should be no lower than 15%. RIA Novosti, 05.11.2011. [Рентабельность оборонных предприятий должна быть не ниже 15% – Путин] https://ria.ru/20110511/373027693.html.

[29]Act 1465 On the State Regulation on the Costs on Defense Related Products. [Постановление 1465 ПОЛОЖЕНИЕ О ГОСУДАРСТВЕННОМ РЕГУЛИРОВАНИИ ЦЕН НА ПРОДУКЦИЮ, ПОСТАВЛЯЕМУЮ ПО ГОСУДАРСТВЕННОМУ ОБОРОННОМУ ЗАКАЗУ] http://www.consultant.ru/cons/cgi/online.cgi?req=doc&base=LAW&n=284195&fld=134&dst=100013,0&rnd=0.7531740697956884#02569870398459546.

The actual profit is sometimes considerably smaller. For example, in 2016 Motovilikha Factories, a producer of artillery systems, complained of state armaments orders profits of just 1.6%.[30]

The main method of determining prices for the Ministry of Defense are calculations based on producer-supplied information that confirms the real cost of production. The process is organized as follows: The Defense Ministry's Department of State Defense requests pricing materials from enterprises.

The Ministry of Defense must take the level of profitability into account in accordance with the president's 2010 decision, supplemented by subsequent decisions made by the Cabinet of Ministers.[31]

Accurate pricing for the most complex and expensive weapons (such as nuclear submarines, rockets, and aircraft) was of the greatest importance to the implementation of GPV 2020, and at the same time the biggest roadblock. Pricing transparency was difficult to obtain, given the scale of the participating enterprises. Enterprises across the board were asked provide their price calculations to the MoD for detailed analysis. However, many failed to submit their estimates in a timely fashion, which led to contract delays for state defense orders.

The system of placing and executing state defense orders also changed, with these functions moved under the control of a core business department. It is assumed that in such a system there is much less room for corruption, as all necessary materials and prices have to be submitted in accordance with a set of regulations.

Military campaign in Syria started by Russia in 2015 served as source of valuable experience for the Russian defense industry development unfluencing the MoD approach to procurement at the same time. The Russian military tried to use the Syrian theater as a test ground for as many systems and platforms as possible including the ones under development. The prototypes of the Russian 5th generation Su-57 figthers were sent to Syria for 2–3 days in February 2018 and later in 2019 and conducted strikes against enemy targets with new types of bombs and missiles.[32]

The MoD has claimed that combat use in Syria lead to improvement of over 300 types of weapons and equipment while the development and production of 12 types was discontinued because of the unsatisfactory performance. Personnel of over 70 defense industrial enterprises was posted to Syria to assess the

---

[30] Machine Industry. The results of the year in Kama region. Kommersant 25.12.2018 [Машиностроение. Промышленные итоги года в Прикамье] https://www.kommersant.ru/doc/3842533.

[31] The work on the MoD suggestions for the State Armament order are on the finishing phase. The National Defense 11.07.2011 [«Формирование предложений Минобороны в проект гособоронзаказа на 2012–2014 годы находится в завершающей стадии». Национальная оборона. 11.0.2011] http://www.nationaldefense.ru/includes/periodics/maintheme/2011/1107/18327630/print.shtml.

[32] Su-57 used new types of bombs and missiles in Syria [На Су-57 в Сирии испытали новые типы бомб и ракет] TASS 24/12/2019, https://tass.ru/armiya-i-opk/7413645.

performance of their products and help with improvements.[33] Syrian theater was used to develop the Russian military requirements for various ummanned combat systems including 'Uran' series unmanned ground vehicles (Uran-6 mine clearing vehicles and Uran-9 unmanned tanks).[34] The first and so far the only operational Russian MALE-class UCAV 'Orion' was also battle tested in Syria conducting 38 combat and reconnaissance sorties.[35]

Input factors: Financial resources for Russian defense innovation

Boosts to the Russian defense budget started soon after the grand military reform began. Defense spending started at a relatively low level of 1.5% of GDP in 2010, reached 2.7% of GDP in 2012, and peaked in 2015 with expenditures (taking into account mid-year cuts) reaching 3.8% of GDP. Defense expenditures then gradually declined. They were at 3.4% of GDP in 2017. By 2019 they declined to 2.9% and in 2020 were supposed to be at 2.87%.[36]

There are alternative views on the actual amount of Russian defense expenditures, sometimes bringing it to 6% of GDP and above. Such high numbers are achieved by lumping together expenditures on law enforcement, security, border protection, intelligence, and even disaster relief services as military, which makes it difficult to use such numbers for cross-country comparison and policy analysis.

The initial rise in the defense budget was caused by the need to quickly conclude a number of large-scale R&D projects and boost the production capacity of some major defense industrial enterprises that had been underperforming for decades. By the end of 2014, internal structural problems in the Russian economy and a collapse in the price of commodities led to a significant economic downturn that was exacerbated by Western sanctions. The Russian economy declined by 2.8% in 2015 and by 0.225% in 2016. It emerged from the crisis in 2017, but growth has remained sluggish (1.5% in 2017, 2.3% in 2018 and 1.3% in 2019).

The Russian government implemented a number of defense budget cuts at the beginning of the crisis to stave off an even worse decline. Some of the cuts were predictable. A number of R&D programs (such as the fifth-generation fighter and new families of ground combat vehicles) had fallen

---

[33] Shoigu told about upgrades on more than 300 types of weapons as result of Syrian operations. [Шойгу сообщил о доработке более 300 единиц оружия по итогам операций в Сирии] Interfax-AVN 29/09/2019, https://www.militarynews.ru/story.asp?rid=1&nid=517895&lang=RU.

[34] Russia Tested Combat Robots in Syria [Россия испытала в Сирии боевых роботов], RG.RU 05/05/2018 https://rg.ru/2018/05/05/reg-cfo/rossiia-ispytala-v-sirii-boevyh-robotov.html.

[35] Orion strikes against militants were shown on videos. [Удары Ориона по боевикам показали на видео], RG.RU, 22.02.2021 https://rg.ru/2021/02/22/udary-bespilotnika-orion-po-boevikam-v-sirii-pokazali-na-video.html.

[36] Russia will cut the defense expenditure in 2020, says Putin. RIA Novosti, 20.06.2020 [Россия сократит военные расходы в 2020 году, заявил Путин. РИА Новости, 20.06.2019]https://ria.ru/20190620/1555746205.html.

behind schedule for technical reasons, while others (construction of new frigates, procurement of two Mistral class assault ships from France for 1.2 billion euros) were victims of the crisis in relations between Russia and the West. For example, Germany quit providing naval diesel engines for Russia's smaller naval combat ships, and Ukraine stopped selling naval gas turbines to Russia, which caused multi-year delays and significant cuts in the programs to build Project 1135.6 and 2235.0 frigates.

Further cuts were implemented in the development of the new State Armament Program 2018–2027 (*Gosudarstvennaya Programma Vooruzheniy*, GPV 2027), which was signed by Russian President Vladimir Putin in February 2018. Work on the program was delayed to address the new, more difficult economic conditions. The scale of the GPV 2027 in nominal terms will be the same as the scale of GPV 2020: 19–20 trillion rubles.[37] With inflation factored in, however, the program's budget has declined by almost 37%. Recall also that almost three-quarters of the projected cost of GPV 2020 consisted of preliminary planning for the second period. The actual procurement expenditures for 2018–2022 may be more limited.

The Russian media has identified the Barguzin railroad-based ICBM and new lightweight ground mobile ICBM (RS-26 Rubezh) as among the programs that were subject to cuts. The government has reportedly decided to concentrate efforts on development and production of the new silo-based liquid fuel ICBM (Sarmat) and new hypersonic weapon systems.[38]

It appears that the long overdue renewal of the Russian Navy's aging fleet of major surface combatants is postponed again, as the GPV 2027 most likely will make additional cuts in naval programs According to then Deputy Defense Minister Yuri Borisov (later promoted to his current position of vice prime minister in charge of the defense industry), the priorities of the naval part of the program will be littoral ships armed with cruise missiles as well as SSBN and multipurpose submarines.[39]

The new GPV will fund most of the breakthrough technologies such as hypersonic and laser weapons and other highly ambitious, disruptive innovations. Putin named a number of such systems during his address to the Russian Parliament on 1 March 2018. These included the already-mentioned Sarmat ICBM, which is expected to have unlimited range and to be able to attack the United States from the south. Other items on the list were the Avangard hypersonic reentry vehicle for ICBMs (initially expected to be

---

[37]19 trillions for the weapons. Kommersant 15.11.2017 [19 триллионов принимают на вооружение, «Коммерсант," 15.11.2017], https://www.kommersant.ru/doc/3467573.
[38]'Barguzin' is excluded from the State Armament Program for 'Sarmat' and 'Rubezh', TASS 08.12.2017 [«Баргузин» исключили из ГПВ ради «Сармата» и «Рубежа»], http://tass.ru/armiya-i-opk/4787839.
[39]Priorities in maritime part of state armament program will be ships with guided missiles and nuclear submarines [Приоритетом морской части новой Госпрограммы вооружения станут корабли с высокоточными ракетами и атомные подводные лодки] Ministry of Defense website, 29.11.2017 https://structure.mil.ru/structure/forces/navy/news/more.htm?id=12152815@egNews.

deployed on the UR-100NUTTH/SS-19 Mod.1 Stiletto ICBM, later on Sarmat); the Kinzhal ('Dagger') intermediate range air-launched hypersonic cruise missile; the Peresvet ground-based laser air/missile defense system; Poseidon unmanned autonomous nuclear submarines; and a previously unknown system—a nuclear-powered cruise missile known as Burevestnik (Petrel).

Aside from the nuclear weapon delivery systems and nuclear submarines, known priorities under the GPV 2027 include strategic air defense and missile defense systems, new space reconnaissance satellites, command and control systems for all services, unmanned aerial vehicles (UAVs), and land-based robotic systems. The Ground Forces, which had the smallest share of the previous programs among the services, will be the biggest beneficiary of the new GPV.[40]

The emergence of a 'non-nuclear strategic deterrence capability' is the result of considerable progress in the development and production of cruise missiles. As Chief of the General Staff Valeriy Gerasimov stated in November 2017, Russia now has a planning and organization system for targeting of the long-range cruise missiles, with a range of up to 4,000 km.[41] The development of non-nuclear strategic capabilities can be expected to remain among the priorities.

These procurement cuts were made possible to some extent because some of the GPV 2020 goals were more or less met. For example, although the original goal was to reach a 70% share of advanced weapons, the percentages achieved were 58.9 for the armed forces in general, 74 for the strategic nuclear triad, 72 for the Air Force, 66 for the Strategic Rocket Force, 53 for the Navy, and 44 for the Ground Forces.[42] The shipbuilding part of the GPV 2020 is generally considered a failure, especially with regard to surface combatants.

Organizations: Defense industrial commission, advanced research foundation the ministry of defense innovation infrastructure, arms exports related agencies

Russia tries to implement an aggressive policy of simultaneous promotion of civil and military modernization which to certain extent echoes the Chinese civil-military fusion policies although no public reference to the Chinese experience has ever been made by the Russian officials. The relative weakness

---

[40]L. Nersysyan. How the Russian military will be armed in the next 10. Regnum 17.11.2017 [Леонид Нерсисян. Как будут вооружаться Вооруженные силы России в последующие 10 лет?] https://regnum.ru/news/2346188.html.

[41]Valerii Gerasimov. Respected force. What was done for the military after the President's May Decrees. Defense Industry Courier, 14.11.2017 [Валерий Герасимов. Уважаемая сила. Что сделано в армии после майских указов президента.] https://vpk-news.ru/articles/39882.

[42]Shoigu's 5 years [«Пятилетка Шойгу»], http://rusplt.ru/policy/pyatiletka-shoygu-31356.html; Russian military has summarized the results of the last five years [«Российская армия подвела итоги пятилетки"], http://vestikavkaza.ru/material/214352.

of the civilian high technology sector of the Russian economy in comparison to the defense industry lead to the defense industry being considered as the driver as modernization which in turn expanded the ambitions of the ministry of defense to play greater role in the national technological modernization policies in general.

To certain extent such situation is caused by the ongoing crisis in the Russian civilian science and technology management with Russian Academy of Sciences and ministry of science and higher education frequently finding themselves amid scandals and controversies.[43] At the same time the defense industrial establishment has enjoyed greater attention from the Russian political leadership after the beginning of the Ukrainian crisis in 2014. The Defense Industrial Commission which leads the developmet of the industry and which used to be chaired by one of the vice-premiers since that time was headed by the Russian president Vladimir Putin himself. That means that the leader is personally involved in the process of development of the key industrial and technological policies and supervising their implementation. DIC also has authority over development and implementation of arms export policies and controls[44]

The commission has one deputy chair, the vice prime minister responsible for the defense industry.[45] Its membership includes the heads of the key economic ministries (Finance, Economics, and Trade and Industry) as well as the most important defense industry leaders (the CEOs of Rostech, Roscosmos, and Rosatom); the president of the Russian Academy of Sciences; ministers of defense and internal affairs; chiefs of the Federal Security Service and Foreign Intelligence Service; the commander of the National Guard; among others.[46]

This setup allows the Russian leadership to regularly review the status of its main defense programs and take decisions quickly once problems emerge. The huge concentration of power in the hands of the president in the Russian system makes it possible for Putin to act as supreme arbiter if the government agencies and the defense industry companies are unable to resolve their differences.

The Ministry of Defense has a special department responsible for formulating and implementing innovation policies: the Chief Directorate of Research and Development and Technological Support of Advanced Technologies. The directorate is responsible for tracking the development of defense science

---

[43] See for example 'Russian Academy of Sciences is showing instability', Nezavisimaya Gazeta 18.12.2019 [Россияйская академия наук демонстрирует неустойчивость] https://www.ng.ru/science/2019-12-18/100_221717122019.html.
[44] Presidential Decree on the Military-Industrial Commission of the Russian Federation. `[Указ президента Российской Федерации о Военно-промышленной комиссии Российской Федерации], http://static.kremlin.ru/media/events/files/41d5041c78a6da8cf5ad.pdf.
[45] Previously it was Dmitriy Rogozin; since May 2018 the position has been filled by former Defense Minister Yuri Borisov.
[46] Russian Defense. [Оборона России] http://www.ros-oborona.ru/.

and technology abroad, organization and support of certain development projects, and support for practical applications of new technologies in the military.[47] In general, the directorate serves as the key representative of the Russian military to the R&D community. It does not work with information technology, which falls under a separate department.[48]

In the second year of GPV 2020 development Russia created a separate government agency responsible for identifying breakthrough innovation programs—the Advanced Research Foundation (ARF). The agency was officially established in October 2012.

According to the law establishing the ARF, the foundation is supposed to 'encourage the implementation of high-risk breakthrough research in the interest of State defense and security'. The foundation can conduct economic activities only in areas designated by the relevant law and should use all of the received profit for the support of advanced research. Other state agencies have no right to intervene in foundation activities and cannot influence ARF decisions about which research should be supported.

The experts working for the ARF are supposed to identify critical technological threats to national security and choose how to neutralize such threats. The ARF management identifies the companies and research institutions that will conduct the relevant research. The intellectual property rights for research results belong to ARF. ARF can transfer these property rights to defense industry companies. ARF prepares three-year research programs that are subject to yearly reviews. Projects to be included in the programs are chosen by the ARF Council on Science and Technology and then confirmed by the ARF board, which consists of the ARF director general and his deputies in charge of various research areas.[49]

The foundation appears to finance a wide set of technologies, many of which are similar to known US priorities. These include robotics, including fully robotic combat platforms; hypersonic systems; additive technologies; advanced underwater technologies; cyber security; and cognitive technologies.[50] For example, projects on 'advanced underwater systems' are supposed to help develop advanced unmanned underwater vehicles for both warfighting and natural resources exploration, create new underwater tracking technologies, and find

---

[47]The main directorate of the R&D activities and advanced technologies support [Главное управление научно-исследовательской деятельности и технологического сопровождения передовых технологий], https://structure.mil.ru/structure/ministry_of_defense/details.htm?id= 11376@egOrganization.

[48]The main directorate for the development of the information and telecom technology of the Ministry of Defense [Главное управление развития информационных и телекоммуникационных технологий министерства обороны], https://structure.mil.ru/structure/ministry_of_defense/details. htm?id=11737@egOrganization.

[49]Excerpts from the 'Regulation of the Main Directorate for Research Activities and Technological Support of the Advanced Technologies of the MoD,' http://doc.mil.ru/documents/quick_search/more.htm?id= 11919505@egNPA.

[50]ARF website data, http://fpi.gov.ru/about/areas/physics/bisokoskorostnie_sredstva.

ways to reduce the acoustic detectability of underwater objects.[51] Russia also has active rail gun and directed energy weapons programs.[52] Recently ARF is increasingly involved into the dual use technologies such as air traffic control systems for the UAVs[53]

The ARF and the Ministry of Defense choose future programs primarily by monitoring global trends in technological development and listening to guidance from the Russian military, intelligence, and law enforcement agencies, which are also represented on the foundation board.

Other important players include the Federal Service for Defense Industrial Cooperation, the government agency responsible for regulation of the arms export and the Rostech corporation which currently is by far the largest Russian defense industrial corporation controlling the Russian arms export monopoly – Rosoboronexport. Since arms exports remain a significant source of revenue for the industry, the export considerations do influence the industrial policies for the industry to a significant extent.

The trend toward greater participation of the MoD science and technology departments, ARF and the defense industrial corporations such as Rostech in implementation of wider industrial policies of the Russian government aimed at modernization of the Russian economy as a whole will likely continue for the foreseeable future as Russia tries to implement a number of high profile projects in the fields of digital economy, telecom and urban development. For example, Rostech is playing a leading role in the 'Safe city' (Russian version of 'smart city) project which is supposed to create a massive disaster prevention, environmenta monitoring and surveillance infrastructure in every Russian city.[54]

Conclusion

Two events, the 2002 US withdrawal from the ABM Treaty and the 2008 war with Georgia, played catalytic roles in the rise of defense innovation in Russia. Russia started to pay serious attention to defense innovation after the US withdrawal from the ABM Treaty, looking primarily at the technologies and

---

[51] ARF website data, http://fpi.gov.ru/about/areas/physics/perspektivnie_podvodnie_tehnologii.
[52] On railguns, 'Россия создаст свой рельсотрoню' ['Russia Is to Build Its Own Railgun'], *Rossiyskaya Gazeta*, 31 May 2016, https://rg.ru/2016/05/31/rossiia-sozdast-svoj-relsotron.html. On directed energy weapons, see, for example, the well-known Sokol-Echelon airborne laser program, https://rg.ru/2014/10/31/boevoilazer-site.html.
[53] Tomsk University of Flight Control Systems and Radioelectronics has created a UAV flight control system demonstrator prototype. [ТУСУР создал облик прототипа системы управления воздушным движением беспилотников], Tomskaya Internet Gazeta, 26/04/2021, https://gt-tomsk.ru/news/tusur-sozdal-oblik-demonstratora-sistemy-upravleniya-vozdushnym-dvizheniem-bespilotnikov/?utm_source=yxnews&utm_medium=desktop&utm_referrer=https%3A%2F%2Fyandex.ru%2Fnews%2Fsearch%3Ftext%3D.
[54] Rostech Will Develop the Safe City.[Ростех спроектирует безопасный город] Kommersant 23.10.2020, https://www.kommersant.ru/doc/4541307.

systems affecting strategic stability. From the beginning, Russia decided to concentrate resources on the development of a limited number of very ambitious and risky breakthrough projects at the expense of current force capabilities.

Since at least 2008, Russia's political leadership has increasingly considered military modernization as vital to the survival of Russia and the current Russian political system. The Russian government worked hard to develop a defense reform strategy in 2006–2007, but moved to implement it only after the military conflict with Georgia in 2008. Once military reforms started to show results, Russia boosted investment in weapons procurement. That process started in 2010 and peaked in around 2015. After 2015 the Russian important in the military operations in Syria continued to serve as an important source of experience which influenced the Russian approach to defense innovation.

The turn toward active modernization required the Russian leadership to restructure the institutions responsible for the control of the defense industry and military procurement. The most difficult part of this effort was the creation of a working pricing mechanism, which required the Russian government to find a new balance between industry and military interests.

By 2017, Russia had largely managed to overcome the consequences of its military decline (1992–2008) when the procurement of conventional weapon systems was extremely limited. The only exceptions are the Ground Forces, which still rely heavily on Soviet platforms and weapon systems, and the surface Navy, which traditionally has been the lowest priority for the Russian military leadership when the country is encountering a crisis.

The Russian defense industry was capable to retain a significant portion of its old technological and innovative capabilities in the period of decline by boosting exports to countries such as China and India.

After the significant rise of inputs in the defense sector in the first half of the 2010s, the defense budget started to stabilize in the mid-2010s. The Russian government is trying to maintain defense expenditures at a comfortable level of 2.5 to 3% of GDP by sacrificing or postponing high-profile programs that are not vital (for example, the new generations of carriers, frigates, and destroyers and some of the strategic weapons projects).

Russia can maintain and increase its military power by concentrating its limited resources in a few select areas, such as the ICBM force, SSBNs, non-nuclear strategic deterrence, air defense, and selected ground force systems while ignoring those areas that are less relevant from its current strategic point of view. Russia seems to be sacrificing long-range power projection capabilities, with both its amphibious fleet and heavy transport aircraft fleet being produced and upgraded very slowly.

The Russian government holds pessimistic views on the future of the international relations and expects Russia to face increasingly complex and sophisticated military and security threats. While the priorities for the coming years will be the rearmament of the ground forces, further modernization of the nuclear triad, and upgrades to strategic air and missile defenses, increasing attention is being paid to emerging technologies such as artificial intelligence, directed energy weapons, hypersonic weapons, and robotics.

The long-range projects supported by the Advanced Research Foundation and the MoD will play key roles in this future military revolution and in the development of the Russian economy in general. Both the MoD and the defense industries seek the primary role in determining national innovation and industrial policies.

The general preference to give high priority to ambitious projects that are expected to 'revolutionize' warfare can be expected to continue. The key challenge is to develop the necessary expertise in the areas where the Soviet and Russian R&D and production base has been historically weak—electronic components, UAVs, and the like.

Being an advanced developed regime, Russia has major differences from the other countries of the group. The key difference is the structure of the Russian economy where innovative activities are concentrated in the defense industry and a number of dual use industries (nuclear, space) with the important exception of the information technology. No other developed economy now is looking at the defense industry as the main driver of the general technological organization while in Russia it is increasingly the case.

Russia and before the Soviet Union used to operate in hostile environment and under different degrees of isolation for much of their history which resulted in self reliance strategy and sometimes – in extreme technonationalism of the Russian military and defense industry establishment. The growing confrontation with the US and deep feeling of insecurity in the Russian elite resulted in the growing role of the military factors in the Russian foreign policy in general, creating strong motivation to revive the defense innovation.

As a player on the international arena Russia is constantly punching above its' weight engaging in political rivalry and defense technological competition against the US while having about 20% of the US GDP in purchasing power parity terms. Russia is trying to deal with this disparity by carefully choosing the priorities and concentrating resources on some sectors of defense technology while underfunding others.

By now the Russian military has managed to achieve significant results in boosting the domestic defense innovation which already lead to significant growth of the capabilities of the Russian military. That in turn has already produced major strategic and political effects wich could be felt globally. While the current Russian defense posture appears to be economically sustainable, the key factor which will define the Russian long term defense industrial and technological capability is the ability to implement the structural changes in the economy revitalizing the civilian high tech industries.

Disclosure statement

No potential conflict of interest was reported by the author(s).

Bibliography

Achasov, O.B., S.S. Smirnov, and A.Y. Pronin, 'Main Directions of the Technological Development of the Russian Armed Forces Weapons Systems', *Armaments and Economics* 1/34 (2016). [О.Б.Ачасов, С.С.Смирнов, А.Ю.Пронин. Основные направления технологического развития системы вооружений Вооруженных Сил Российской Федерации. Вооружение и Экономика. 1 (34), 2016, стр. 9–19].

Barabanov, M., 'Russia's New Army'. Center For Analysis of Strategies and Technologies. 2010. [М.Барабанов. Новая армия России. Центр Анализа Стратегий и Технологий, 2010]. http://cast.ru/books/novaya-armiya-rossii.html (accessed 14 Oct. 2020).

Mikhail, Barabanov, Konstantin Makienko, and Ruslan Pukhov, 'Military Regorm. On the Path Towards Thew New Layout of the Russian Army'. Valdai Discussions Club. 2012. [М.Барабанов, К.Макиенко, Р.Пухов. Военная реформа. На пути к новому облику российской армии. Дискуссионный клуб Валдай, 2012].

Pankov, S.E., I.I. Borisenkov, S.S. Smirnov, and R.V. Reulov, 'Planning of Basic and Applied Research in the Defense and Security Areas in the Current Conditions', *Armaments and Economics* 2/39 (2017). [С.Е.Панков, И.И. Борисенков, С.С. Смирнов, Р.В.Реулов. Планирование фундаментальных и прикладных исследований в области обороны и безопасности государства в современных условиях. Вооружение и Экономика. 2 (39), 2017, стр. 43–54].

Varshavsky, A.E. and Y.A. Makarova, 'The Analisys of the Defense Industrial Complex R&D Financing during the Growth and Contraction of the Military Expenditure', *National Interests: Priorities and Security* 18/255 (2014), 2–16. [А. Е. Варшавский and Ю. А. Макарова, Анализ особенностей финансирования сферы НИОКР оборонно-промышленного комплекса на этапах роста и сокращения военных расходов. Национальные интересы: Приоритеты и безопасность. 18 (255) 2014, стр. 2-16.].

Examining India's defence innovation performance

Laxman Kumar Behera

ABSTRACT
India has expended a great deal of energy and resources to set up a vast defence economy to innovate state-of-the-art weapon systems. However, the performance of the defence economy has been largely suboptimal. An examination of the causes of poor performance exhibits a number of shortcomings related to India's both 'hard' and 'soft' innovation capacities. Lack of strong support from higher political leadership, meager research and development (R&D) and procurement budgets, inefficiency of the main R&D and manufacturing players, poor management of human resources and a weak acquisition system, among others, leave India's defence innovation in a poor state.

India is the fifth largest economy in the world, and aspires to become a $5 trillion economy by 2024. Faced with security concerns arising primarily due to unresolved border disputes with Pakistan and China, Beijing's encirclement of India through a growing military and strategic presence in the Indian Ocean Region and cross-border terrorism sponsored by the western neighbour, protecting its vast economic ambition is a chief task for national leaders.[1] Prime Minister (PM) Modi's Make in India initiative and *Atma Nirbhar Bharat Abhiyan* (self-reliant India campaign) aim to galvanise Indian innovation to meet 21st-century challenges, such as the use of the space, cyberspace, artificial intelligence and quantum computing in modern warfare. As a near-term goal, PM Modi has also challenged the defence industry to grow to $26 billion by 2025 with an export turnover of $5 billion. Will these targets materialize, and more importantly, does the Indian defence innovation ecosystem have what it takes to meet the national and emerging challenges?

---

[1]The article builds on author's previous work. See Laxman Kumar Behera, 'Defence Innovation in India: The Fault Lines'.

For sure, India has spent a great deal of energy and resources in setting up a vast defence economy to innovate and produce state-of-the art weapon systems for use by the armed forces.[2] To the credit of this defence economy, India is one of the few countries in the world to have achieved a credible, multi-level nuclear deterrence, besides being one of the few countries to have designed, developed and produced a fourth generation combat aircraft, a main battle tank, and a nuclear powered submarine. It is also one of the select four countries to have successfully tested an anti-satellite (ASAT) missile. With an active Ballistic Missile Defence (BMD) program, and an array of other high-profile research and development (R&D) projects that include, among others, a range of missile systems, airborne surveillance system and unmanned aerial vehicle, India's defence innovation image looks at first glance quite impressive.

However, behind these feats lie many gaping holes, resulting in the country's overwhelming dependence on external sources for conventional arms, and earning the dubious distinction of being one of the largest arms importers in the world. According to the Stockholm International Peace Research Institute (SIPRI), India, with a share of 9.5% in global arms import during 2016–20, was the second largest importer behind Saudi Arabia.[3] This, in turn, raises the key questions about the efficiency and efficacy of defence innovation system, and as to whether India could ever achieve its long-cherished self-reliance goal in defence procurement.

The article attempts to evaluate India's defence innovation performance. In so doing it also looks at country's progress in defence science, technology and manufacturing capacity, and the key hurdles encountered in achieving its larger objective of self-reliance.

How does the Indian government define innovation?

India's Draft National Innovation Act of 2008 characterises innovation as technological advancement leading to economic benefits. The Act defines innovation as a 'process for incremental or significant technical advance or change, which provides enhancement of measurable economic value'.[4] The Act adds that the accrued benefits of innovation result from a number of factors arising out of introduction of better goods and services; or implementation of new or improved operational, organisational and managerial processes.

Innovation, however, goes beyond the techno-economic connotations, and refers to all new ways and means to accomplish any particular task. The broad nature of innovation can be understood from the way the term

---

[2]For a recent review of India's defence economy, see Laxman Kumar Behera, *India's Defence Economy: Planning, Budgeting, Procurement and Industry*.
[3]Peter D. Wezeman et al, 'Trends in International Arms Transfers 2019'.
[4]Ministry of Science and Technology, 'The National Innovation Act of 2008'.

is defined in the field of defence and security. Close observers of security-related innovations identify three types of innovations: strategic, military and defence. While strategic and military innovation refer to 'grand strategy' and the 'military's ability to prepare, fight and win war,' respectively, defence innovation is viewed as the 'transformation of ideas and knowledge into new or improved products, processes and services for military and dual-use applications'.[5]

Defining innovation is one thing – measuring its outcome objectively and precisely is another. The Indian Innovation Act of 2008 provides four parameters to measure innovation performance: 'increase in market share, competitive advantage, improvement in the quality of products and services and reduction of costs'. However, using these objective parameters to measure the innovation success, particularly in the Indian defence field, is difficult, in view of the lack of credible data, and the secrecy that surrounds many defence programmes. To overcome such a problem, the paper uses an indirect approach that essentially deals with the Indian defence economy's capability to innovate.

For a country to innovate it must have certain attributes such as political vision and support, R&D and manufacturing infrastructure, human capital, access to foreign technology and financial resources to name a few. This article examines these innovation attributes through an analytical framework developed by Cheung. In essence, the framework assesses innovation attributes through hard and soft innovation capabilities, which are then examined through seven functional factors: catalytic, input, institutional, organisational, networks and subsystems, contextual and output.[6]

India's ad hoc approach to innovation

Unlike the step-by-step approach followed by some developing countries aspiring to become major powers in science and technology (S&T), India has followed, by and large, what can be termed an *ad hoc* approach towards defence innovation. The only segment in which it has followed innovation in some disciplined manner is warship building in which the indigenous capability has moved from imitating British designed warships during 1960s to independently designing frigates, destroyers, corvettes and even a nuclear submarine and an aircraft carrier. With a focussed approach to building its own warships, it has also achieved a high degree of component innovation – to the extent of more than 80% in latest versions of frigates and destroyers.

---

[5]Tai Ming Cheung, 'A Conceptual Framework of Defence Innovation'.
[6]Cheung, 'A Conceptual Framework of Defence Innovation'.

India has not seriously followed reverse engineering as a primary springboard for its defence innovation. In contrast, China has been quite successful in absorbing foreign technology and improving it through its own R&D efforts. The only highly visible technology that India has reverse engineered (through legal means) is the Bofors artillery gun acquired in late 1980s. The *Dhanush* howitzer gun, as it is named, is an improved version of the original Swedish Bofors gun, with many improved features pertaining to range, calibre, precision and handling. However, the development of *Dhanush* commenced more than three decades after the technology was first acquired and was initiated after repeated efforts to import another gun were met with failure.

A comparison with China illustrates India's *ad hoc* approach further. As succinctly observed by Cheung, Beijing has painstakingly gone through various innovation ladders beginning with 'duplicative imitation' and progressively moving to other higher forms of innovation such as 'creative imitation', 'creative adaptation', 'incremental innovation', 'architectural innovation', 'component innovation' and finally to what looks like 'radical innovation.[7] Beijing has made steady progress in innovation capability, growing initially from imitating foreign-designed technologies to improving them through a dose of indigenous R&D, to finally independently designing disruptive technologies. As a result of moving to higher forms of innovation, China has increasingly transformed itself from being a major arms importer to a big exporter.

Instead of moving on the innovation ladder one rung at a time, India attempted to quickly jump to the higher forms of innovation at the very beginning while its basic innovative capabilities were rudimentary. Predictably, when the outcome was not to the government's liking, it abandoned the higher forms of innovation to settle for mere assemble or license production of foreign designed weapons. With its pride hurt, and hugely dependent on arms imports, India again attempted some higher forms of innovation, while continuing simultaneously with lower forms of innovation. By and large, India seems to have abandoned higher forms of innovation especially that relate to big military platforms such as fighter aircraft, tanks and submarines. This *ad hoc* approach to defence innovation can be seen from different models that India has followed in its quest for self-reliance since independence.

Immediately after independence, India's defence innovation approach was characterised by self-sufficiency, which was in fact the overall principle behind India's chosen path for scientific and industrial development. Although India was nowhere close to meeting its defence requirement from domestic sources, an attempt was nevertheless made to create an eco-system under the direct control and supervision of the Ministry of Defence (MoD). Several companies – Mazagon Dock Ltd (MDL), Garden Reach Shipyard and Hindustan Aircraft Ltd (later

---

[7]For a detailed understanding of the various ladders of innovation, see Cheung, 'The Chinese Defense Economy's Long March from Imitation to Innovation', 327.

renamed Hindustan Aeronautics Ltd (HAL) – were brought under the MoD's direct control besides setting up a new company, Bharat Electronics Ltd (BEL), with French assistance for manufacture of various electronics for defence use. These companies came to be known as Defence Public Sector Undertakings (DPSUs), the number of which has increased to nine over the years. While setting the foundation for defence production, the government also established the Defence Research and Development Organisation (DRDO) to undertake technology and product development.

These DPSUs and DRDO labs along with 18 Ordnance Factories (OFs), which India inherited from the British, formed the core of defence R&D and manufacturing base. They were put firmly under the control of the MoD, with the private sector denied any direct role in defence production. The hallmark of the phase, which ran from independence to mid-1960s, was India's ambitious effort to design and manufacture a combat aircraft, HF-*Marut*. The design effort, which began in 1956 was truly ambitious, not least because of India's previous experience in designing any flying object was limited to a primary trainer. The innovation efforts of Marut can truly be categorised under the radical innovation as India was at that time 'one of the four or five countries to proceed with the development of a supersonic fighter aircraft' and except for the US, none of the countries had 'settled down for role-specific aircraft rather than a multi-role combat aircraft'.[8]

The humiliating defeat at the hands of Chinese forces in the 1962 border war brought a major setback to India's defence innovation efforts. In a move to quickly strengthen its defence preparedness, India moved away from the path of indigenous design and development of major weapon systems towards direct import and license-based production, the latter of which has become a major feature of India's defence production ever since. The only major exception to this license-based production post-1962 war was the Main Battle Tank (MBT) Arjun, the design and development of which was sanctioned in 1972.

The foundation for the license-based production, which became the primary innovation tool for the industry, was laid with the MiG-21 aircraft. However, unlike China, which reverse engineered several Soviet fighters and fielded its own versions, Indian efforts were limited to part-production of the aircraft with limited absorption of technology. It not only brought several successive generations of Russian weapons but also required Moscow's assistance to upgrade them, as it was done for the MiG aircraft, to name just one.

---

[8] Lorne J. Kavic, *India's Quest for Security: Defence Policies, 1947–1965*, 136; and Jasjit Singh, *Indian Aircraft Industry*, 128.

Realising the pitfalls of overdependence, India made another attempt to return to the path of innovation. A major beginning was made in early 1980s, when the government augmented the resources of the DRDO and sanctioned a number of high-profile projects, namely the Integrated Guided Missile Development Programme (IGMDP) – for development of five missile systems – and a light combat aircraft. Subsequent to these, the government has also sanctioned a number of other projects to be undertaken by the DRDO.

It is, however, to be noted that most of these projects are not intended to be fielded as frontline equipment of the armed forces, implicitly implying that the indigenous innovation efforts are not good enough to meet the high-end requirements of the defence forces. In fact, one broader survey of the current procurement plans of the armed forces do indicate that when it comes to such platforms as fighters, submarines, tanks, helicopter and even small arms like carbines and assault rifles, direct import or, at best, license production, is the preferred option.

Since the DRDO/DPSUs/OFs driven efforts have not been adequate to meet the growing requirements of the armed forces, India has moved to two other models of self-reliance: one of collaboration with foreign partners, and the other of greater participation of Indian private sector. The foundation of the co-production model was laid in 1998 when India and Russia signed an Inter-Governmental Agreement for development of *BrahMos* supersonic cruise missile. A number of other high-profile projects have been added to the list, including for missiles (in collaboration with Israel), fifth generation fighter aircraft and transport aircrafts (Russia). However, India's role in these projects has been that of a junior partner with all the key technologies being supplied by the foreign collaborator. In the BrahMos missile for instance, key technologies such as seeker, booster and ramjet engine are directly supplied by Russia.

Along with the co-production model, the government has since the turn of this century been trying, though with limited success so far, to boost defence innovation though increased participation of private sector. In a major policy change in 2001, the government liberalised the defence production and threw it open to the private sector which was hitherto barred from manufacturing defence items. Subsequent to the liberalisation, the government also brought in a host of other measures including an offset policy and a host of domestic industry friendly procurement guidelines to incentive private participation.

It is, however, to be noted that until now the private sector's contribution has been marginal. Practical barriers such as difficulty in obtaining a license (or official permission to start manufacturing a defence item), lack of level playing field vis-à-vis the state-owned entities, complexities surrounding procurement procedures and a host of tax and payment related anomalies ensured that private sector's participation remains only a policy objective for much of the post-2001 liberalisation period. The Make in India initiative and *Atma Nirbhar Bharat Abhiyan* (self-reliant India campaign) launched by the Modi government have attempted to remove some of these barriers. However, the tardy procurement process and budgetary constraints have limited the utility of the Modi government's reform measures. Suffice it to say that except for one 155 mm/52 calibre Tracked Self-Propelled Gun contract, no other major contract has been awarded to the Indian private sector until now under the Make in India regime which was launched in 2014.

Besides, the private sector is also not considered a major player in the innovation system. It is increasingly being contemplated to be license manufacturer of major platforms, a role traditionally being played by the state-owned entities without much value addition. This is amply evident from the new 'Strategic Partnership' model that the MoD announced in May 2017. Under the model, the MoD plans to designate a number of private companies as strategic partner and whose primary responsibility would be to manufacture, under technology transfer, a number of high-end platforms, which at present are identified under four categories, fighters, helicopters tanks and submarines.

Assessing India's innovation capabilities

For sure, India has expended a great deal of efforts to cultivate both hard and soft innovation capabilities. The hard capabilities include a network of R&D and manufacturing establishments, a large pool of scientists, engineers and other workforce, a significant procurement and R&D budget, and access to foreign knowhow and technology. The soft capabilities include both the institutions and processes pertaining to higher decision making, planning and acquisition. However as explained in the succeeding sections, both the hard as well as soft capabilities, examined through seven functional categories (catalytic, input, institutional, organisational, networks and subsystems, contextual and output) encounter numerous challenges, limiting the innovation potential of Indian defence economy and leading to and perpetuating India's arms import dependency.

Catalytic factor

The role of higher political leadership

The higher political leadership has a vital role in driving defence innovation in a number of ways – by setting out key strategic goals, monitoring the progress of major developmental projects, removing obstacles by way of bringing timely reforms, and providing adequate resources for procurement and R&D. In India, however, the role of the political leadership in defence innovation pertaining to conventional weapons system (as opposed to strategic ones) does not often go beyond paying lip-service. Though the self-reliance goal has been cherished by successive leaders since independence, it has not yet been mandated in any policy document sanctioned by the highest political authority. In fact, unlike many other countries, such as the United States, the United Kingdom, France and China, India does not issue either a national security strategy or defence whitepaper, highlighting, among others, the key targets for the innovation players to achieve the intended national security goals. The only policy document that is available until recently is a four-page defence production policy issued by the Department of Defence Production (DDP)[9] in 2011. The policy was though very ambitious in its objective of achieving 'substantive self-reliance in design, development and production' of arms, it lacked any authority and means to achieve the same. Besides, the policy didn't articulate any specific projects for the Industry to execute. The policy was such a lacklustre that it prompted the government to relook the document afresh. In late 2018, the MoD released a revised draft defence production policy which went another round of revision before an integrated defence production and export promotion policy draft was announced in 2020 for public comments.[10] The draft has not seen final form (until March 2021) for unknown reasons. In the meantime, the MoD has announced a list of 101 items banned for import. The negative list is intended to reserve the featured items for production by the domestic industry.[11]

The lack of policy focus on defence innovation from the higher political authority is also visible from the fact that defence was not part of India's 5-year national Plan, which has now been discontinued with the abolition of the soviet-era Planning Commission and its replacement by the Niti Ayog as a think tank of the government. On the other hand, the internal plan documents of the MoD, which are formulated keeping in view three different time horizons (annual, five year and 10 year) are more of procurement oriented, and without any concrete national tasks for defence economy to achieve. Without any strong policy or concrete plan that can be monitored by the higher leadership, various projects are sanctioned in an *ad-hoc* manner.

The lack of interest of political leadership in defence innovation is particularly visible on the various reform fronts. Key reforms suggested in the past are either ignored, or implemented in extremely slow pace, negating any benefit that could accrue in a timely manner. In the past decade or so, numerous committees and task forces have been appointed by the government to examine some of the fundamental weakness afflicting the defence economy's

---

[9]DDP is one of the five departments of the MoD, with others being the Department of Defence, Department of Defence R&D, Department of Ex-Servicemen Welfare and the newly created Department of Military Affairs.

[10]PIB, 'MoD releases draft Defence Production and Export Promotion Policy 2020'.

[11]PIB, 'MoD's big push to Atmanirbhar Bharat initiative; Import embargo on 101 items beyond given timelines to boost indigenisation of defense production' and PIB, 'MoD notifies 'Second Positive Indigenisation List' of 108 items to promote self-reliance & defence exports'.

main players – DPSUs, DRDO and the OFs. However, the recommendations such as those pertaining to the revitalisation of the DPSUs, corporatisation of the OFs, and restructuring of DRDO have hardly been implemented in true letter and spirit. It is only recently that the Modi government has taken few concrete steps to revitalise the state-owned/controlled defence production entities by way of listing some of DPSUs in the stock exchanges and announcing corporatisation of the OFs, in a move to unlock their true business potential and enhance their corporate governance. This much overdue reform notwithstanding, the government is yet to articulate a reform plan for the other players. Moreover, the government seems to be backtracking on its promised reform of BEML, which manufactures heavy transport vehicles for the defence forces. After announcing a plan to privatise it, it has now deferred its own decision.

Finally, the leadership's lack of unflinching support to defence innovation is clearly visible on the resource front. In the last several years, the share of defence procurement and R&D in the defence budget has been on a constant decline, largely due to increase in manpower cost owing to hike in salary and pensionary benefits. There is however no concrete plan to stem the manpower cost or find resources to keep the innovation amply funded. As a result, procurement and R&D budget which was 44% of the defence expenditure in 2004–05, has been reduced to 34% in 2020–21. With such a dwindling share of the resources, it is only natural that indigenous projects remain fund constrained.

Input factors

R&D expenditure

Although India has often cherished the goal of self-reliance in design, development and production of military equipment, it has hardly backed up with adequate resources. Compared to the US and China which spend in excess of 10% of their defence budget on R&D, India's current spending is around six per cent.[12] Even the present share in defence budget came only after 1980s before which the allocation on R&D was negligible: about one per cent of the defence budget in 1960s, rising to about 2% in early eighties.[13] This low share in the defence budget together with India's relatively smaller defence budget means that defence R&D budget in absolute terms is minuscule in comparison to other major countries. In absolute terms, DRDO's 2021–22 budget of INR 204.57 billion (US$ 2.8 billion) amounts to a mere three percent of the US Department of Defence's over $ 100 billion R&D budget.

---

[12]International Institute for Strategic Studies, *Military Balance 2013*, 262; and MoD, *Defence Services Estimates 2013-14*.
[13]SCoD, 10th Lok Sabha, *Defence Research and Development: Major Projects*, 4.

The low share of defence budget for DRDO has an unintended consequence on the type of projects the organisation can take up. This is revealed through the present project portfolio of the DRDO. Of the total 400 ongoing projects (excluding strategic ones) valued INR 695.95 billion as of 2019, much of them are spent on either Mission Mode (MM) projects or Technology Demonstration (TD) projects which are applied in nature, leaving a mere 1.5% for Science and Technology (S&T) projects.[14] Although the S&T projects are crucial for generating new technologies for future use and hence vital for India's defence innovation point of view, DRDO's limited budget does not allow much priority to them.

To compound the problem of meagre funding for DRDO, the defence industry has done very little by way of stepping its own R&D expenditure. As explained later, the lack of R&D funding by the defence industry can be attributed to lack of R&D culture in most of India's government owned companies. It may be highlighted that until recently, R&D was not a mandatory function of the state-owned enterprise. It is only in 2011 that government brought a set of guidelines, requiring the state-owned entities to spend a certain percentage of their profit on R&D. Post articulation of the guidelines some of the DPSUs have stepped up their R&D, but given the low base to start with, the overall expenditure remains miniscule.

Civil military integration

Civil-military integration (CMI) is a week aspect in India's innovation system because of administrative and other barriers between the defence and civilian entities engaged in R&D and manufacturing. Surprisingly, this has not yet been fully appreciated among the policy circles. Unlike some other countries, particularity the United States and China which have a CMI strategy, India is yet to articulate one such. In the absence of a clear-cut strategy, the CMI has been left to be pursued in an ad-hoc manner. Among the defence innovation players, the DRDO has some kind of arrangement through which its taps expertise across a network of civilian sector entities for its developmental projects. For the defence manufacturing players, on the other hand, the efforts are largely restricted to outsourcing parts and component manufacturing to the civilian industry. Even then, the full potential of the civilian sector has not been tapped. As Joshi notes, capabilities existing in the civil sector such as those relating to common materials, design and analysis software (for modelling and analysis of designed components), manufacturing process (tolling, machining, forgings and castings and heat treatment) and testing and inspection methods are some of the areas where the military can benefit immensely.[15]

---

[14]DRDO, *Annual Report 2019*, 3–4.
[15]Keertivardhan Joshi, 'Win-Win: How Integration of Civilian and Military Technology Can Boost Defence Indigenisation'.

Poor human resource management

Defence economy provides direct employment to nearly 175,000 in the state-owned R&D and production centres alone. However, management of this workforce has been a major issue. On one hand there is shortage of high-quality scientists, engineers and designers and at the same time there is surplus of workers at the shop floor. The latter is evident from the low productivity of the state-owned entities. In case of the DPSUs, the average per employee sales is less than one-fifths of their global peers.[16] The shortage of high-quality workforce is a particular problem in the DRDO, which is supposed to be at the heart of India's defence innovation. It is of note that number of scientists at DRDO has not increased since 2001, although number of projects has been increased exponentially, with the organisation pursing 61 large projects (each costing over INR 1.0 billion) worth Rs. 707.40 billion.[17]

Besides shortage of skilled workforce, the DRDO also battles the low educational qualification of its scientific workforce. The Rama Rao Committee which reviewed the functioning of the DRDO and submitted a report to the government in February 2008, was greatly perturbed to see the predominance of first degree holders in DRDO's scientific cadre. It had noted that only 10% of the scientific manpower had higher qualification of Ph.D. To make the matter worse, majority of the workforce were not research trained, observed the Committee.

It is, however, to be noted that low education and lack of training is an aspect that is common to other high-end R&D organisations like the Indian Space Research Organisation (ISRO) and atomic energy department, and even to manufacturing establishments such as HAL. A major reason for this is the class room teaching orientation of most of Indian universities which themselves are far behind the global peers. However, to overcome the quality constraints, organisation like ISRO and atomic energy department have devised their own methods. ISRO, for instance, runs a dedicated university, Indian Institute of Space Science and Technology (IIST) that taps talent at very early age and provides graduate, post-graduate and doctoral programme in areas of space science and technology. There is no such dedicated university for defence, although the requirement is far greater than in ISRO. According to one estimate, the aerospace industry in its three verticals – R&D, manufacturing, and maintenance, repair and overhaul (MRO) – alone will require an additional manpower of over 1,85,500 by 2022, justifying the necessity to set up a dedicated defence technology university.

---

[16]Laxman Kumar Behera, *Indian Defence Industry: An Agenda for Making in India.*
[17]MoD, *Annual Report 2018-19*, 96.

Access to foreign technology

Since independence, India has had continuous access to foreign technology for its armament requirements. With the time, the source of access has only grown with the list of suppliers now constituting almost all major global arms exporters except China. In addition to the traditional suppliers such as Russia, France and the United Kingdom, India's weapons procurement of late is heavily dependent on countries such as Israel and the US, the latter having bagged more than $20 billion worth of arms contracts between 2008 and 2020.[18] India's access to foreign technology has typically been in the form of direct import of arms and/or transfer of technology (ToT) for local production. The ToT has been a preferred route in many procurement cases so as to allow the domestic industry to overcome the shortcomings of indigenous R&D and produce state-of-the art technology. Tacitly, it is also understood that access to foreign technology will help the local industry to learn 'know-how' and the 'know-why' of the latest technology which in turn would help them in their own design and production efforts. However, as seen in most cases, ToTs have hardly served in furthering the innovation efforts of the industry. On the other hand, whatever ToTs have been received have not been absorbed in its entirety in a prescribed timeframe, leading to continued import of critical components.

There are several factors that are responsible for partial absorption of ToTs. Among them, there are some which are beyond the control of the domestic industry. The blacklisting of foreign vendors after the ToT contracts are signed due to the corruption allegations (as is the case with 130 mm Cargo Ammunition contract with Israel), or the foreign suppliers' reluctance to transfer the agreed designs (as seen in T-90 Tank contract) are among few examples where the industry could do little to absorb the technologies. The most important factors for partial absorption are, however, lethargy on the part of the receiving agencies, and lack of foresight on the part of decision makers. As mentioned earlier, the ToT obtained during the Bofors gun purchase in 1980s was left unused for almost three decades. Though the OFB has now been able to use the ToT to design an upgraded version of the original gun, crucial time period lost has prevented organisation from undertaking any innovation efforts for a contemporary gun of higher calibre (155×52mm) which the Army wants in most of its new guns. In case of T-90 Tank, the OFB took nearly six years to translate the design documents, leading to delay in commencement of the indigenous production and the planned indigenisation.

The lack of foresight on the decision makers to use ToT to achieve intended indigenisation is best seen in license production of Su-30 fighter aircraft by the HAL. Between 2000 and 2012, the Indian government signed three agreements with Russia to locally produce 222 Russian fighters. Of the total number, 64 aircrafts were to be assembled from ready-to-assemble kits

---

[18]U.S. Department of State, 'U.S. Security cooperation with India'.

and from semi knocked down (SKD) and complete knocked down (CKD) kits, while 138 units were to be produced from 'Phase-IV' stage, which involves manufacturing the entire aircraft including its airframe, components and main assemblies from raw materials. The plan was, however, later revised, with the number of aircrafts to be produced from raw material stage being reduced to 84. The reason for resorting to higher number of aircrafts to be assembled from CKD/SKD was the delay in commencement of domestic production and the depleting squadron strength of the IAF. No attempt was, however, made to remove the production and other bottlenecks and expedite local production, which would have helped HAL to benefit from the 'learning curve' of larger unit of production. As mentioned later, after more than a decade of production, only 40% of aircraft has been indigenised.

Compared to Indian approach of partial absorption of ToT and continued dependence on foreign supplier, China has used ToT to attain complete independence. The Su-27 Flanker fighter that China produced under license from Russia is a clear example of how Beijing has used foreign technology to build its own capability. China produced around 100 Su-27s during 1998–2005 to not only absorb the technology but to use the technology to successfully produce its own version of the aircraft, which it named J-11B. Interestingly, China used the J11B to cancel negotiations with Russia to produce more Su-27s.[19] Such an approach towards absorption of foreign technology is never heard of in India's defence innovation set up.

Institutional factor

Defence procurement procedures

Since early 1990s, India has attempted to evolve a set of guidelines to not only expedite arms procurement but to do so through greater participation of domestic R&D and production agencies. The evolved guidelines are captured in a document, known Defence Acquisition Procedure (DAP), the successor of the the erstwhile Defence Procurement Procedures (DPP). The document sets out the rules for arms acquisition and assigns responsibility among various procurement organs of the MoD. First articulated in 1992, the document has been revised several times with the latest revision being carried out in 2020 by the Modi government. Reflecting the *Atma Nirbhar Bharat Abhiyan* of the government, the DAP-2020 emphasises on the domestic manufacturing with higher indigenous content, technology transfer, foreign investment and export of arms through offset route, among other features.[20]

---

[19]Tai Ming Cheung, 'Remaking Cinderella: The Nature and Development of China's Aviation Industry'.
[20]Laxman Kumar Behera, 'Defence acquisition procedure 2020: Imperatives for further reforms'.

The periodic improvements in the DPP/DAP notwithstanding, the document, owing to various reasons, has not proved very effective in promoting higher forms of innovation, especially those related to big conventional weapon systems. The guidelines are themselves not linked to any strategic plan with clear defence innovation targets. In the absence of such a plan, it has been convenient for the procurement authorities to target lower forms of innovation through ToT arrangements with foreign partners. Moreover, the implementation of the document has been anything but smooth for procurement in general and promotion of innovation in particular. Various functions of the acquisition, such as identification of technical and performance requirement, the R&D and production, quality assurance, contracting and finance are handled by diverse group of officials (in both civilian military bureaucracy) which not only lack expertise for their tasks but are also not centrally accountable to one administrative head. The lack of expertise and accountability entails an element of risk-averseness among the procurement officials besides making whole procurement system highly compartmentalised and bureaucratic.

Organisations

DRDO

The DRDO is nearly synonymous with India's defence R&D and is the principal agent behind India's defence innovation. Formed in 1958, it is primarily responsible for design and development of state-of-the-art weapons systems for the armed forces. At the time of its inception, DRDO was a small organisation with only 10 laboratories. Over the years DRDO has grown into a huge organisation, presently consisting of 52 research laboratories and establishments spread across the country, with a workforce of 24,732, including 7329 scientists/engineers, 9105 technical staff, and 6255 administrative and allied staff.[21] It caters virtually to all possible dimensions of defence technology. By December 2017, the cumulative production value of all DRDO-developed items (inducted or in the induction process) has exceeded INR 2,076.63 billion ($32 billion) – a significant increase compared to less than INR 60 billion in early nineties.

DRDO's contribution to defence innovation is perhaps best described by several of its high profile projects' global comparison. The latest to join the list is the ASAT weapon which was successfully demonstrated in March 2019. As has been highlighted by the DRDO and its chief in various forums, India is:

> one of the four countries in the world to have a multi-level strategic deterrence capability; one of the five countries of the world to have its own ballistic missile defence (BMD) program and underwater missile launch capability; one of the

[21]MoD, *Annual Report 2018-19*, 95.

seven countries to have developed its own main battle tank (MBT) and an indigenous 4th generation combat aircraft; one of the six countries of the world to have developed a nuclear powered submarine; one of the select few countries of the world to have its own electronic warfare and multi-range radar program.[22]

DRDO's above international comparison is however to be read with caution as not all the above mentioned projects are matured enough or have passed through the developmental phase for production and deployment. Among all the above listed programmes, one programme where the DRDO has achieved a high degree of success is in strategic deterrence capability, consisting especially of Agni-series of ballistic missiles. With a range of more than 5,000 km, the Agni-V missile, which can be launched from a canister on a road mobile launcher, provides India its most credible land-based nuclear strategic deterrence. In other programmes, however, the success is mixed. The BMD programme, for example, still years away from effective deployment. Moreover, the projects which have passed through developmental phase for production are not necessarily 100% indigenous as many key components and technologies used in them are imported. For instance, the power pack, gun control and fire control systems of the MBT Arjun and the engine of the LCA are sourced from abroad, indicating the lack of depth in component innovation. The technological shortcomings in the LCA are further illustrated in published list of 121 systems (pertaining to avionics, electronics, hydraulic, landing gear and propulsion) that the Aeronautical Development Agency (ADA) – the agency responsible for the design and development of LCA- wants to indigenise through the participation of Indian vendors.[23]

DRDO's technological gap in frontline military technologies, especially in comparison to advanced countries is perhaps best illustrated in the list of 33 critical technologies listed for acquisition from abroad by the organisation through the MoD's defence offset guidelines that stipulate a minimum 30% re-investment (through technology transfer and other means) from the foreign arms suppliers into the domestic industry. The list includes seeker technology, jet engine above 90KN, stealth technology, single crystal blade manufacturing process and shock hardened sensors, among others.[24]

DRDO's lack of original innovation is also partly illustrated in its Intellectual Property Rights (IPR) portfolio. It is noteworthy that the organisation is the biggest R&D spending organisation among all the scientific agencies in India (in 2017–18, it accounted for 32% of total R&D expenditure of major scientific organisations, distantly followed by the Department of Space (19%), Department of Atomic Energy (11%) and CSIR (9.5%), among other

---

[22]VK Saraswat, 'Harbingers of Change'.
[23]Aeronautical Development Agency, 'Indigenous Development of Line Replaceable Units (LRU's) for LCA-Tejas'.
[24]MoD, *Defence Acquisition Procedure 2020*, 130.

agencies).[25] However compared to its large funding, it has lesser IPR to its credit. For instance, in comparison to CSIR which maintains a portfolio of over 7000 patents, including around 4500 granted abroad, DRDO's IPR portfolio consists of less than 2000 patents, copyrights, designs and trademarks. In 2017, it was granted only 78 patents.[26]

DRDO's technological shortcomings notwithstanding, the organisation has often attempted to grab as many R&D projects as possible. However, many a time, the organisation is constrained to complete the projects and achieve the technological deliverables within the sanctioned timeframe and budgetary provision. This has often led to mid-way cancellation of projects. For example, a 1989 review of all DRDO projects led to closure of as many as 618 projects (out of total 989 projects).[27] Although resource crunch that time was cited as the primary reason behind the short-closure of projects, it nonetheless showed organisation's inability in developing the technologies of the projects it had pursued originally. It also shows absence of a strong approval mechanism which would have examined the feasibility of the programmes before they are taken up. A 2007 report of the parliamentary Standing Committee on Defence (SCoD) takes note of abandonment of several developmental projects (including those of airborne surveillance platform, cargo ammunition, 30 mm fair weather towed air defence gun system) undertaken by the organisation.[28] A 2012 Report the Comptroller and Auditor General of India (CAG) is also critical of the failure of DRDO in several projects in which the progress was dismal.[29]

Almost all of DRDO's flagship projects including the MBT Arjun, LCA and Kaveri Engine (for LCA) have witnessed significant time and cost overrun, besides eliciting poor user response. The cost overrun of MBT Arjun (the development of which was closed in 1995 as against the originally envisaged bulk production by 1984) was a whopping 1884%.[30] Although Arjun has now been inducted into the Army the number does not inspire confidence. As against the inventory of over 2000 Vijayanta tanks which the Arjun was supposed to replace, orders for 248 tanks have so far been placed, indicating the user's lack of confidence on the indigenous tank. A 2008 parliamentary committee report also talks of Army's displeasure of the Arjun which reportedly 'performed very poorly' in a winter trial.[31] With the Army planning to buy 1770 light tanks of foreign design, the DRDO's attempt to filed an upgraded Arjun is all but over. Similar is the fate with the LCA. Sanctioned in early 1983 for replacement of MiG fighters, the aircraft got the final operational clearance (FOC) in 2019, over three-and-a-half decade later.

---

[25]Ministry of Science and Technology, *Research and Development Statistics at a Glance 2019-20*, 4.
[26]DRDO, *DRDO News Letter*, 7.
[27]SCoD, 10th Lok Sabha, *Defence Research and Development: Major Projects*, 8.
[28]SCoD, 14th Lok Sabha, *Defence Research and Development Organisation*, 39–40.
[29]Comptroller and Auditor General of India (CAG), *Union Government (Defence Services): Army and Ordnance Factories*, 54–67.
[30]Public Accounts Committee, 13th Lok Sabha, *Design and Development of Main Battle Tank Arjun*.
[31]SCoD, 14th Lok Sabha, *Demands for Grants 2008-09*, 75.

Like the MBT Arjun, LCA has also got few orders so far. As against 870-odd MiG-series of aircraft which the LCA was intended to replace, some 120 units have been ordered for production by the HAL.[32] The poor user satisfaction is also evident from IAF's decision to deploy the initial lots of LCA in southern India far away from the active borders of China or Pakistan.[33]

Networks and subsystems

India's defence innovation performance is greatly hampered by lack of synergy among the major stakeholders. The critical functions of procurement, R&D and production are handled by three distinct departments within the MoD, with each of them enjoying a fairly high degree of autonomy in their decision making. Since there is no common thread binding them together in the form of a clearly articulated innovation targets, each of them tend to pursue goals independent of each other. The lack of synergy is further aggravated by mistrust and antinomy among the stakeholders, especially between the users on one side and development and production agencies on the other. The lack of unity of purpose has prevented timely decision-making, performance trade-offs which are crucial for developmental projects. Barring few projects such as *Dhanush*, and *Brahmos*, in which all the stakeholders worked as a team, in most other projects, R&D and/or production agencies work separately from the users which have a deep suspect towards the former. In some cases, suspicion is such that they tend to put hurdles by way of articulating stringent performance parameters to be achieved by the developer/producer. For instance in the Arjun MBT, the Army stipulated as many as nine performance parameters that are were stringent than available with T-90 tanks with which the Arjun was put to a comparative field trial.

In comparison to the conventional weapons in which the users have a decisive role by way of having the authority to articulate the technical parameters, in strategic programme, the developers have greater freedom. This is probably the single biggest reason why nuclear, ballistic missiles and even space programmes have seen greater success while almost all major conventional weapon programmes continue to struggle.

Contextual factors

The historical legacy of state-led planning and a weak civilian S&T, and industrial base have also been responsible for the poor performance of Indian defence innovation system. Since India's independence, major players in the defence innovation system – DRDO, DPSUs and OFs – have all been

---

[32]PIB, 'Delay in Manufacturing of Tejas by DRDO'.
[33]'First LCA squadron to be stationed in Sulur: DRDO'.

functioning under the state control. As explained elsewhere, the state-led innovation model has however been found to be inefficient. This has promoted the government to set up a number of task forces and committees to suggest improvements in the functioning and governance structure of these entities. However owing to lack of political conviction, very little worthwhile reforms have been implemented, leaving these players to function at a sub-optimal level, and limiting their innovation potential.

The poor innovation performance of main defence innovation players has further been accentuated by the general backwardness of India's wider S&T and industrial base. Except for a few pockets of excellence, especially in the domain of pharmaceuticals, automobiles and software, the depth of India's overall innovation base is rather poor. The *Economic Survey 2017–18*, a flagship publication of the Ministry of Finance, has mapped some of the manifestations of this backwardness vis-à-vis other comparable countries through an in-depth analysis of key innovation inputs and outputs. As succinctly brought out by the *Survey*, India is way behind many countries in a range of innovation parameters such as R&D spending, patents, scientific publication and advance qualification in science, technology, engineering and mathematics (STEM), which together indicate how scientifically advanced a country is.[34] Among all these indicators, one indicator that is most striking is India's overall R&D spending, 'the most studied component for innovation'. With an estimated budget of $16 billion, India's total R&D budget of 2016–17 is little more than what one South Korean company, Samsung, spends in a year. In comparison, China's R&D spend in 2017 is $280 billion, or 15 times bigger than India's. What is of greater significance is that India is gross under-spender in comparison to its own level of economic development. Unlike many counties which have increased their R&D expenditure with the increase in their economic development, India has reduced its R&D spend. Moreover, as a percentage of GDP, India's R&D of 0.6% is the lowest among a select countries such as Israel (4.3), South Korea (4.2), the United States (2.8) and China (2.1). The most pressing issue, therefore, is to double the R&D spend to broad base India's innovation potential.

Output factor

Manufacturing base

As a producer of major armaments Indian defence industry is a vital cog of India's defence innovation system. The main players are the state-owned entities, particularly the nine Defence Public Sector Undertakings (DPSUs) and 40-odd Ordnance Factories (OFs). Apart from these there is a small but growing number of private companies. Compared to the private sector companies which were barred from producing defence items until the 2001 defence industrial reforms,

---

[34] Ministry of Finance, *Economic Survey 2017-18: Vol. I*, 119–130.

the DPSUs and OFs are the traditional payers and still dominate India's defence production. Employing nearly 143,000 people their turnover reached INR 576.41 billion in 2018–19.

The vastness of the Indian defence production base is, however, in stark contrast with its poor innovation record. Measured in terms of key innovation parameters such as R&D spending, patents, in-house design and development, technology assimilation and indigenisation, the defence industry is often found wanting. Going by the number of patents and copyrights, which is by far the most the common yet powerful indicator of innovation, the DPSUs and OFs are way below their global peers. By March 2012, they together held a mere 23 patents. The number has although increased in recent years for the some of the entities due to government push through the Mission Raksha Gyan Shakti, it is not so impressive. For instance, HAL, the biggest defence company has an IPR portfolio of 56 as of 2016–17. In comparison, the US-based aerospace major, Boeing claims over 1000 patents in a single programme, the 787 Dreamliner.[35]

Barring HAL and BEL, which have dedicated R&D centres and spend 6–8% of their turnover on R&D, other defence enterprises have what is termed by India's former defence minister a 'miserly attitude' towards R&D spending. The lack of in-house R&D in most of the enterprises make them perpetually dependent on others, either DRDO or foreign companies for technology for production. In the case of the OFs, the largest and oldest departmentally run organisation in India, the in-house developed products contribute only 7.5% of its turnover.

The separation of R&D from the production agencies has however created a unique problem in Indian context. As observed by a former chief of the DRDO, since most of Indian production agencies, 'do not speak R&D language, it leads to difficulty in [absorption of technology and] transforming research designs into manufacturing'.[36] The difficulty is often manifested in the form of undue delay in production programme of the concerned entities. The delay in construction of Scorpene class submarines by the MDL with transfer of technology from France is one example of how the lack of R&D could lead to 'teething problems' in absorption of technology.[37] The undue delay in the production of MBT Arjun is partly due to the OF's problem in absorption of technology given by the DRDO.

In terms of in-house design and development, the capability of the Indian industry is largely limited to HAL and BEL. Even these two enterprises' capability is way behind their globally peers. HAL, India's biggest defence enterprise, is the classic example of innovation backwardness of Indian defence industry. Notwithstanding its ambitious mission and vision statements of becoming a 'significant global player in the aerospace industry' and achieving 'self-reliance

---

[35]'Guarding the "Gold"'.
[36]V.S. Arunachalam, 'In Season of Blame: A Defence'.
[37]PIB, 'Scorpene Submarine'.

in design, development, manufacture and upgrade of aerospace equipment', HAL is at best a fringe player in the global aerospace sector. Its capability for designing aircrafts seems to have drastically reduced from that of fighter aircraft to trainers and helicopters. In the 1960s, HAL had shot into global prominence with the successful development of HF-24 *Marut*, which was rated by experts as a good fighter that time. Now, the company plays a second fiddle to others, either the DRDO for indigenous fighter aircraft development or the foreign companies for co-development and license manufacturing of such planes. Even when HAL is a co-developmental partner, its role is limited. For instance, in the case of FGFA, which is not abandoned for all practical purpose, HAL's contribution was believed to be around 15–25%.[38]

Even though HAL's design capability has been reduced to helicopters and trainers, the company is still constrained to translate such capability into successful product in a reasonable timeframe, leading to import of similar system from abroad. A case in point is Indian Air Force's (IAF's) changing inventory of trainers. At one point of time, the IAF's entire trainer inventory was consisted of HAL-designed planes such as the HPT-32 (for basic training) and Kiran Mk-I and Mk-II (for stage-II and III training).[39] With ageing of these trainers and HAL making no credible replacement in time, the IAF's entire current inventory of trainers is now filled up with imported ones. It bears emphasising that the IAF has already inducted the British Hawk trainer for advanced training and Swiss Pilatus for basic flying training.

HAL's hope to meet a part of the IAF's trainer requirement rests with HTT-40. However, the IAF was not initially interested in the HTT-40 and was, in fact, wanted more of Pilatus for basic training.[40] The MoD was also not inclined towards HTT-40 initially on high cost ground, though it has now agreed for procurement of 116 units after certification and operationalisation of the HAL-made trainer.[41]

Intermediate Jet Trainer (IJT), another plane being developed by the HAL as replacement of Kiran has seen inordinate delays. The project, sanctioned in 1999, has not yet got initial operational clearance (as against the planned induction from 2005 onwards), causing frustration in the IAF, which once had threatened to use Pilatus for the IJT's role.[42]

HAL's seemingly poor state of the design capability is also equally matched by its poor record in technology assimilation and indigenisation or component innovation. The company is overwhelmingly dependent on foreign sources for

---

[38] Ajai Shukla, 'India to Develop 25% of Fifth Generation Fighter'; and 'AK Antony to take up issues related to FGFA project with Russia'.
[39] Kiran Mk I & Mk II HPT 32 were developed in 1968, 1976 and 1977, respectively. MoD, *Annual Report 2010-11*, 60.
[40] Ajai Shukla, 'Indian Air Force at war with Hindustan Aeronautics; wants to import, not build, a trainer'.
[41] Ajai Shukla, 'MoD Rejects HAL's Proposal to Build Basic Trainer'; and PIB, 'DAC approves procurement proposals worth Rs 8,722.38 crore, including 106 Basic Trainer Aircraft for IAF'.
[42] SCoD, 14th Lok Sabha, *In-Depth Study and Critical Review of Hindustan Aeronautics Limited*, 39–41; SCoD, 13th Lok Sabha, *Demands for Grants 2003-04*, 19th Report, 53; Ajai Shukla, 'IAF Laments HAL Delays in Delivery of Intermediate Trainer'; and Biswarup Gooptu, 'HAL to Work for Quicker Clearance of Defence Programmes'.

production inputs (raw materials, parts and components, etc). Suffice it to say that in terms of the materials consumed for production, the share of import is a whopping 82–95% in the last 10 years.

Significantly, high import dependence is for both indigenously developed products and products manufactured under the license. For example, as reported by a 2010–11 report of the Comptroller and Auditor General of India, import content in HAL's indigenously developed Advanced Light Helicopter, *Dhruv* (the design and development of which started in 1984, with the production beginning from 2000 to 2001) is 90% as against 50% envisaged originally.[43] The high import dependency in license manufacturing is best amplified in SU-30 MKI, which the HAL is manufacturing in four different phases since 2004–05.[44] Although the HAL has commenced the last phase of manufacturing of the aircraft from the 'raw materials stage' (supposed to be the highest form of indigenisation), the maximum indigenisation it has achieved so far is about 40%.

Conclusion

Barring a few successes especially in missile and other strategic programmes and warship building, India's defence innovation performance can at best be described as lacklustre. This is amply evident from India's continued high import dependency for major conventional arms, apart from poor component level innovation. The poor innovation performance can be attributed to a number of factors, related to both hard and soft innovation capabilities.

One thing for sure is that for a country of India's size, geo-strategic location, economy and international influence could little afford to perpetually depend on the foreign arms. It has to perforce equip its defence forces with arms of its own make, if it desires to be recognised as a true major power in the international system. Fortunately, its defence innovation set up has the necessary building blocks. Only thing that is required is a revamp, albeit a major one, to put it on a right course.

The framework, developed by Cheung and put to use in this study for examining India's innovation performance, is a useful tool for the Indian policy makers to set its defense innovation eco-system on right course. It identifies the areas where greater focus is required. To begin with, the policy makers would have to emphasis on the catalytic factors in terms of providing a strong vision for the innovation enterprises, monitoring the progress of key projects and fixing accountability. The Make in India initiative and *Atma Nirbhar Bharat Abhiyan* launched by the Modi government do have the necessary political will and vision to transform India's defense innovation performance. But they need to be pursued in right earnest and supported by other measures.

---

[43]CAG, *Performance Audit of Activities of Public Sector Undertakings*, 23–25.
[44]PIB, 'Indo-Russian Defence Deal'; and MoD, *Annual Report 2004-05*, 78.

India do have a large military budget, a huge pool of human resource, access to technology from diverse external sectors and a large civilian industrial base. These input factors need to be exploited further by devolving a greater share of the defense budget for R&D, creating a dedicated and more qualified S&T force, absorbing imported technology in a time bound manner and articulating a CMI strategy.

It needs no emphasis that the procurement decision-making especially in relation to buy or make plays a vital role in developing and sustaining a credible indigenous arms enterprise. This vital institutional factor as codified in India's defense procurement manual needs a sharp focus on indigenous design and development of large military platforms rather than on license manufacturing of imported designs, which has been case so far.

Organisationally, the DRDO, which is at the heart of India's defense innovation set up, would have to play a much larger role to put India in the global innovation map. It has to be however more accountable and focus on development of frontline technologies in a time bound manner. Its performance would, however, depend on how the Indian policy makers reform the networks and subsystems, contextual and output factors. The government would perforce create an environment where the stakeholders – users, developers and producers – work as a team and not at cross-purposes. The government also needs to relook at state-led planning and the state of wider civilian S&T base. Reforming the public sector enterprises and providing the private sector a greater role in R&D and manufacturing would go a long way in creating a strong innovation set up.

Disclosure statement

No potential conflict of interest was reported by the author.

Bibliography

Aeronautical Development Agency, 'Indigenous Development of Line Replaceable Units (Lru's) for LCA-Tejas', http://www.ada.gov.in/ADA-IND.pdf

'AK Antony to Take up Issues Related to FGFA Project with Russia', *The Economic Times*, 17 Oct. 2013.

Arunachalam, V.S., 'In Season of Blame: A Defence', *Deccan Chronicle*, 09May 2013, http://www.deccanchronicle.com/130509/commentary-dc-comment/commentary/season-blame-defence

Behera, Laxman Kumar, 'Defence Innovation in India: The Fault Lines', IDSA Occasional Paper, No. 32 (New Delhi: IDSA 2014).

Behera, Laxman Kumar, *Indian Defence Industry: An Agenda for Making in India* (New Delhi: Pentagon Press 2016).

Behera, Laxman Kumar, 'Defence Acquisition Procedure 2020: Imperatives for Further Reforms', ORF issue Brief, Issue No. 440, Feb. (2021), https://www.orfonline.org/wp-content/uploads/2021/02/ORF_IssueBrief_440_DAP2020.pdf (accessed 20 Mar. 2021).

Behera, Laxman Kumar, *India's Defence Economy: Planning, Budgeting, Procurement and Industry* (London: Routledge 2021).

CAG, 'Performance Audit of Activities of Public Sector Undertakings', Report No. 10 of 2010-11 for the period ended March 2009, https://cag.gov.in/cag_old/sites/default/files/audit_report_files/Union_Performance_Commerical_Activities_Public_Sector_Undertakings_10_2010.pdf.

CAG 2012, 'Union Government (Defence Services): Army and Ordnance Factories', Report No 16 of the Year 2012-13. (New Delhi: CAG)

Cheung, Tai Ming, 'Remaking Cinderella: The Nature and Development of China's Aviation Industry', Testimony before the U.S.-China Economic and Security Review Commission, 20 May 2010, https://www.uscc.gov/sites/default/files/5.20.10%20Cheung.pdf.

Cheung, Tai Ming, 'The Chinese Defense Economy's Long March from Imitation to Innovation', *The Journal of Strategic Studies* 34/3 (June 2011), 325–354.

Cheung, Tai Ming, 'A Conceptual Framework of Defence Innovation', *The Journal of Strategic Studies*, DOI: 10.1080/01402390.2021.1939689.

DRDO, *DRDO News Letter*, 38/2. (February 2018).

DRDO (2020), *Annual Report 2019*. (New Delhi: DESIDOC).

'First LCA Squadron to Be Stationed in Sulur: DRDO', *Zee News*, 21 Sept. 2011, http://zeenews.india.com/news/nation/first-lca-squadron-to-be-stationed-in-sulur-drdo_732796.html

Gooptu, Biswarup, 'HAL to Work for Quicker Clearance of Defence Programmes', *The Economic Times*, 7 Feb. 2013.

'Guarding the 'Gold'', *Boeing Frontiers*, May 2010, http://www.boeing.com/news/frontiers/archive/2010/may/i_eot.pdf

International Institute for Strategic Studies. 2013, *Military Balance 2013*. (London: Routledge).

Joshi, Keertivardhan, 'Win-Win: How Integration of Civilian and Military Technology Can Boost Defence Indigenisation', 17 Oct. 2017, https://swarajyamag.com/defence/win-win-how-integration-of-civilian-and-military-technology-can-boost-defence-indigenisation

Kavic, Lorne J., *India's Quest for Security: Defence Policies, 1947-1965* (Berkeley: University of California Press 1967).

Ministry of Finance. 2018, *Economic Survey 2017-18: Vol. I*. (New Delhi: Government of India Press).

Ministry of Science and Technology, 'The National Innovation Act of 2008', http://www.dst.gov.in/draftinnovationlaw.pdf

Ministry of Science and Technology. 2020, *Research and Development Statistics at a Glance 2019-20*. (New Delhi: Department of Science and Technology).
MoD. 2005, *Annual Report 2004-05*. (New Delhi: Government of India).
MoD. 2011, *Annual Report 2010-11*. (New Delhi: Government of India).
MoD. 2019, *Annual Report 208-19*. (New Delhi: Government of India).
MoD. 2013, *Defence Services Estimates 2013-14*. (New Delhi: Government of India Press).
PIB, 'Scorpene Submarine', 14 Mar. (2011)
PIB, 'Delay in Manufacturing of Tejas by DRDO', 20 Mar. 2013, https://pib.gov.in/news ite/erelcontent.aspx?relid=94068 (accessed on October 28, 2021).
PIB, 'Indo-Russian Defence Deal', 18 Mar. 2013, https://archive.pib.gov.in/archive2/erelease.aspx (accessed on October 28, 2021)
PIB, 'DAC Approves Procurement Proposals Worth Rs 8,722.38 Crore, Including 106 Basic Trainer Aircraft for IAF', 11 Aug. 2020, https://pib.gov.in/PressReleaseIframePage.aspx?PRID=1645092 (accessed on October 28, 2021).
PIB, 'MoD Releases Draft Defence Production and Export Promotion Policy 2020', 03 Aug. 2020, https://pib.gov.in/PressReleaseIframePage.aspx?PRID=1643194 (accessed on October 28, 2021).
PIB, 'MoD's Big Push to Atmanirbhar Bharat Initiative; Import Embargo on 101 Items beyond Given Timelines to Boost Indigenisation of Defence Production', 09 Aug. 2020, https://www.pib.gov.in/PressReleasePage.aspx?PRID=1644570 (accessed on October 28, 2021).
Public Accounts Committee, 13th Lok Sabha, *Design and Development of Main Battle Tank Arjun*, 5th Report (New Delhi: Lok Sabha Secretariat 2000).
Saraswat, VK, 'Harbingers of Change', Iinterview, *Engineering Watch*, March 2013.
SCoD, 10th Lok Sabha, *Defence Research and Development: Major Projects*, 5th Report (New Delhi: Lok Sabha Secretariat 1995).
SCoD, 13th Lok Sabha, *Demands for Grants 2003-04*, 19th Report (New Delhi: Lok Sabha Secretariat 2003).
SCoD, 14th Lok Sabha, *Defence Research and Development Organisation*, 14th Report (New Delhi: Lok Sabha Secretariat 2007).
SCoD, 14th Lok Sabha, *In-Depth Study and Critical Review of Hindustan Aeronautics Limited*, 17th Report (New Delhi: Lok Sabha Secretariat 2007).
SCoD, 14th Lok Sabha, *Demands for Grants 2008-09*, 29th Report (New Delhi: Lok Sabha Secretariat 2008).
Shukla, Ajai, 'India to Develop 25% of Fifth Generation Fighter', *Business Standard*, 6 Jan. 2010, http://www.business-standard.com/article/companies/india-to-develop-25-of-fifth-generation-fighter-110010600047_1.html
Shukla, Ajai, 'MoD Rejects HAL's Proposal to Build Basic Trainer', *Business Standard*, 19 Dec. 2012.
Shukla, Ajai, 'IAF Laments HAL Delays in Delivery of Intermediate Trainer', *Business Standard*, Feb. 05, 2013.
Shukla, Ajai, 'Indian Air Force at War with Hindustan Aeronautics; Wants to Import, Not Build, a Trainer', *Business Standard*, 29 July 2013.
Singh, Jasjit, *Indian Aircraft Industry* (New Delhi: Knowledge World 2011).
U.S. Department of State, 'U.S. Security Cooperation with India', *Fact Sheet*, 20 Jan. 2021, https://www.state.gov/u-s-security-cooperation-with-india/ (accessed 20 Mar. 2021).
Wezeman, Peter D. et al., 'Trends in International Arms Transfers 2019', *SIPRI Fact Sheet*, March 2021, https://sipri.org/sites/default/files/2021-03/fs_2103_at_2020_v2.pdf (accessed 18 Mar. 2021).

ⓐ OPEN ACCESS

North Korea's nuclear and missile programs: Foreign absorption and domestic innovation

Stephan Haggard and Tai Ming Cheung

ABSTRACT
North Korea's strategic weapons innovation system is exemplary of an authoritarian mobilization model. The top leadership prioritizes the program and mobilizes the country's science, technology, and heavy industrial resources around key programs. Key to success are investments in a defense industrial infrastructure that runs from basic research and development to applied R&D, product development, and linked production capability. Although foreign borrowing is important, the country's nuclear and missile programs would not have gelled in the absence of complementary domestic investments.

The international community has consistently underestimated North Korean nuclear and missile capabilities. How has an economically impoverished, technologically backward, and internationally isolated state been able to establish robust and increasingly competent nuclear weapons and ballistic missile programs? Has the Democratic People's Republic of Korea (DPRK) achieved this on its own, as it proudly claims, or has it been predominantly reliant on foreign sources and if so to whom and in what ways?

This essay synthesizes what we know about the development of North Korean nuclear and missile capabilities, which together makes up the country's strategic weapons complex. In the typology of defense innovation ecosystems presented in the introductory essay to this volume, the North Korean strategic weapons complex is a rapidly catching up regime that has made concerted progress over the past two decades in moving up the innovation ladder. This highly secretive apparatus is the most technologically advanced, innovative and privileged segment of the North Korean national economy.

The security challenges that North Korea faces – some of its own making – have clearly been important motives in the regime's pursuit of a nuclear capability as have blackmail or pecuniary motives. We focus here, however,

---

This is an Open Access article distributed under the terms of the Creative Commons Attribution-NonCommercial-NoDerivatives License (http://creativecommons.org/licenses/by-nc-nd/4.0/), which permits non-commercial re-use, distribution, and reproduction in any medium, provided the original work is properly cited, and is not altered, transformed, or built upon in any way.

not on these well-known dynamics but on the input, institutional, and organizational factors that have facilitated the adaptation of foreign technologies. As with other developing countries with nuclear ambitions – from Pakistan and India, to Libya, Iraq and Syria – nuclear and missile development rests on importing, absorbing and developing preexisting stocks of foreign technology. This activity is not always considered 'true' innovation. But this judgment is misleading as it has been a key component of economic latecomers more generally. Successful emulation ultimately rests on the development of complementary local capabilities, and that capability varies: Pakistan and India clearly exhibit superior capacity in this regard than Libya and Iraq. The case of North Korea is interesting precisely because it combines a surprisingly low level of economic development with rapid technological advance.

What role did foreign sources play in this process? It is often thought that official support from the Soviet Union/Russia and/or China was instrumental, and there are points at which these relationships proved crucial. Yet the record also suggests that these two patrons were wary of North Korean ambitions, and that their assistance was indirect or achieved only through unofficial or even illicit channels of transfer that were outside the control of the country's two main patrons, including not only Iran and Pakistan but through aggressive use of open sources of information as well.

The central point of this essay is that the effectiveness of North Korea's strategic weapons innovation system ultimately rests on the steady accretion of domestic capabilities under what we call an authoritarian mobilization model. This is a highly centralized, state-led and top-down 'big engineering' approach that consists of the following core elements:

- The top leadership prioritizes the program, and the state mobilizes and concentrates the country's science, technology, and heavy industrial resources on a select – but in North Korea's case an ever-widening– number of programs.
- The regime invests in a wide-ranging defense industrial infrastructure that runs from basic research and development (R&D) to applied R&D, product development, testing, linked industries devoted to the production of relevant inputs, manufacture of components and subassemblies and final output.
- The leadership simultaneously places priority on research institutions and trading entities tasked with securing technology and needed inputs from abroad through both official, informal and illicit channels.

One of the core messages of the essay is that as a result of this strategy, the barriers to dismantling North Korea's nuclear program are substantial, and not only because of the perennial bargaining problems that confront any such effort. The North Korean military-industrial complex is not only incredibly large but has become a political mainstay of the regime. It enjoys an increasingly privileged status and representation at the highest levels of the state, party and military apparatuses, and its accomplishments are consistently used to legitimize the regime politically.

The analysis will proceed in four steps, beginning with a brief overview of the current institutional structure in which the programs are embedded and some estimates of their size in the Kim Jong Un era. We then turn to the nuclear program and missile programs respectively, tracing exemplary developments of the catch-up model. Our purpose is not a contemporary assessment of capabilities but rather a demonstration of the long arc of North Korea's efforts and their deeper strategic and institutional implications.

The current institutional structure

How decisions actually get made in North Korea remains opaque. Yet two features of the system are imminently clear. First, it has been highly centralized around the three Kims – Kim Il Sung (1948–1994), Kim Jong Il (1994–2011) and Kim Jong Un (2011-present) – who, outside of brief transitional periods, have typically held the top positions in the party, the state apparatus and the military. Centralization of power facilitates the ability to prioritize and coordinate activity across institutions that may be located in the party, state or military. Second, the system is state socialist, meaning that all units involved in the research, development, production and operation of the defense-industrial complex fall under the direct control of the party-state. The principal-agent problems and potential inefficiencies of such command-and-control systems are well-known, but as the Soviet and Chinese innovation systems show, they can effectively mobilize organizational resources around particular tasks.

While the system looks hierarchical, however, it is at the same time highly personalist. Informal networks play a key role: ad hoc special committees, leading small groups, and on-the-spot guidance tours that bring together top members of the political and military leadership and the scientitic, technical and industrial infrastructure. In addition, key officials often occupy multiple overlapping roles. A consideration of the career of Gen. Ri Pyong Chol provides insight into these networks. Nominally a retired air force officer, Ri has held a number of important party and state posts related to military and defense industrial affairs. They include as a senior deputy department director (presumably of the Munitions Industry Department) of the Korean Workers Party (KWP) Central Committee, which ultimately oversees the ballistic missiles program, and memberships of the KWP's Central Military Commission and National Defense Commission under Kim Jong Il. In 2020, Ri was promoted to the KWP Politburo Presidium – the pinnacle of party power – to vice chairmanship of the Central Military Commission, and to the rank of Marshal of the KPA. He also is a KWP vice chairman and a member of Kim Jong Un's Executive Policy Council (政務局), the body from which he formally rules. He simultaneously serves as the director of the Munitions Industry Dept, also known as the Machine-Building Industry Department and is a top member of key state bodies as well, including the State Affairs Commission and the Supreme People's Assembly. As Ri's career and appointments show, leadership at the top fuses party, state, and military leadership positions.

Figure 1 reproduces an attempt to outline the formal organization of the nuclear infrastructure as of 2017,[1] and shows how elements of the program are spread across state, party and military institutions. In our view, Bermudez wrongly situates Kim Jong Un's authority as arising from his position on the State Affairs Commission and underplays the central role of the party; in all Communist systems, the party dominates the state and military and in any case Kim Jong Un sits at the apex of all three. Yet the diagram is nonetheless useful in showing the sprawling nature of the nuclear weapons complex.

On the left are several key state institutions: supporting ministries that fall under the Cabinet, such as the Ministries of Chemical Industry and Extractive Industry that provide relevant inputs (for example, reprocessing technology and uranium). The Ministry of Atomic Energy Industry has in various iterations acted as the external face of the program since formed in 1986. The State Academy of Sciences is involved in both basic and applied R&D, and is responsible for training scientists, technicians and support personnel. It also oversees the science departments in the major universities that are also effectively instruments of the program and even run some production facilities.

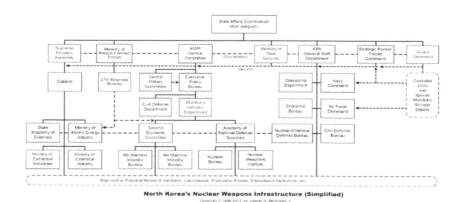

Figure 1. North Korea's nuclear weapons infrastructure.

---

[1] Joseph Bermudez, 'Overview of North Korea's NBC Infrastructure', *US-Korea Institute*, June (Johns Hopkins School of Advanced International Studies 2017), p. 14, Figure 2.

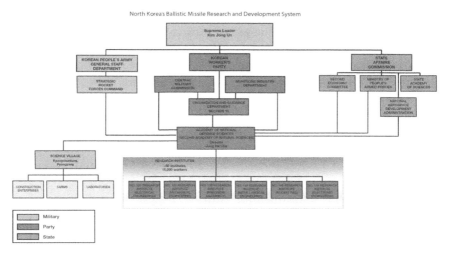

Figure 2. North Korea's ballistic missile research and development system.

However, the party is the dominant institution and a second important cluster of bodies fall directly under it. Most notable in this regard is the Munitions Industry Department, below which sit the Nuclear Bureau, Nuclear Weapons Institute, the Academy of National Defense Sciences – specifically devoted to weapons-related research–and the all-important Second Economic Committee, which oversees the defense-industrial complex. A sign of the significance of the Second Economic Committee – and of the coalitional foundation of the regime–is that its chair was a member of the National Defense Commission under Kim Jong Il, the remainder of which was made up entirely of high-ranking military and internal security personnel.[2] The 4th and 5th General Bureau of the Second Economic Committee are devoted to the missile and nuclear industries respectively, and thus sit atop a network of production facilities associated with those two programs. The Second Economic Committee also has an External Economy Department that was in charge both of missile sales during their heyday and has been involved in both the sale and procurement of relevant inputs.

Finally there is the military and security apparatus itself – again, subordinate to the party through the Central Military Commission as much as the Ministry of State Security–including the Strategic Rocket Forces Command. Although we cannot assess their influence with great confidence, these end-users do not appear to have played a central role in the development of strategic weapons capabilities, suggesting that the innovation system is 'technology push' rather than 'military pull' in nature.

---

[2] Stephan Haggard and Marcus Noland, *Hard Target: Sanctions, Inducements and the Case of North Korea* (Stanford: Stanford University Press 2017).

The organization of the missile program shows some significant overlap with the organization of the nuclear infrastructure just described, but a few differences are worth underlining. First, the missile program rests on a different set of research institutes that are primarily under the Academy of National Defense Sciences (also known in the past as the Second Academy of Natural Sciences). Second, the missile program involves an ongoing manufacturing component and the entire complex of work units that provide inputs to it as we will see. But these differences are less significant than the fundamentally hierarchical nature of the weapons complexes and the capacity of the top leadership to direct the entirety of the research, development and production supply chains.

How large is this infrastructure? With respect to the nuclear program, Bermudez[3] argues for a range of 100–150 'entities' and 9,000–15,000 personnel directly involved in the research, development, testing or production of nuclear weapons. The size of the missile infrastructure is much harder to gauge because of the manifold linkages with a variety of heavy industries noted above. South Korean media reports and articles by defecting North Korean missile researchers indicate that there are around 50 research institutes within the missile complex. The most important of these provide a sense of the reach of the complex: the No.120 (electrical engineering), No.122 (mechanical engineering), No.130 (precision machinery), No.144 (metallurgical engineering), No.166 (rocket R&D), and No.185 (electronic engineering) institutes. Yet the scope of actual production facilities is larger still and include linkages to other heavy industries: steel, non-ferrous metals, machine tools, electronics, chemicals and even automotive vehicles (for example, modified trucks for transporter-erector launchers) and shipbuilding (for the growing submarine fleet). If we narrow our metric to the dedicated missile research, development, and engineering community it is estimated to number around 15,000 personnel, of which around 3,000 are believed to be scientists and engineers.[4]

The growing significance of the programs is not just a question of formal institutions and personnel. It can also be measured by the attention given to them by Kim Jong Un from the outset of his assumption of power. Of particular significance in this regard was the roll-out of the *byungjin* line at the plenum of the Workers' Party Central Committee and the Supreme People's Assembly (SPA) meetings in March-April 2013.[5] The new policy line – 'On Consolidating the Position of Nuclear Weapons for Self-Defense'–

---

[3]Bermudez, *Overview of North Korea's NBC Infrastructure*.
[4]'North Korean "Missile Researcher" Lays Bare Missile Development by the North Korean Military,' *Shindong-A*, 9 (March 2015).
[5]'Report of Plenary Meeting of WPK Central Committee, 'KCNA 31 March 2013 and 'Seventh Session of the 12th SPA of DPRK Held', 1 April 2013 and on nuclear weapons in particular: 'Law on Consolidating Position of Nuclear Weapons State Adopted', KCNA 1 April 2013 and particularly 'Nuke and Peace 1 and 'Nuke and Peace 2', KCNA 26 and 27 April 2013.

committed the country to *both* economic reconstruction and the pursuit of its nuclear program. A separate edict committed the country to its space program, and set up a Space Development Bureau. The new policy was followed by the announcement of a five-year weapons modernization schedule in 2014 that included an increasing focus on modernization of the defense industrial base.[6] Particularly in 2016–17, as tensions with the United States escalated, his guidance visits included tours of weapons manufacturing facilities, exhortation to modernization and praise for successful completion of plan targets.

To get some sense of the emphasis on the military industrial complex, we surveyed conventional and strategic weapons-related inspection visits that Kim Jong Il conducted between 1994 and 2011 and compared them with Kim Jong Un's on-the-spot guidance inspections (Figure 3) between 2012 and 2017, the year before the onset of the summit era and the testing moratorium. Kim Jong Il made 45 publicized site visits to strategic weapons facilities during his 17 years in power, an average of 2.6 trips annually. He made 122 visits to conventional weapons-related facilities. Between 2012 -his first full year in power- and December 2017, Kim Jong Un made 57 trips to strategic weapons sites, an average of nearly six visits annually and more than twice the frequency of his father.

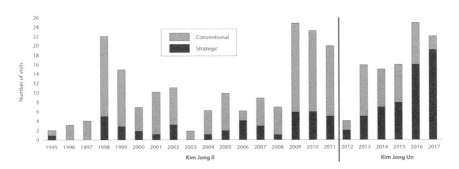

Figure 3. Site visits by Kim Jong Il and Kim Jong un to strategic vs. Conventional weapons facilities, 1994-July 2017.Source: News reports of Korean Central News Agency, collected and archived at NK Pro (https://kcnawatch.co).[7]

---

[6]Suk Lee, ed, *The DPRK Economic Outlook: 2016* (Seoul: Korea Development Institute 2017), 131–132.

Figure 4. North Korean missile launches. (Source: NKPro, North Korea Missile Tracker at https://www.nknews.org/tag/missiles/?t=1589231586629).

How did we get here? We turn to that question next by providing a reconstruction of the authoritarian mobilization model with respect to the nuclear and missile programs. The main objective of this history is to underline it's long arc and the sustained commitment of the regime to acquiring these capabilities.[7]

The nuclear program

It is surprisingly hard to determine when Kim Il Sung decided to pursue a nuclear weapons program. The interest in nuclear technology was a virtual constant from the mid-1950s forward, but these early efforts were arguably associated with an economic and prestige interest in nuclear *power*. Denisov[8] claims that the final decision on developing a weapons capability was not taken until the 1970s and others such as Bodansky[9] even push it into the second half of the 1980s. Yet it is highly plausible that the ability of the United

---

[7]Conventional weapons sites include munitions factories, military research centers, artillery factories, ammunition factories, military-related universities, some precision machinery factories, KPA unit factories, and machine plants inter alia. Strategic weapons sites include a group of munitions factories rocket test facilities, chemical weapons factory/ research centers, strategic rocket forces sites, aerospace facilities, the National Defense university, bio-chemistry research centers, the State Academy of Science, Hamhung Research Center and related facilities.

[8]Valery I. Denisov, 'Nuclear Institutions and Organizations in North Korea', in James Clay Moltz and Alexandre Mansourov (eds.), *The North Korean Nuclear Program: Security, Strategy, and New Perspectives from Russia* (New York: Routledge 2000), 22.

[9]Yoseff Bodansky, *Crisis in Korea* (New York: Spi Books 1994), 113.

States to wield nuclear threats during the Korean War and in the armistice negotiations had a profound influence on Kim Il Sung's interest in nuclear weapons from the 1950s, as demonstrated by Hayes[10] and Mazaar[11] (see Dingman[12] for information on the threats themselves).

A range of evidence suggests the emergence of a nuclear weapons ambition as early as the first half of the 1960s at the latest (see Szalontai and Radchenko[13] for a review of others reaching this conclusion). This evidence includes the first articulation of the *byungjin* line of simultaneous national defense and heavy-industrialization objectives at that time; a pattern of seeking to evade Soviet limits on the transfer of nuclear technology; the emergence of parallel acquisition tracks; and statements emanating from the leadership itself, now made available through the opening of the Soviet and Eastern European archives (for example, Szalontai and Radchenko[14]; Clemens[15]).

The manufacture of nuclear weapons requires capabilities in three discrete stages of the nuclear fuel cycle: the mining of uranium for the milling of fuel rods or for enrichment; the production of fissile material through reprocessing and/or enrichment; and the making of weapons themselves. With the partial exception of the uranium component of the nuclear fuel cycle, we see a common pattern of aggressive borrowing from foreign sources coupled with the development of complementary domestic capabilities.

Fueling the weapons drive: The uranium piece

One early suggestion of North Korean interest in developing a nuclear program came from a 1948 request from the Kim Il Sung regime to the Soviets as early as 1948 for assistance in prospecting, a request the Soviets sought to defer.[16] These requests persisted, and resurfaced in the early 1960s when the drive for a nuclear program gained steam.[17] According to

---

[10] Peter Hayes, *Pacific Powderkeg: American Nuclear Dilemmas in Korea* (Lexington: Lexington Books 1991), 3–16.
[11] Michael J. Mazaar, *North Korea and the Bomb: A Case Study in Nonproliferation* (New York: St. Martins 1995), 15–21.
[12] Roger Dingman, 'Atomic Diplomacy during the Korean War', *International Security*, 13/3 (Winter, 1988–89), 50–91.
[13] Balazs Szalontai and Sergey Radchenko, 'North Korea's Efforts to Acquire Nuclear Technology and Nuclear Weapons: Evidence from Russian and Hungarian Archives', *Cold War Internationial History Project*, Working Paper #53, Aug. 2006, 24.
[14] Szalontai and Radchenko, 'North Korea's Efforts to Acquire Nuclear Technology and Nuclear Weapons'.
[15] Walter Clemens, 'North Korea's Quest for Nuclear Weapons: New Historical Evidence', *Journal of East Asian Studies* 10 (April 2010), 127–54.
[16] See Protocol No. 61 of a meeting of the special committee under the Council of Ministers of the USSR (excerpt). Wilson Center Digital Archive at http://digitalarchive.wilsoncenter.org/document/110597.
[17] For example, the North Koreans reportedly communicated the interest in mining uranium and extracting large amounts of it to the Soviet ambassador Vasily Moskovsky in September 1963 (Clemens 2010, 129).

Yoon,[18] the two main mining sites came online between 1976 and 1981, both believed to be under the direct control of the military and both developed largely independently of the Soviets. In a pattern visible in other parts of the nuclear weapons and missile production chains, efforts at exploration and processing were supported by a cluster of universities that developed specialized expertise on both prospecting and separation of uranium.[19]

A key development in this part of the nuclear fuel cycle emerged as a result of the Soviet refusal to supply fuel to the 5MWe reactor that North Korea developed in the 1980s outside of Soviet control. The demand for fuel both for the 5MWe reactor and two much larger reactors in the planning stages was the motive for the construction of a complex devoted to uranium conversion and the milling of fuel rods.[20] Work on the Yongbyon fuel fabrication plant began in 1980–81 and according to declarations made to the IAEA operated from 1983–1986 before being decommissioned.[21] This facility produced the fuel rods that were ultimately discharged from the 5MWe and stored in 1994 before being reprocessed in 2003, the defining event in the onset of the second nuclear crisis. These spent fuel rods also generated the fissile material believed to have powered the 2006 and subsequent tests.

Under Kim Jong Un, the regime has signaled heightened interest in the uranium segment of the nuclear fuel cycle, perhaps as a signal of capability to fuel its new light water reactor and to pursue renewed enrichment activities. This interest has been reflected both in new mining activities[22] but also in the evidence of a new fuel fabrication plant.[23]

The drive to nuclear power – and fissile material

The training of scientists and technicians and the development of research capabilities were initially cast in terms of an interest in developing nuclear power. A failed effort to establish a North Choson Central Research

---

[18]Edward Yoon, 'Status and Future of the North Korean Minerals Sector', *Nautilus Institute for Security and Sustainability* (January 2011).

[19]Kim-Chaek Engineering University, Chongjin Mining and Metal University, the University of the Chemical Industry, Sariwon Geology University and the Yongbyon nuclear technical college described in more detail below.

[20]International Institute for Strategic Studies (IISS), *North Korea's Weapons Programmes: A Net Assessment*, (London: 2004), 33–34.

[21]This facility was subsequently converted to the enrichment operation that was revealed in 2010 to a visiting group of American scientists (Hecker 2010).

[22]International Atomic Energy Agency (IAEA), 2011, 7. Andrea Berger, 'What Lies Beneath: North Korean Uranium Deposits,' NKNews, Aug. 28 2014. https://www.nknews.org/2014/08/what-lies-beneath-north-koreas-uranium-deposits/ and Jeffrey Lewis, 'Recent Imagery Suggests Increased Uranium Production,' 38North, Aug. 12 2015. http://www.38north.org/2015/08/jlewis081215/.

[23]Nick Hansen, 'Major Development: Reactor Fuel Fabrication Facilities Identified at Yongbyon Nuclear Complex,' 38North, Dec. 23 2013. at http://www.38north.org/2013/12/yongbyon122313/#_ftn2/.

Institute[24] was followed in quick succession by the establishment of Kim Il Sung University in 1946, the Kimchaek Industrial University in 1948 and the Academy of Science of the DPRK in 1952, which in turn exercised control over a number of other research institutes related to the nuclear program. For example, in 1963 the Pyongsong Institute of Science (also called P'yongsong Scientific University) established a nuclear curriculum and from 1983 housed the Nuclear Physics Research Institute.[25] The dependence of these institutions on Soviet training was substantial, but by no means absolute. Kim Il Sung personally directed a peninsula-wide census of scientists, and managed to attract (or abduct) a number to seed these new institutions, most with degrees from Japanese institutions and some teaching in the South.

Formal bilateral agreements with the Soviet Union on educational and scientific cooperation respectively in 1952 and 1956 coincided with the opening in the Soviet Union of the United Institute for Nuclear Research in Dubna, designed as a hub for the sharing of nuclear technology between the Soviet Union and its allies. As we will see throughout the analysis of North Korean programs, external developments–North Korean participation in activities at Dubna – were matched by the development of an array of new departments and laboratories at North Korean universities and research institutes.[26] For example, a nuclear physics laboratory established under the new Academy of Sciences in 1955 became the nucleus of the Yongbyon complex under a 1959 bilateral agreement with the Soviet Union on cooperation on peaceful uses of nuclear energy.

Khruschev's secret speech and the emergence of the Sino-Soviet split played into North Korean nuclear developments. The split between North Korea's two communist patrons force the regime to balance its relations with the two countries in the alliance treaties of 1961. Not coincidentally, the evidence of an active interest in nuclear weapons technology first becomes unambiguously evident from the Soviet and Eastern European archives.[27] In September 1961, following Kim Il Sung's public commitment to pursue nuclear power, a Nuclear Power Committee was established under the Central Committee of the KWP largely to facilitate international cooperation on the issue. The Nuclear Power Research Center was launched at around this time at Yongbyon and ultimately completed in 1967. A new nuclear physics

---

[24]Kang Ho Je (강호제), *History of Science and Technology in North Korea* (북한과학기술형성사) (Seoul: Son In (선인) 2007).
[25]Joseph Bermudez, 'Exposing North Korea's Secret Nuclear Infrastructure I', *Jane's Intelligence Review*, July 1999.
[26]Alexander Zhebin, 'A Political History of Soviet-North Korean Nuclear Cooperation', in James Clay Moltz and Alexandre Mansourov (eds.), *The North Korean Nuclear Program: Security, Strategy, and New Perspectives from Russia* (New York: Routledge 2000), 29.
[27]Szalontai and Radchenko, 'North Korea's Efforts to Acquire Nuclear Technology and Nuclear Weapons', 27–30. Clemens, 'North Korea's Quest for Nuclear Weapons', 130.

laboratory was housed at the site in addition to another eight laboratories covering virtually the entire fuel cycle, including the production of fissile material.[28] Complementary developments occurred at nominally academic physics departments at Kim Il Sung and Kimchaek Industrial Universities.

The Soviets ultimately overcame their nervousness about sharing nuclear technology more directly and in June 1963, construction on the IRT2000 experimental reactor began and was completed in 1965 under Soviet aegis. But in a sign of the indigenous capabilities clustered at Yongbyon, this reactor was expanded to 4MWt in 1973 and 8MWt in 1998 without Soviet assistance.[29]

In January 1974, North Korea enacted a Nuclear Power Law and in September North Korea became a member of IAEA. The IAEA opened another important foreign channel of technology transfer. Choe Hak Gun, the ambassador to IAEA from 1974 to 1978, appears to have collected resources on nuclear technology through the IAEA. Not coincidentally, North Korea acquired its first reprocessing capabilities around this time. The IRT2000 experimental reactor was the site for early experimentation with the separation of plutonium in 1975. These efforts were ultimately scaled up at the Yongbyon 'radiochemistry laboratory', the country's main reprocessing facility, drawing on designs from a European consortium.[30] Construction of the radiochemistry laboratory probably began in 1984–85, and by the end of 1993, shortly before the facility was frozen according to the Agreed Framework, was 70–80% completed; nonetheless, the two lines in the plant were more than adequate to the task of reprocessing available spent fuel.[31]

There can be little question that North Korea's crowning nuclear achievement was the successful construction of the 5MWe reactor at Yongbyon (1979–86), another development that demonstrated the ability of the North Korean nuclear establishment to bypass the Soviets and exploit publicly available foreign scientific information.[32] The indigenous reactor was modeled after the U.K.'s Calder Hall 'Magnox' reactor – another European connection–designed by the UK Atomic Energy Authority (UKAEA) in the early

---

[28]Bermudez, 'Exposing North Korea's Secret Nuclear Infrastructure I'. Bill Streifer and Sang S. Nam. 2012. 'In a North Korean Nuclear Defector's Own Words', *KPA Journal* 2/11 (November 2012).
[29]National Threat Iniative, 'IRT 2000 Nuclear Research Reactor' at http://www.nti.org/learn/facilities/767/.
[30]Eurochemic was a consortium owned by thirteen European countries that ran a plant dedicated to the reprocessing of spent nuclear fuel from 1966–1974; it disseminated developed technologies widely. See Olli Heinonen, 'North Korea's Nuclear Enrichment: Capabilities and Consequences' at http://www.38north.org/2011/06/heinonen062211/.
[31]David Albright, 'North Korean Plutonium Production', *Science and Global Security* 5 (September 1994), 63–87. International Institute for Strategic Studies (IISS), *North Korea's Weapons Programmes*, 36–39.
[32]New reseach based on the Hungarian archives suggested that North Korea was openly seeking assistance in the consruction of reactors (Szalontai and Rachchenko 2006). On the indirect British role, Douglas Hogg, a Conservative minister, admitted in a written parliamentary reply in 1994 that the Yongbyon reactor had 'generic similarities to the reactors operated by British Nuclear Fuels' and that 'design information of these British reactors is not classified and has appeared in technical journals.'

1950s.[33] The design was perfect for local endowments: fueled by natural uranium, a capability that North Korea had developed as we have seen; cooled by a carbon-dioxide gas cooling system that does not require heavy water technology; and moderated by graphite, also plentiful in the country.

The Agreed Framework reached in the wake of the first nuclear crisis ultimately froze construction on two other reactors: a 50MWe reactor at Yongbyon and the 200MWe reactor at Taechon, for which the 5MWe reactor was planned as a prelude. It is revealing that these two reactors were modeled after the French G-2 reactor, which France also developed in the 1950s primarily for plutonium production. While smaller in size, the 5MWe reactor was adequate for North Korea's fissile material needs given the parallel development of reprocessing capabilities. Although shut down in 1994 by the Agreed Framework, the reactor was restarted in 2003 when that agreement collapsed, shut down again four years later as a result of agreements reached under the Six Party Talks, but restarted again in mid-2013 with likely discharge and reprocessing of plutonium in 2016.

The second path to fissile material is through enrichment, and provides a case study in how illicit transfers fueled indigenous developments.[34] The onset of the second nuclear crisis in 2002 was the direct outgrowth of American intelligence that the DPRK was experimenting with a uranium enrichment programme. The origins of this program date to 1993–94 and North Korea's insertion into the A.Q. Khan network. In his memoirs, Pervez Musharraf[35] revealed that two dozen P1 and P2 centrifuges and measuring equipment had been transferred to North Korea, enough to begin trial enrichment. Moreover, there was ongoing technology transfer following a more formalized agreement in 1996 before it was reversed under Musharraf after 2001.[36]

Subsequent illicit activities that were required to access critical inputs for the program, such as maraging steel and aluminum, became a central focus of sanctions efforts and have been well-documented by many including Albright and Brannan.[37] These activities required a trading front, a role played by the Nam Chongang Trading Company and other companies subsequently spun off from it.

---

[33]The name 'magnox' came from the alloy used to clad the fuel rods, a technology that the North Korean also appropriated.
[34]David Albright, *Peddling Peril: How The Secret Nuclear Trade Arms America's Enemies* (New York: Free Press 2010). David Albright and Paul Brannan, 'Taking Stock: North Korea's Uranium Enrichment Program', *Institute for Science and International Security*, Oct. 2011) at https://isis-online.org/uploads/isis-reports/documents/ISIS_DPRK_UEP.pdf. Siegfried S. Hecker, 'A Return Trip to North Korea's Yongbyon Nuclear Complex', *Center for International Security and Cooperation*, Nov. (Stanford University 2010) at https://fsi-live.s3.us-west-1.amazonaws.com/s3fs-public/HeckerYongbyon.pdf.
[35]Pervez Musharraf, *In the Line of Fire* (New York: Free Press 2006), 296.
[36]Albright and Brannan, 'Taking Stock: North Korea's Uranium Enrichment Program'.
[37]see note 37 above.

In response to sanctions imposed in 2009, North Korea openly acknowledged the program and even invited a group of American scientists to visit in 2010.[38] The sophistication of the program – with 2000 centrifuges arranged in six cascades with a capacity of 8000 separative work units (SWU) per year – was far beyond what at least some in the intelligence community had estimated. The visit provided strong circumstantial evidence that North Korea maintained a second, secret site where its enrichment capability was piloted or ran in parallel, perhaps even during the Agreed Framework period; by 2016, evidence from satellite imagery and defectors suggested a location for this site at an underground aircraft manufacturing plant.[39] But of equal importance to our purposes here, the visit implied a massive industrial infrastructure for *manufacturing* of centrifuges, which would have included, inter alia, a number of complex technologies in addition to the input of UF_6: vacuum pumps; ring magnets; frequency inverters; maraging steel and particularly machine tools, up to and including computer numeric controlled flow-forming machines.[40]

Weaponization

Despite the fact that North Korea has conducted six nuclear tests, the weapons development phase of the cycle is obviously the most opaque. North Korea first announced that it had nuclear weapons in 2003.[41] and first tested a small device on 6 October 2006 at the Punggye-ri test site. The question is how far back we can push the start date of an actual weapons program. The 101 Nuclear Physics Chemistry Institute is believed to have conducted nuclear weapons research as early as the 1970s; the fact that the unit is housed inside a mine in the vicinity of Yongbyon is suggestive of the secrecy and security surrounding its operation. At that point, however, North Korea was still not close to having the fissile material for a weapon.

It is more likely that the push toward weaponization occurred in the second half of the 1980s when fissile material was more plausibly in sight. By the early 1990s, a cluster of reports suggested elements of a weaponization program, including test explosions at Yongbyon from the early 1990s that are consistent with development of an implosion device. Moreover, defector testimony has claimed a bomb-building program and even actual

---

[38] Hecker, 'A Return Trip to North Korea's Yongbyon Nuclear Complex'.
[39] David Albright, 'North Korea's Suspect, Former Small-Scale Enrichment Plant', ISIS 21, Sept. 2016. at http://isis-online.org/uploads/isis-reports/documents/North_Koreas_Pilot_Enrichment_Plant_21Jul2016_Final.pdf
[40] Early suspect firms involved in the program are believed to be the Ryonha Machinery Joint Venture Corporation in Pyongyang, the Kusong Machine-Tool Plant in North Pyongan Province, and the Huichon Machine Tool Factory in Huichon city (Albright and Brannan, 'Taking Stock: North Korea's Uranium Enrichment Program', 2010, 21).
[41] 'Statement of DPRK government on its withdrawal from NPT', KCNA, Jan.10 2003.

weapons in the early 1990s.[42] Yet as the earlier description of the facilities housed at Yongbyon suggest, the first investments in these capabilities came decades before the first test.

With the tests, the debate about weaponization has shifted from whether North Korea *could* engineer a device to whether they can miniaturize it for delivery on a warhead and how far down the boosted or hydrogen weapons path they can go. This debate goes somewhat beyond our purposes here; it is only worth noting that the assessments of how long it will take North Korea to achieve these capabilities has fallen steadily and for military planning purposes, the existence of the capability is now effectively assumed.

The missile infrastructure

Until the Kim Jong Un years, the North Koreans pursued five overlapping missile programs: the Scud, Nodong, Musudan, Taepodong and KN-02 programs, with the complementary Taepodong or Paektusan programs generating satellite launch vehicles. Even before the accelerated testing and second 'big push' of the Kim Jong Un years, the missile inventory had thus already grown in size, implying a range of discrete development programs corresponding to missiles of different ranges and involving different production processes and even facilities. Although early phases of the program are clearly phased, a striking feature of North Korea's missile development is a big push to extend ranges beginning in the late-1980s and persisting to this day.

The second big push came during the Kim Jong Un years and saw unanticipated developments along a number of fronts. Strategically, the most important developments are those that increase survivability and lower launch times: road mobile missiles of extended range, solid fuel capabilities, and completely new programs such as the pursuit of a SLBM capability.

How do we understand these developments? With respect to virtually each system, there is a robust debate in the open source literature on the extent to which direct transfers of whole systems, foreign designs and technical assistance as well as parts and components played into particular missiles (see particularly Shiller 2012[43]). At one end are those who see strong reverse engineering and subsequent innovation capabilities. A second possibility is a 'licenced production' model in which North Korea is working off foreign designs and inputs. A third possibility is the existence of various mixed models of acquisition involving both foreign and domestic capabilities. And at the more skeptical end are those who believe that at least some

---

[42] AFP, '"Test Explosions" at DPRK Nuclear Facility,' June 28 1991; Crisis Group, 'Asia Report No. 168: North Korea's Nuclear and Missile Programs', June 2009, 9–11; and David Albright and Kevin O'Neill, *Solving the North Korean Nuclear Puzzle* (Washington DC: ISIS Press, 2000).
[43] Markus Schiller, *Characterizing the North Korean Nuclear Missile Threat* (Santa Monica: RAND 2012).

systems reflect little more than outright purchase of existing stocks, most likely from Russia. Finally, a fifth interpretation – at least for some systems – cannot be ruled out: that development efforts represented bluffs or strategic attempts to mislead foreign intelligence agencies about capabilities.

This debate cannot be fully resolved, but we can gain some perspective by considering some of the similarities and differences with the nuclear story. The nuclear program rests on a fairly discrete set of steps required to get from uranium to fissile material to weapons. The effort could thus be focused on single facilities at each stage, for example, the fuel fabrication plant, the reactors, the reprocessing facility, and device and bomb-making. A partial exception to this generalization is the enrichment program, which implied an industrial-scale effort to manufacture centrifuges.

Missile development and production similarly involves basic and applied R&D and the acquisition or manufacture of a number of inputs and subassemblies. But it does so on a serial production basis that requires underlying process engineering and systems integration capability. This is particularly true when we consider that the program enjoyed a brief but extremely significant commercial phase when North Korea was not simply manufacturing missiles for its own use but for export as well.[44]

Perhaps the best way to sort out this debate between foreign dependence, absorption, and indigenization is to acknowledge that North Korea pursues all these different approaches simultaneously and opportunistically. Nonetheless, the most important feature of the model is the ability to absorb foreign inputs, reverse engineer, and add domestic improvements to allow for constant upgrading. This sequence can be called the Acquistion, Digestion, Engineering, and Re-innovation (ADER) model.[45] Acquisition means the purchase, theft or other transfer of foreign technologies and know-how. Digestion refers to the processes required to collate, assess, and diffuse the acquired foreign capabilities internally. Engineering is the ability to turn this absorbed knowledge and technology into output, of which reverse engineering is a key method. The actual output appears thus as a kind of re-innovation.

Developing domestic capabilities in munitions

From independence, North Korean engineers went to the Soviet Union to receive technical training in the production of weapons, for which demand expanded dramatically once the war broke out. A number of military factories

---

[44]Joshua Pollack, 'Ballistic Missile Trajectory: The Evolution of North Korea's Ballistic Missile Market', *Nonproliferation Review* 18/2 (June 2011), 411–429.
[45]Tai Ming Cheung, 'Innovation in China's Defense Technology Base-Foreign Technology and Military Capabilities', *Journal of Strategic Studies* 36 (September 2016), 5–6.

date to the war or early postwar period.[46] The wider scope of the military industrial complex as it has evolved since then can be seen in the fact that while the 4th and 5th Bureau of Machine Industry of the Second Economic Committee are involved in the missiles and the WMD program respectively, the Committee oversees a total of seven such bureaus as well as a trading company, with one estimate in the mid-2000s counting 134 separate factories.[47]

By the mid-1960s, the leadership's focus was still overwhelmingly on other conventional weapons systems rather than missiles. In 1962, North Korea received an SA-2 surface-to-air missile from the Soviet Union, but at that juncture had no domestic capability. Yet as with respect to the nuclear program, the regime invested simultaneously in domestic capabilities. In 1963, the Hamhung Military Academy – now the Defense University–was built for the explicit purpose of developing advanced weapons.[48] The Defense University became an important feeder for the Academy of National Defense Science, or the Second Academy of Natural Science, that was established in 1964. A recent report on the Academy of Defense Science shows how it grouped a number of specialized bodies together, bodies that came under the Munitions Industry Department at the time of the formation of the Second Economic Committee. In 1993, Kim Il Sung ordered that all such research institutes would fall under the Academy of National Defense Science and they included a wide array of engineering capabilities: metals, electronics; engines; satellites, electronic warfare and so on.

Most importantly, grouped under these research institutes are so-called 'middle factories' located in Pyongyang city and the Hamkyong and Pyongan provinces that constitute the effective production infrastructure. A combination of defector testimony and satellite imagery has expanded the public source tracking of this infrastructure; for example, the NTI database[49] lists no fewer than 21 facilities that are engaged either directly

---

[46]Heavy material industry of North Korea, North Korea Information, searched in 17 October 2017, http://nkinfo.unikorea.go.kr/nkp/overview/nkOverview.do?sumryMenuId=EC212.
[47]First Bureau, firearms and general logistics equipment; Second Bureau, tanks and armored vehicle; Third Bureau, artillery; Sixth Bureau, shipbuilding; Seventh Bureaa, aircraft and communications equipment. Hong Song-pyo, 'North Korea's Military Science and Technology,' *Kunsa Nontan*, Apr. 29 2005. See also Dan Pinkston, *The North Korean Ballistic Missile Program* (Carlisle: Strategic Studies Institute 2008) 15, 41–2.
[48]SBS news, http://news.sbs.co.kr/news/endPage.do?news_id=N1004383078 Another important educational and research initiative was the creation of the Science University in 1967 in Pyongsong. Falling under the Academy of Science, it was tasked with training scientists and engineers who earn the privilege of study abroad and subsequently work at the Academy of Defense or Academy of Science.
[49]At http://www.nti.org/learn/countries/north-korea/facilities/.

in missile manufacture or in linked industries. But given the incentive to put such facilities underground and hide them, this should be taken as a lower bound of the production infrastructure.

Technology transfer, reverse engineering and innovation: An overview of the programs under Kim Il Sung and Kim Jong Il[50]

It is far beyond the scope of this paper to provide a thorough analysis of the development of all of the main missile systems.[51] However, it is possible to consider the evolution of several systems – the early Scud variants, the Nodong and Taepodong – as a way of demonstrating the operation of the ADER model. Several points bear emphasis. First is the wide variety of foreign channels that the North Koreans have used to advance the program: from direct state-to-state transfers and technology cooperation agreements, to purloined foreign designs, illicit scientific cooperation and the aggressive exploitation of global product and technology markets, including for goods that nominally face strict dual-use export restraints. The second point to make is that the debate over foreign or domestic influences is to some extent misleading, as even absorption of foreign technology and information requires domestic capabilities.

These domestic capabilities start with duplicative imitation or direct copying with no local refinements but is followed by creative imitation in which the same foreign platform is subjected to moderate levels of domestic modification. In the most advanced phases of imitation, creative adaptation demonstrates significant levels of domestic improvement. A big question is whether North Korea's missile innovation system remains at this advanced imitation level or has crossed over into homegrown innovation, in which the platform is primarily locally designed and developed. It is doubtful that North Korea has reached this step if the metric is an entire missile system some core designs of which are clearly inherited. But we can't rule out innovation in some subsystems nor in systems integration.

As with the nuclear program, the missile story also commenced in earnest in the 1960s. Following a brief period of Soviet-DPRK stress that interrupted arms transfers and cooperation, North Korea reached an agreement with the Soviet Union on military cooperation in 1965 that included provision of the

---

[50] In addition to the works referenced below, this section relies on two websites that provide high-quality information on the programs: the National Threat Initiative at http://www.nti.org/learn/countries/north-korea/delivery-systems/ and the CSIS Missile Threat Initiative at https://missilethreat.csis.org/country/dprk/.

[51] An extensive literature now exists on these programs. See Bermudez, 1999c, Bermudez, 'Going Ballistic: North Korea's Advanced Missile Capabilities', *Jane's Intelligence Review*, Mar. 2009; IISS, *North Korea's Weapons Programmes*; Pinkston, *The North Korean Ballistic Missile Program*; Wright 2009; Schiller, *Characterizing the North Korean Nuclear Missile Threat*; and Postol and Schiller, 'The North Korean Ballistic Missile Program', *Korea Observer* 47/4 (December 2016), 751–806.

S-2 Sopka (SSC-2b SAMLET) coastal-defense cruise missile, P-20 (SS-N-2 STYX) anti-ship missile, and the 3R10 Luna-2 (FROG-5) artillery rocket as well as TELs and other equipment. The Soviet Union was not the only source of early missile technology, however. In the late 1960s, Soviet-DPRK relations again soured and Moscow held back further weapons transfers. North Korea reached an agreement with China in 1971 that allowed it not only to acquire another cluster of missile technologies[52] but to reorganize its Soviet-related programs.

This early Soviet and Chinese training – including assembly, test and maintenance – no doubt expanded North Korean capabilities. However, we can also assume that the systems that North Korea received were also sent to the Academy of National Defense Science for reverse engineering which the North Koreans had probably achieved with respect to at least some of these systems (including the Chinese HQ-2 and HY-1) by the mid- to late-1970s.

The next generation of missiles, and the first ballistic missiles, arose in the face of limitations on support from both the Soviet Union and China. When Kim Il Sung visited Beijing in 1975 he sought deepened missile cooperation but just as the Cultural Revolution was unfolding. It was at this juncture that the regime launched a more concerted missile program and entered into a new partnership with Egypt in 1976.

Although there is some controversy about the timing,[53] Egypt subsequently sent North Korea Soviet R-17E (SS-1 C Scud B), MAZ-543 TELs, and other equipment in return for technical support in developing joint Egyptian and North Korean capabilities.[54] It was the reverse engineering of these transferred weapons that led to the Hwasong-5, key to which is a long-standing Russian engine design that was relatively easy to mass produce and highly reliable.[55] The first tests of this missile were not undertaken until 1984, however, and half failed. The speed with which they subsequently achieved a low failure rate – perhaps three years to reverse engineering and another three years to mass production–leads Schiller[56] to conclude that the 'pure reverse engineering plus innovation' hypothesis is probably not correct: there was either substantial outside help that is not visible or some of the Hwasong 5's (and subsequent generations) could even have been purchased from retired Soviet inventories.

---

[52]These systems were themselves modified versions of Soviet designs. See Bermudez 1999c, 3–4.
[53]Pinkston, *The North Korean Ballistic Missile Program*, 15.
[54]On expansion of the Musudan-ri facility during the 2000s, see Digital Globe, 'Musudan-ri Missile Test Facility North Korea, 15 February 2002–26 March, 2009   . at https://fas.org/nuke/guide/dprk/facility/musudan-ri.pdf.
[55]Theodore Postol and Markus Schiller, 'The North Korean Ballistic Missile Program', *Korea Observer* 47/4 (December 2016), 767.
[56]Schiller, *Characterizing the North Korean Nuclear Missile Threat*.

Whatever assistance North Korea might have received, however, it was also precisely at this time that the North began selling missiles to Iran. Most clients were not probably involved in significant co-development (Syria, Egypt, Libya) because they lacked the capabilities. But the rapid expansion of demand, information gleaned from Iraqi Scud variants provided by Iran[57] and the sharing of other information with the Iranians almost certainly deepened North Korean capabilities[58] What followed was the heyday of the North Korean missile export program – roughly from 1987–1993–after which demand began to contract and become more erratic.[59] At the peak of serial production, North Korea was producing as many as 8–10 missiles a month.[60]

These capabilities were subsequently leveraged into the first important incremental innovation of the North Korean missile program. The Hwasong 6 (Scud C) could have reflected a number of incremental technological adjustments of the Hwasong 5 (Scud B) without any fundamental breakthroughs: reduction in warhead weight, lightening of the airframe (thanks to imports of specialty steel from Russia), modifications to the Hwasong 5 propellant and oxidizer tanks and guidance systems. Wright and Kadyshev[61] suggest that the key innovation in expanding range was probably incremental improvements in the Russian engines, with Chinese assistance. The Scud ER (Hwasong 9) represented a further iteration, with development beginning in 1991 and the first flight test in 1993.

The end of the Cold War was a particular shock for North Korea, and the opportunities for state-to-state collaboration with both Russia and China rapidly disappeared. But these state-to-state links were quickly replaced by a range of new scientific and technical networks. These included the recruitment of Russian and even Japanese scientists and the Iran and Pakistan connections. According to Kim Kil-son, a defector, engineers from the Soviet Union, Pakistan and Iran were working at laboratories under the Academy of National Defense Science from 1991. The Russian connection seems to have been particularly important, first recruited through a solid-state physicist Anatoliy Rubtsov and ultimately

---

[57]Pinkston, *The North Korean Ballistic Missile Program*, 17.
[58]Joseph Bermudez, 'A History of Ballistic Missile Development in the DPRK', *Center for Nonproliferation Studies Occasional Paper #2*, Nov. 1999, 18–19.
[59]Pollack, 'Ballistic Missile Trajectory'.
[60]Bermudez, 'A History of Ballistic Missile Development in the DPRK', 13–15.
[61]Wright and Kadyshev, 'An Analysis of the North Korean Nodong Missile', *Science & Global Security* 4/2 (1994), 129–60.

involving as many as 60 scientists.[62] A smaller contingent of Korean-Japanese scientists associated with the pro-North Korean Chongryon (or Chosoren in Japanese) also have been implicated, working at the University of Tokyo Institute of Industrial Science and probably contributing to the development of missile engines.[63]

These patterns of foreign involvement were also clearly evident in the next major missile program: the Nodong. The timing of the initiation of the Nodong program in 1988, roughly contemporaneous with the Hwasong 6, suggests that it was probably the first missile that was designed with nuclear ambitions from the outset, overlapping with the early evidence of weaponization efforts described above. The development of the Nodong remains even more controversial than the early Scud variants because of the paucity of flight tests and apparent technical problems (2008, 19). But it is possible North Korea was securing information from tests of similar or even identical Iranian Shahab 3 and Pakistani Ghauri/ Hatf 5 missiles[64]

The way in which prior capabilities provided the foundation for subsequent ones is most clear in the initiation of the Taepodong (in Korean Paektusan) program in the early 1990s, which generated the Taepodong 1 and 2 and became the foundation for the subsequent Unha satellite launches (in April 2009 and April 2012, which failed, and in December 2012 and February 2016 that succeeded). In both cases, the main strategic objective was clearly to extend range as well as payload. For our purposes, though, the most important feature of these systems is the way in which they leveraged the Scud variants and Nodong programs. This new program included two- or three-stage missiles with a Nodong variant as the first stage and a Hwasong variant in the second. The system was first tested in spectacular fashion in satellite mode in August 1998 in the first test that overflew Japan. The 1998 test ultimately generated a moratorium that held from September 1999 until

---

[62]Two more groups of Russian experts planning to travel to North Korea were intercepted in 1992, one of missile engineers the other associated with the country's nuclear program, but it is not known how many got through. Not until late 1993 was North Korean Major General Nam Gae Wok, stationed in Moscow as a recruiter, finally expelled from Russia. See *Yonhap* (Seoul), 23 April 1994; in JPRS-TND-94-011, 16 May 1994, 51–52. UPI, 10 February 1993, in *Executive News Service*, 10 February 1993. Mikhail Popov, *Rabochaya Tribuna*, (Moscow) 11 February 1993, 3; in JPRS-UST-93-002, 8 April 1993, 52. *KBS-1 Radio Network* (Seoul), 21 December 1992; in JPRS-TND-93-001, 7 January 1993, 6. *Itar-Tass*, 4 February 1993; in JPRS-TND-93-005, 12 February 1993, 14–15. UPI, 10 February 1993; in *Executive News Service*, 10 February 1993. *Itar-Tass*, 24 February 1993; in FBIS-SOV-93-035, 24 February 1993, 11–12. *Armed Forces Journal International*, April 1993, 9.
[63]Tsutomu Nishioka, 'Researchers in Japan helped N. Korea develop Nuclear Missiles', Japan Institute for National Fundamentals, Apr. 7 2016. https://en.jinf.jp/weekly/archives/4308.
[64]Wright and Kadyshev, 'An Analysis of the North Korean Nodong Missile', 129–60, missing in the references. Joseph Bermudez, 'Going Ballistic: North Korea's Advanced Missile Capabilities', *Jane's Intelligence Review*, Mar. 2009.

July 2006,[65] but no one believed that the North Koreans were sitting still during this period. Following the tests of July 2006 it became clear that a variety of new programs had been initiated, including most significantly the further extensions of the Hwasong noted above as well as the Musudan[66] and the KN-02, a shorter-range missile that was nonetheless programmatically significant for its use of solid fuel.

Into the Kim Jong Un era

As we noted in the introduction, it has become abundantly clear that the commitment to the nuclear and missile programs has become a defining feature of the Kim Jong Un regime. The acceleration of missile tests from the onset of his rule up to the flurry of tests in late 2017 and the period of 'fire and fury' with the US tells the story. But outside of a pause on testing, the short-lived period of nuclear diplomacy – running roughly from the PyeongChang Winter Olympics in February 2018 through the failed Hanoi summit a year later – did not succeed in making a dent in the developments described here. To the contrary, the failure to secure sanctions relief has probably led to another moment of acceleration in the effort to deepen capabilities.

From our perspective, however, the important development of the Kim Jong Un years is not quantitative but qualitative. In particular, five objectives of Kim Jong Un's big push have forced either important innovations in existing systems or altogether new programs.[67] Our understanding of the source of the technologies that undergird them is very much a work in progress, and it is not our objective to provide a full inventory of capabilities. But each is worth noting briefly as they clearly rest on prior developments.

- Extending the range of the strategic rocket force. The most striking feature of the 2017 tests was what appeared to be unprecedented jumps in range, mirrored in the debate over whether North Korea had an ICBM capability (tests of the Hwasong 12 [May, August], Hwasong 14 [twice in July] and Hwasong 15 [October]). These tests also revived the question of the plausibility of purely domestic development, with suspicion focusing on the acquisition of a high-performance liquid-propellant engine from illicit networks in Russia and Ukraine.[68] A military parade in

---

[65].See for example Philip Maxon, 'Official Estimates of the TP-2 , 38North, Jan. 28 2011 for a thorough review of the US intelligence estimates of the Taepodong's capabilities at http://www.38north.org/2011/01/estimates-of-taepodong-2/.

[66]Markus Schiller and Robert Schmucker, 'Explaining the Musudan: New Insights on the North Korean SS-N-6 Technology', May 2012.

[67]Joel S. Wit and Sun Young Ahn, 'North Korea's Nuclear Futures: Technology and Strategy', *U.S. Korea Institute at SAIS*, Feb. 2015.

[68]Michael Elleman, 'The Secret to North Korea's ICBM Success', *International Institute for Strategic Studies*, Aug. 2017.

October 2020 appeared to reveal yet another generation, a surprisingly large two-stage liquid propelled ICBM that was quickly dubbed a Hwasong-16.
- The quest for road-mobile missiles with greater ranges in order to achieve survivability and a credible second-strike capability, with demands not only on the missile program but on transporter-erector-launcher technology as well.
- Closely related, the development of solid-fuel rocket technology, most notably to extend the range of the Russian KN-02 SRBM design that could be deployed both on mobile land launchers and as an SLBM capability. Tests in 2017 included the first flight test of KN-15, a land-based version of the KN-11 and every test since that time has used solid propellants.

- The pursuit of naval platforms and a submarine launched ballistic missile capability, with a new variant revealed shortly after President Biden's inauguration, also motivated by achieving a credible second-strike.
- Continuing pursuit of the satellite and space launch vehicle program that increasingly appears to be a component of the ICBM program.

As of this writing, long-range missile tests have been on pause. Even the failure of the Hanoi Summit in February 2019 did not lead to a reversal of the test moratorium. However, North Korea is clearly continuing to develop its missile capabilities, resumed testing of short-range missiles shortly after the breakdown of the Hanoi summit and continued such tests into the Biden administration. The Trump administration admitted that the regime continued to generate fissile material under its watch.[69] An important Central Committee meeting in 2018 signaled the 'completion' of the strategic nuclear and missile forces. Similar signals have been sent since, not only through work reports of important meetings – such as the Fifth Plenum of December 2019 and the 8th Party Congress of January 2021 – but in the display of missiles of clearly inter-continental design at the military parade in October 2020.[70]

The big push under Kim Jong Un and the test successes suggest that the North Korean nuclear and missile programs have reached a critical juncture in the country's move up the innovation ladder. The missile sector has already

---

[69] For example, 'U.S. Spy Agencies: North Korea is Working on New Missiles', *Washington Post*, July 30 2018; and Reuters, 'North Koreaw Making Bomb Fuel Despite Denuclearization Pledge,' July 25 2018 at https://www.reuters.com/article/us-northkorea-usa/north-korea-making-bomb-fuel-despite-denuclearization-pledge-pompeo-idUSKBN1KF2QT.

[70] Vann H. Van Diepen and Michael Elleman, 'North Korea Unveils Two New Strategic Missiles in October 10 Parade', 38North, Oct 10 2020 at https://www.38north.org/author/vann-h-van-diepen/.

reached the stage of advanced imitation where most if not all of its programs demonstrate a significant level of domestic improvement on existing designs, and as we have emphasized here, the capacity to produce.

Conclusions: The vital ingredients of the North Korean model for nuclear weapons and ballistic missile development

The story of how the DPRK built a nuclear weapons and intercontinental ballistic missile capability appears to go against all geo-strategic, economic, and technological odds. Indeed, it is a test case for how even the poorest, most backward, and isolated states can engage in the development of potent defense innovation capabilities if the leadership is willing to prioritize the effort, build complementary domestic capability and exploit the many holes in the nonproliferation architecture. The features of the authoritarian mobilization approach to catch-up are worth reiterating.

- A unified and single-minded leadership with long time horizons that is able to mobilize the entire resources of the country for an extended period of time to pursue its strategic goal regardless of economic and social costs at home and isolation abroad. This is especially the case under Kim Jong Un, who has shown a laser-like focus and dedication to the development of strategic weapons capabilities far greater than his father.
- Significant access to foreign technology and knowledge, especially in the formative stages of research and development, and the continuing ability to acquire critical foreign technologies at later phases. This requires a well-connected and well-funded international network of suppliers and collaborators as well as an effective intelligence collection system.
- A well-trained, experienced, and wide bench of scientists and engineers across the full range of scientific, technological, and engineering disciplines needed for nuclear weapons and ballistic missiles. Even if foreign scientists have contributed, the claims of official propaganda carry an important germ of truth: that the strategic weapons complex ultimately rests on the training of North Korean scientists, technicians and production managers and workers. On this dimension, North Korea appears to differ most sharply from the less comprehensive efforts of Libya, Iraq, Syria and even Iran.
- An effective systems integration capability that is able to manage all the diverse and complex design, research, development, and engineering processes involved in the absorption and reverse engineering of foreign technologies and marrying this with domestically developed technologies.

- An institutional culture that is willing to take risks, learn from mistakes, be flexible and adaptive, and to learn while doing. These characteristics seem to be at odds with the highly ideological, risk-adverse, and tightly regimented norms that appear to characterize the North Korean political system. But such clichés mislead, as the system proved highly flexible and adaptive at the top.

The implications of this story for how to manage North Korea go far beyond our purposes. However, the findings of this essay clearly have a number of implications for the effort of the Biden administration to revive negotiations with North Korea. The country not only has a deployed nuclear weapons capability but also a very large workforce of highly skilled strategic weapons scientists and engineers. In addition to the complexities of negotiating a pause, let alone a rollback, of this capability negotiations will need to consider the deeper implications of the system we have outlined here. The international community must grapple not only with North Korean weapons, but with the entire strategic weapons complex we have described and the difficulty – if not impossibility – of rolling it back.

Finally and returning to the theme of defense innovation, the North Korean case study provides an example of the rapid catch-up variant put forward in the introductory chapter. In this model, catalytic factors motivate technological and industrial development, which has clearly happened in North Korea where top level leadership intervention has been shaped by acute external threat environment. Yet threats are not enough; other attributes of successful catch-up states need to be in place including effective absorption of foreign technologies and the highly targeted mobilization of limited national resources. The question going forward is whether, at least in the defense sphere, North Korea will remain locked in the catch-up category or can make the transition and become an advanced and sustainable military technological regime. Given the country's ability to advance despite significant sanctions headwinds, the possibility can no longer be ruled out.

Acknowledgement

The authors wish to acknowledge the invaluable research assistance from Taseul Joo, who compiled key data sources and conducted extensive reviews of Korean language sources and Daniel Pinkston for detailed comments on earlier drafts.

Disclosure statement

No potential conflict of interest was reported by the author(s).

Funding

This work was supported by, or in part by, the U.S. Army Research Laboratory and the U.S. Army Research Office under contract/grant No. [W911NF-15-1-0407]. Any opinions, findings, and conclusions or recommendations expressed in this publication are those of the author(s) and do not necessarily reflect the views of the U.S. Army Research Office.

Bibliography

Albright, David, 'North Korean Plutonium Production', *Science and Global Security* 5 (September 1994), 63–87. doi:10.1080/08929889408426416.

Albright, David, *Peddling Peril: How The Secret Nuclear Trade Arms America's Enemies* (New York: Free Press 2010).

Albright, David and Paul Brannan, 'Taking Stock: North Korea's Uranium Enrichment Program', *Institute for Science and International Security*, Oct. 2011. https://isis-online.org/uploads/isis-reports/documents/ISIS_DPRK_UEP.pdf

Albright, David and Kevin O'Neill, *Solving the North Korean Nuclear Puzzle* (Washington DC: ISIS Press 2000).

Bermudez, Joseph, 'Exposing North Korea's Secret Nuclear Infrastructure I', *Jane's Intelligence Review*, July 1999a.

Bermudez, Joseph, 'A History of Ballistic Missile Development in the DPRK', *Center for Non-Proliferation Studies Occasional Paper #2*, Nov. 1999b.

Bermudez, Joseph, 'Going Ballistic: North Korea's Advanced Missile Capabilities', *Jane's Intelligence Review*, Mar. 2009.

Bermudez, Joseph, 'Overview of North Korea's NBC Infrastructure', *US-Korea Institute*, June (Johns Hopkins School of Advanced International Studies 2017).

Bodansky, Yoseff, *Crisis in Korea* (New York: Spi Books 1994).

Brugge, Norbert, 'The North Korean/Iranian Nodong-Shahab Missile Family', 2017. http://www.b14643.de/Spacerockets/Specials/Nodong/index.htm

Cheung, Tai Ming, 'Innovation in China's Defense Technology Base-Foreign Technology and Military Capabilities', *Journal of Strategic Studies* 36 (September 2016), 5–6.

Clemens, Walter, 'North Korea's Quest for Nuclear Weapons: New Historical Evidence', *Journal of East Asian Studies* 10/1 (April 2010), 127–54. doi:10.1017/S1598240800003246.

Crisis Group, *Asia Report No. 168: North Korea's Nuclear and Missile Programs*, June 2009.

Denisov, Valery I., 'Nuclear Institutions and Organizations in North Korea', in James Clay Moltz and Alexandre Mansourov (eds.), *The North Korean Nuclear Program: Security, Strategy, and New Perspectives from Russia* (New York: Routledge 2000).
Dingman, Roger, 'Atomic Diplomacy during the Korean War', *International Security* 13/3 (Winter 1988-89). doi:10.2307/2538736.
Elleman, Michael, 'The Secret to North Korea's ICBM Success', *International Institute for Strategic Studies* (August 2017).
Haggard, Stephan and Marcus Noland, *Hard Target: Sanctions, Inducements and the Case of North Korea* (Stanford: Stanford University Press 2017).
Hayes, Peter, *Pacific Powderkeg: American Nuclear Dilemmas in Korea* (Lexington: Lexington Books 1991), 3-16.
Hecker, Siegfried S., 'A Return Trip to North Korea's Yongbyon Nuclear Complex', *Center for International Security and Cooperation*, Nov. (Stanford University 2010). https://fsi-live.s3.us-west-1.amazonaws.com/s3fs-public/HeckerYongbyon.pdf
International Atomic Energy Agency (IAEA) 2011.
International Institute for Strategic Studies (IISS), *North Korea's Weapons Programmes: A Net Assessment* (London 2004).
Je, Kang Ho, (강호제), *History of Science and Technology in North Korea (북한과학기술형성사)* (Seoul: Son In (선인) 2007).
Lankov, Andrei, *Crisis in North Korea: The Failure of De-Stalinization 1956* (Honolulu: University of Hawaii Press 2007).
Lee, Suk, (ed), *The DPRK Economic Outlook: 2016* (Seoul: Korea Development Institute 2017)
Mazaar, Michael J., *North Korea and the Bomb: A Case Study in Nonproliferation* (New York: St. Martins 1995).
Musharraf, Pervez, *In the Line of Fire* (New York: Free Press 2006).
Pinkston, Dan, *The North Korean Ballistic Missile Program* (Carlisle: Strategic Studies Institute 2008).
Pollack, Joshua, 'Ballistic Missile Trajectory: The Evolution of North Korea's Ballistic Missile Market', *Non-Proliferation Review* 18/2 (June 2011), 411-29.
Postol, Theodore and Markus Schiller, 'The North Korean Ballistic Missile Program', *Korea Observer* 47/4 (December 2016), 751-806.
Schiller, Markus, *Characterizing the North Korean Nuclear Missile Threat* (Santa Monica: RAND 2012).
Schiller, Markus and Robert Schmucker, *Explaining the Musudan: New Insights on the North Korean SS-N-6 Technology* May 2012.
Streifer, Bill and Sang S. Nam, 'In a North Korean Nuclear Defector's Own Words', *KPA Journal* 2/11 (November 2012).
Szalontai, Balazs and Sergey Radchenko, 'North Korea's Efforts to Acquire Nuclear Technology and Nuclear Weapons: Evidence from Russian and Hungarian Archives', *Cold War Internationial History Project*, Working Paper #53, Aug. 2006.
Warrick, Jo, 'On North Korean Freighter, A Hidden Missile Factory,' *Washington Post*, 14 Aug. 2003a. https://www.washingtonpost.com/archive/politics/2003/08/14/on-north-korean-freighter-a-hidden-missile-factory/164efb6b-c1d8-4fa5-8634-f33b8e83597c/?utm_term=.f2e58d82523e
Warrick, Jo, 'N. Korea Shops Warily for Nuclear Arms Gear,' *Washington Post*, 15 Aug. 2003b. https://www.washingtonpost.com/archive/politics/2003/08/15/n-korea-shops-stealthily-for-nuclear-arms-gear/d8eaa322-f629-4a41-aa90-a90deaeac034/?utm_term=.2a26036ec4f5

Wit, Joel S. and Sun Young Ahn, 'North Korea's Nuclear Futures: Technology and Strategy' *U.S. Korea Institute at SAIS*, Feb. 2015.

Wright, David, 'North Korea's Missile Program', *Union of Concerned Scientists*, Apr. 2009.

Wright, David, 'Re-Entry of North Korea's Hwasong-15 Missile', *Union of Concerned Scientists, at All Things Nuclear*, 2017. http://allthingsnuclear.org/dwright/reentry-of-hwasong-15

Wright, David, 'Markus Shiller's Analysis of North Korea's Unha-3 Launcher', *Union of Concerned Scientists, at All Things Nuclear*. http://allthingsnuclear.org/dwright/markus-schillers-analysis-of-north-koreas-unha-3-launcher

Wright, David C. and Timur Kadyshev, 'An Analysis of the North Korean Nodong Missile', *Science & Global Security* 4/2 (1994), 129–60. doi:10.1080/08929889408426397.

Yoon, Edward, 'Status and Future of the North Korean Minerals Sector', *Nautilus Institute for Security and Sustainability*, Jan. 2011.

Zhebin, Alexander, 'A Political History of Soviet-North Korean Nuclear Cooperation', in James Clay Moltz and Alexandre Mansourov (eds.), *The North Korean Nuclear Program: Security, Strategy, and New Perspectives from Russia* (New York: Routledge 2000).

Military-technological innovation in small states: The cases of Israel and Singapore

Richard A. Bitzinger

ABSTRACT
Both Israel and Singapore engage in military-technological innovation in areas deemed critical to strategic sovereignty. Both countries have consistently championed high levels of funding for military R&D and for maintaining and nurturing indigenous defense industries. Both countries have, to a varying degree, also strongly supported the cultivation of local S&T, including the spin-on of commercial high-technology breakthroughs into the defense sector. Israel has been more successful when it comes to military-technological innovation, mostly because it *has* to: its strategic situation is much more tenuous than Singapore's. Singapore, on the other hand, faces much less of an existential threat, and so its military-technological innovation activities are more one of desire than necessity.

On the surface, Israel and Singapore share many characteristics when it comes to security and defense.[1] Both are small countries with relatively small populations and no strategic depth, ostensibly surrounded by a metaphorical sea of adversaries or potentially hostile neighbors. Both rely heavily upon sizable conscript armies, drawn from (more or less) universal national service and long reservist obligations. Both have military expenditures that are relatively high for countries their size, and their armed forces – air, sea, ground, and other – are generally equipped with the most advanced weaponry that is readily available (and kept in a high state of readiness).

Moreover, both Israel and Singapore place a great deal of importance on advanced military technologies for national defense. In both countries, technology is viewed to be a critical force multiplier when it comes to national security and defense, and the idea of leveraging advanced military-

---

[1]The author would like to thank Tai Ming Cheung, Yoram Evron, Shannon Brown, and an anonymous reviewer for their comments on earlier drafts of this article.

technological capabilities as much as possible is an inarguable one. In conjunction with this approach, achieving a high degree of self-sufficiency in sophisticated armaments has long been a priority for both countries. As such, both countries have, by design, created and nurtured a clutch of indigenous defense industries, with the intention of meeting – as much as it is financially and technological feasible – national requirements for the acquisition of advanced weapons systems and other types of military equipment.

In this regard, both countries are fortunate in that they are islands of superior economic and technological development within their respective regions, boasting considerable industrialization, state-of-the-art high-technology sectors (including private and state-owned companies, laboratories, universities, technology incubators, and the like), and highly educated workforces. They therefore possess many indigenous capacities and competencies that can be exploited for advanced military-technological innovation and development. This has, theoretically at least, bolstered their faculties for advancing self-reliance in research and development (R&D) and manufacture of cutting-edge – or even novel – military equipment.

And yet, when we more closely examine the individual experiences of each country, we see a marked gap in achievement when it comes to military-technological innovation. In particular, Israel has been much more pioneering when it comes to original and state-of-the-art military systems. This is self-evident in a number of examples: drones, stand-off precision-guided weapons, missile defenses, electro-optical systems, systems for command, control, communications, computing, intelligence, surveillance, and reconnaissance (C4ISR), etc. In comparison, most of the indigenous weapons systems coming out of Singaporean arms factories are remarkably prosaic in terms of technology and function; only rarely do Singaporean military systems approach the state-of-the-art.

The question to ponder, therefore, is what factors account for the vast differences in these two nations' approaches and outcomes? In more closely examining the nature and dynamics of military-technological innovation in Israel and Singapore, it appears that two influences are the strongest: one exogenous and strategic – that is, relating to the immediate external security environment in which these countries must exist – and the other domestic and societal – that is, having more to do with the nature of society and the culture of these countries as it affects their attitudes toward innovation.

In exploring the key factors driving military-technological innovation in Israel and Singapore, we will use the template laid out by Tai Ming Cheung for identifying and categorizing national defense innovation systems.[2] As he points

---

[2]Tai Ming Cheung, 'Critical Factors in Enabling Defense Innovation: A Systems Perspective', Research Brief 2018–2, May (UC Institute on Global Conflict and Cooperation, Study of Innovation and Technology in China 2018).

Table 1. List of key factors driving the defense innovation system, incorporating hard-soft and critical factors categories.

Factor types	Hard innovation factors	Soft innovation factors
Catalytic	Revolutionary product or process breakthrough opportunities	Top-level leadership support; external threat environment
Contextual		Historical legacy; development level; political system
Input	Foreign technology transfers; resource inputs (state budget allocations, capital market investments); human capital (size and quality of workforce, cultivation of top talent)	
Organizational	Corporations; government agencies; research entities; individuals; military organizations	
Networks and subsystems	Procurement subsystem; research and development subsystem	Social networks; professional networks; technology push vs. demand pull; technological diffusion
Institutional	Plans and strategies	Regulatory and standards-based regime; incentives (i.e., intellectual property protection); governance norms
Output	Production process; maintenance; sales and distribution	End-user demand

Source: Tai Ming Cheung, *Critical Factors in Enabling Defense Innovation: A Systems Perspective*, Research Brief 2018–2 (UC Institute on Global Conflict and Cooperation, Study of Innovation and Technology in China, May 2018).

out, "In examining the factors that may account for the success or failure in the operations of these innovation systems, there is an overflowing smorgasbord of drivers, dynamics, and variables to choose from." To make better sense of how these myriad factors affect defense innovation, Cheung sorts these factors into "hard" and "soft" innovation variants, and then categorizes them into "distinctive domains based on their functions."[3] This is visualized in Table 1. Accordingly, this thematic approach will be applied to the cases of Israel and Singapore.

Patterns of military-technological innovation: The case of Israel

Israel subsists in a unique security environment, basically one of a permanent existential threat. In the first place, the country faces "multifarious threats."[4] It is surrounded by openly hostile or potentially hostile forces, comprised of both nation-state and sub-state actors. Second, it is a small country, with little strategic depth – just 85 miles (137 kilometers) across at its widest point and 9 miles (14 kilometers) at its narrowest (based on Israeli's pre-1967 borders) – and a Jewish population of 6.5 million. This geostrategic situation has existed continuously since independence in 1947 and has subsequently guided

---

[3]Ibid.
[4]Marc R. DeVore, 'Commentary on the Value of Domestic Arms Industries: Security of Supply or Adaptive Innovation?' *Defense Studies*, 17/3 (2017), 248.

Israeli national security policy – particularly when it comes to arms manufacturing and the local defense industry.

Israel's defense strategy is based on three historical basic pillars: (1) deterrence (up to and including nuclear deterrence); (2) early warning (strategic and tactical); and (3) rapid military decision (i.e., decisive victory on the battlefield). Any technological innovations, therefore, must somehow meet or contribute to these basic requirements.[5] Moreover, according to Dima Adamsky, Israel's approach to security is driven by a strategic culture characterized by an "obsessive siege mentality" and a "quest for absolute security."[6] As a result, Israeli security policy has long emphasized maintaining a "material technological superiority over its quantitatively superior rivals."[7] Nevertheless, the Israel Defense Forces' (IDF) faith in state-of-the-art technology has grown as an ideal, but at the same time it seeks to complement any technological superiority with a "faith in quantity as a quality." In other words, "what doesn't work with force will work with more force."[8]

During the 1980s, for example, technology revolved around "integrated battle concepts and the acquisition of the most advanced weaponry possible," i.e., modern main battle tanks (the Israeli-made *Merkava* (Chariot), fourth-generation combat aircraft (US-built F-15s and F-16s, as well as the development of the indigenous *Lavi* fighter jet), precision-guided weaponry (e.g., the *Popeye*), airborne early warning (AEW) aircraft (E-2 C and the *Phalcon*), and the first generation of unmanned aerial vehicles. During this period, the IDF also began to experiment with integrated joint operations ("coordinated participation"); for example, during the 1982 Bekaa Valley operations, Israel was able to take out Syrian surface-to-air missile (SAM) sites through the combined usage of drones (for intelligence-gathering, and as lures and decoys), AEW aircraft for detection and jamming, and fighter-bombers with anti-radiation missiles to attack SAM batteries.[9]

Since roughly 2000, current Israeli military operational concepts have revolved around the ideas of the information-technologies-driven revolution in military affairs (IT-RMA). According to Raska, the IDF "pioneered IT-RMA-related capabilities," such as network-centric warfare, stand-off precision-strike, drones, and integrated C4ISR. During the first decade of the

---

[5]Michael Raska, *Military Innovation in Small States: Creating a Reverse Asymmetry* (New York: Routledge 2016), 63–66.

[6]Dima Adamsky, *The Culture of Military Innovation: The Impact of Cultural Factors on the Revolution in Military Affairs in Russia, the US, and Israel* (Stanford, Calif.: Stanford University Press 2010), 125–126.

[7]Yoram Evron, '4IR Technologies in the Israel Defense Forces: Blurring Traditional Boundaries', *Journal of Strategic Studies* (online article, published 7 December 2020), 4; see also Nissim Hania, *Transformations in the Israeli Defense Development and Production System, and the Contemporary Relevance*, The DADO Center for Interdisciplinary Military Studies, Israel Defense Forces (https://www.idf.il/en/minisites/dado-center/vol-6-force-design-a/transformations-in-the-israeli-defense-development-and-production-system) (undated), 1.

[8]Adamsky, *The Culture of Military* Innovation, 114.

[9]Raska, *Military Innovation in Small States*, 73–76.

twenty-first century, RMA capabilities were employed for "sub-conventional warfare," i.e., to combat the Second Intifada (2000–2005) and other low-intensity conflicts. Counter-terror operations during this time began to place greater emphasis on intelligence-gathering and analysis, precision-strike, and special forces, while "effects-based operations" (EBO) concepts were used in attempts to defeat the will of the enemy, via swarmed, networked, and coordinated attacks.[10] During the 2010s, these operational concepts were complemented by a new appreciation for so-called "cyber-kinetic operations" – offensive and defensive cyber strategies set up to protect the IDF's and Israeli national "cyber ecosystem." These operations included cyber-enabled intelligence-gathering, cyber-attacks on enemies (e.g., the Stuxnet computer worm), and kinetic attacks on an adversary's information infrastructures.[11]

This comprehensive strategic vision for the IDF was encapsulated in a 2015 document entitled *Estrategiat Tzahal*. This paper asserted that future warfare could run the gambit from low-intensity conflict up to full-scale war and that the emphasis must be on destroying the enemy's critical military capabilities and various strategic infrastructures, rather than territorial conquest. As such, the IDF shifted its emphasis to improved surveillance and intelligence, precision-fires, swift and stand-off attack, and defending the homeland from kinetic and non-kinetic (e.g., cyber) attacks.[12]

Given this faith in technology as a cure-all, continuous technological innovation has long been a "central tenet" of Israeli security policy.[13] In the first place, this has meant investing "vast resources" in such innovation, reflected in part by high levels of defense research and development (R&D) spending. Just as important has been the creation and nurturing of an "ultrasophisticated and innovative defense industry."[14]

The Israeli defense industry predates statehood, with covert factories established by the *Hagana* Jewish militia to produce small arms and other weapons for the independence movement.[15] After the creation of the state of Israel, the establishment of a self-sustaining domestic arms industry became only more critical. While initially most armaments – and certainly most major weapons platforms – were acquired from abroad, Israel's leaders saw the need for a strong indigenous defense industry, embedded in overall national

---

[10]Raska, *Military Innovation in Small States*, 59, 80–84.
[11]Raska, *Military Innovation in Small States*, 84–89. See also Israel Tal, *National Security: The Israeli Experience* (Westport, CT: Praeger, 2000); and Brig.-Gen. Itai Brun, 'While You're Busy Making Other Plans': The 'Other-RMA' (Jerusalem: DADO Center for Interdisciplinary Military Studies, Israel Defense Forces 2010).
[12]Evron, '4IR Technologies in the Israel Defense Forces', 4–5.
[13]David A. Lewis, 'Diversification and Niche Market Exporting: The Restructuring of Israel's Defense Industry in the Post-Cold War Era', in Ann Markusen, Sean DiGiovanna, and Michael C. Leary (eds.), *From Defense to Development: International Perspectives on Realising the Peace Dividend* (London: Routledge 2003), 130.
[14]Adamsky, *The Culture of Military* Innovation, 125–126.
[15]Uzi Rubin, 'Israel's Defense Industries – An Overview', *Defense Studies* 17,3, 229.

economy, particularly when it came to creating jobs and leveraging technological breakthroughs in the civilian sector.[16] During the 1950s and early 1960s, the country designed, developed, and manufactured many kinds of weapons considered uniquely necessary for Israel's security, including small arms (such as the iconic Uzi submachine gun), the *Gabriel* antiship cruise missile (ASCM), and the *Shafrir*-1 air-to-air missile. Israel's first prime minister, David Ben-Gurion, strongly advocated the idea of self-sufficiency in such an integrated civil-military defense industrial ecosystem: "Ben-Gurion asserted that only through integrating national industrial policy, investments in education and science, the role of the military services and industries, and cultivating strategic international partners could Israel sustain and defend herself."[17] A national strategy of self-reliance and self-sufficient was doubly reinforced by arms embargoes imposed on Israel by Britain and France (initially Israel's main arms suppliers) in the 1960s.[18]

Consequently, the period from roughly 1967–1987 was the height of Israeli "munitions independence."[19] The IDF and the Israeli ministry of defense pursed self-sufficiency in major weapons platforms as a policy priority. During this period, the country undertook the indigenous R&D and manufacture of several categories of large weapons systems, including the *Merkava* main battle tank, the *Sa'ar*-4 and *Sa'ar*-4.5 classes of missile boats (initially armed with the indigenous *Gabriel* ASCM), and many types of tactical missile systems (e.g., the *Popeye* stand-off air-to-surface missile and the *Python* family of air-to-air missiles). Also during this period, Israel manufactured its own combat aircraft, the *Kfir* (Lion Cub), based on the Dassault Mirage-5 (acquired through espionage), and later the *Lavi* (Young Lion), an indigenous effort to design and develop an advanced, fourth-generation multirole fighter jet. Just as important – or perhaps even more important – Israel began to undertake the development of first-generation unmanned aerial vehicles (UAVs), including tactical reconnaissance UAVs (e.g., the *Scout* and *Mastiff*) and loitering anti-radiation drones (e.g., the *Harpy*).

Beginning in the late 1980s, however, it became more and more clear to many Israelis that a strategy of comprehensive autarky in armaments was unsustainable. In the first place, the costs of developing large state-of-the-art weapons systems such as the *Lavi* were becoming increasingly untenable. In the case of the *Lavi*, the United States, which had been underwriting much of its R&D expenses through FMS (Foreign Military Sales) funding, decided to stop supporting this particular program, and the aircraft was subsequently cancelled in 1987. At the same time, then-defense minister Yitzhak Rabin

---

[16]Rubin, 'Israel's Defense Industries – An Overview', 229–231.
[17]Lewis, 'Diversification and Niche Market Exporting', 129.
[18]Yaacov Lifshitz, 'Defense Industries in Israel', in Andrew T.H. Tan (ed.), *The Global Arms Trade: A Handbook* (New York: Routledge 2009), 266–268.
[19]Rubin, 'Israel's Defense Industries – An Overview', 231–232.

argued that such "self-reliance was illusory," since Israeli platforms still relied on foreign sources for propulsion systems (e.g., for combat aircraft, tanks, and missile boats) and "other key components."[20]

Instead, Rabin and his successors began to push a new policy of "focused self-reliance," in which the Israeli defense industry could "develop only such 'force multiplier' systems that are uniquely tailored for the IDF" or unavailable on the global market.[21] Consequently, starting in the late 1980s, domestic arms production priorities began to shift toward supplying "the IDF with force multipliers by means of original, unique technological solutions, while self-sufficiency was relegated to second place."[22] From then on, large military platforms, such as fighter aircraft and corvettes, were to be imported, while the local arms industry was to concentrate on maintaining an indigenous capacity for developing and manufacturing "equipment [Israel] considered critical to strategic sovereignty."[23]

As a result, the Israeli arms industry, which is largely concentrated in three companies – the state-owned Israel Aerospace Industry (IAI) and Rafael Advanced Defense Systems, and the private Elbit Systems Ltd. – began to transform into a specialty manufacturing sector. This strategy permitted it to concentrate on a few niche areas where it has particular core competencies, especially when it comes to long-term evolutionary product development. Key areas for the Israeli defense industry includes drones and UAVs (including armed drones, such as the *Hermes*); air-to-air missiles (*Python, I-Derby*); missile defenses (*Arrow, David's Sling, Barak*, SPYDER); counter-rocket, -artillery, and -mortar (C-RAM) systems (*Iron Dome, Iron Beam*); anti-tank munitions (*Spike*); armored vehicle protective systems (*Trophy, Iron Fist*); C4ISR and targeting systems (LITENING); and electro-optics and systems for electronic and cyber warfare.[24]

As the Israeli arms industry shifted toward a core competencies/niche production business model, overseas sales have taken on a greater urgency. The Israeli defense industrial base today is overwhelmingly export-oriented, and foreign arms sales are crucial to its survival. On average, approximately three-quarters of Israel's defense production (in terms of value) are for overseas customers. During the years 2016–2020, Israel, according to SIPRI, transferred around US$4.14 billion worth of arms to overseas customers, making it the world's eighth largest arms exporter during this period; its biggest customers were India (43% of all Israeli arms exporters), Azerbaijan (17%), and Vietnam (12%).[25]

---

[20]Rubin, 'Israel's Defense Industries – An Overview', 233.
[21]Rubin, 'Israel's Defense Industries – An Overview', 233.
[22]Lifshitz, 'Defense Industries in Israel', 268.
[23]DeVore, 'Commentary on the Value of Domestic Arms Industries,' p. 249.
[24]William F. Owen, 'Punching Above its Weight; Israel's Defense Industry', *Defense Review Asia* (May 2010), 12–16; David Saw, 'The Israeli Defense Industry', *Asian Defense & Diplomacy*, June/July 2011, pp. 26–30; Rubin, 'Israel's Defense Industries – An Overview', 235.
[25]Pieter D. Wezeman, Alexandra Kuimova, and Siemon T. Wezeman, *SIPRI Fact Sheet: Trends in International Arms Transfers, 2020* (Stockholm: Stockholm International Peace Research Institute March 2021), 2.

As a result, over the past three decades or so, Israel's arms industry has transformed itself from an sector oriented mainly to supplying the country's defense forces with critical defense materiel into one that basically exports arms in order to survive. Not only are overseas arms sales essential to keep local defense enterprises in business, but revenues from arms exports in turn provide necessary income to underwrite military R&D programs that help aid Israel's own defense, such as the *Iron Dome* short-range missile defense system.

Further aiding the development and expansion of a high-technology niche-oriented defense business has been the explosive growth of Israel's commercial high-tech sector over the past 30 or so years.[26] Israel today possesses one of the world's most advanced science and technology (S&T) sectors, and it is home to several high-technology companies, in information technologies, computer engineering and cyber, aerospace and space, renewable energy, and biotechnology and pharmaceuticals. Israel spends, on average, about four percent of its gross domestic product on civilian R&D, one of the highest levels in the world.[27] It has also been the recipient of considerable foreign direct investment, by such high-tech companies as IBM and Intel (in 2011, Intel announced an investment of US$2.7 billion to develop a next-generation computer chip at its Israeli plant).[28] Israel also has one of the world's most technology-literate populations, as the result of initiatives pushing S&T education and research in secondary education and national universities, and through the encouragement of public–private partnerships. As a result of all these efforts and endeavors, Israel typically ranks high in various innovation indexes.[29]

Two factors have most affected the process of military-technological innovation in Israel: strategic necessity and a national culture of innovation, competitiveness, and improvisation.[30] The former is well known: as noted earlier, Israel possesses a "siege mentality" and "quest for absolute security," fed by the presence of proximate threats along its borders, along with the country's relatively small size and lack of strategic depth. At the same time, Israeli strategic-military culture is still highly improvisational, characterized by a deliberate aversion to "paradigmatic shifts" in doctrine, organization, and operational concepts.[31] Instead, Israelis prefer to improvise, and thus the IDF

---

[26]Evron, '4IR Technologies in the Israel Defense Forces', 9.
[27]Daphne Getz and Zehev Tadmor, 'Israel', in *UNESCO Science Report: Toward 2030* (Paris: United Nations Educational, Scientific and Cultural Organization 2015), 410.
[28]David Shamah, 'How Intel Came to be Israel's Best Tech Friend', *Times of Israel*, 23 April 2015; Saw, 'The Israeli Defense Industry', p. 29.
[29]Joanna Dyduch and Karolina Olszewska, 'Israeli innovation Policy', *Polish Political Science Yearbook* 47/2 (2018), 265–266.
[30]See, for example, Daphne Getz and Vered Segal, *The Israeli Innovation System: An Overview of National Policy and Cultural Aspects* (Haifa: The Samuel Neaman Institute for Advanced Studies in Science and Technology 2008); also Tal, *National Security: The Israeli Experience*.
[31]Adamsky, *The Culture of Military* Innovation, 116.

has developed a tradition of learning and adapting on-the-fly; consequently, the IDF deliberately does not "do" strategy or planning, and it takes a distinctly problem-solving and anti-intellectual approach to military operations. As Adamsky puts it, the IDF is an institution of "doers, rather than talkers."[32]

These improvisational inclinations have had a substantial impact on Israeli military-technological innovation. Raska argues that the IDF seeks capabilities that operate along the lines of continuous innovation and "multiple adaptations" to fit the contemporary needs of the military. The IDF is not so much interested in disruptive innovations, but rather "relevant adaptive measures" more tailored to IDF requirements at the moment.[33] While innovation is "not a question of choice but a necessity," neither is it dogmatic or theoretical:

> The RMA is not so much about acquiring military-technological capabilities, but developing relevant operational concepts and organizational structures that may effectively utilize these technologies to deal with progressive complexity of security challenges facing Israel.[34]

Adamsky and Raska were mostly talking about innovation on the battlefield ("creative tactical improvisations").[35] However, Israeli military-technological innovation and adaptation has benefited from the country's uniquely non-hierarchical – even *anti*-hierarchical – society. More than one person has observed that Israelis are remarkably casual, informal, assertive, and flexible in their dealings with each other.[36] This is in part out due to the unique nature of Israel being an immigrant society, but it is reinforced by the experience that most young Israelis get by virtue of universal conscription and national service (for women, as well as men):

> The IDF imbues soldiers with a strong bias against hierarchy ... a melting pot, where people from different cultural and economic backgrounds come together to exchange ideas and learn new skills, generating a successful recipe for fostering creativity and innovation. In the IDF, poor Israeli kids who otherwise never would have had an opportunity to operate sophisticated technology get that chance.[37]

This resulting overall informality and absence of hierarchy – together with a "common and collective sense of insecurity" – helps spur innovation, especially in the military-technological realm, by breaking down barriers to

---

[32] Adamsky, *The Culture of Military* Innovation, 119.
[33] Raska, *Military Innovation in Small States*, 59.
[34] Raska, *Military Innovation in Small States*, 60.
[35] Adamsky, *The Culture of Military* Innovation, 126.
[36] Adamsky, *The Culture of Military* Innovation, 117–119; Yaakov Katz and Amir Bohbot, *The Weapons Wizards: How Israel Became a High-Tech Military Superpower* (New York: St. Martin's 2017), 9–12.
[37] Robert Orkand, 'Review: *The Weapon Wizards: How Israel Became a High-Tech Military Superpower*, by Yaakov Katz and Amir Bohbot', Reformjudaism.org, https://reformjudaism.org/jewish-life/arts-culture/literature/weapon-wizards-how-israel-became-high-tech-military-superpower (accessed 2 December 2017).

interaction and subsequently creating an atmosphere that encourages and enables the free exchange of ideas.[38] In short, Israel is simply a society more inclined to engage in high-risk military-technological innovation, because it is deemed essential to national survival.[39]

This improvisational nature resulted in a number of military-technological innovations, including drones, active armor, missile defenses, C-RAM systems, and cyber viruses; it has also driven the process of constant innovation and improvement, such as the evolution of Israeli UAVs from short-range tactical reconnaissance systems to more capable surveillance systems (such as the *Heron* MALE (medium-altitude, long-endurance) UAV, and the *Hermes* attack drone).[40] Finally, such improvisation has been particularly pronounced in Israel's heavy employment of "crash" programs, such as *Iron Dome* (to defend against short-range rockets fired by Hezbollah forces in Lebanon and by Hamas and other groups from Gaza, converting old or captured Soviet tanks into armored personnel carriers, and developing systems that use radar and 3D image-reconstruction algorithms to "see through" walls (given IDF challenges when it came to house-to-house fighting in Lebanon and Gaza).[41]

This stress on technology as a force multiplier and counterweight has only intensified over the years.[42] In Israel's case, it has been complemented by a host of other factors which have aided the spin-on of advanced technologies to the defense industry; these include close relations between the military and academia, the recruitment and training of gifted youth, modes of operation of technological units in the IDF, the relatively tight links between operational units and the defense industry, as well as between the defense sector and local high-tech industries.[43]

Applying Cheung's "hard" and "soft" innovation factors, we can make the following overall observations about Israel's national defense innovation system:

Catalytic and contextual factors

Catalytic and contextual drivers are closely intertwined in Israel. Israeli defense innovation is very much driven by an external threat environment that perceives a very high, ongoing threat to the country's existence. This concern is compounded by the small size of the country and the lack of strategic depth, and this overall sense of insecurity is augmented by the fact

---

[38] Katz and Bohbot, *The Weapons Wizards*, 12.
[39] Raphael Bar-el, Dafna Schwartz, and David Bentolila, 'Singular Factors Behind the Growth of Innovation in Israel', *Athens Journal of Mediterranean Studies* 5/3 (2019), 143–144.
[40] Katz and Bohbot, *The Weapons Wizards*, 12.
[41] DeVore, 'Commentary on the Value of Domestic Arms Industries', 250.
[42] Evron, '4IR Technologies in the Israel Defense Forces', 4.
[43] Evron, '4IR Technologies in the Israel Defense Forces', 11–16.

that Israel has been involved in a series of conflicts since its creation. As a result, the political and military leadership of the country mostly possesses a siege mentality, which in turn places a premium on technology as a "force multiplier."

Input factors

Israel dedicates a high percentage of its GDP (roughly four percent) to R&D, and it actively seeks investments and technology transfers from foreign high-tech firms; most Israeli research universities, for example, have technology transfer offices to encourage joint ventures with overseas firms and draw in outside innovative technologies. National education policies also stress STEM education, and around one-third of all bachelor's degrees awarded in Israel were in fields related to science and engineering.[44] Directly affecting military R&D, it is worth noting that Israel receives nearly 4 USD billion annually in foreign military financing (FMF) from the United States. Moreover, unique to Israel, US foreign military aid to Israel can be applied to indigenous R&D projects; in fact, programs such as the *Merkava* main battle tank and the *Lavi* combat aircraft were mostly funded by US FMF. Moreover, Israel benefits greatly from direct military-technological cooperation with the United States; joint development programs include the *Arrow* antiballistic missile and the Tactical High-Energy Laser (THEL). Finally, the Israel government is giving increasing emphasis to civil-military integration and the exploitation of the country's high-technology commercial breakthroughs for military purposes.[45]

Organizational factors

The Israeli defense industry wields particular influence in the national innovation system. It is the center for national military innovation, and it is responsible for supplying the IDF (or, if not equipping, then maintaining and upgrading) with much of its weaponry and supporting military systems. Parts of the indigenous defense industrial base are still state-owned, but even private Israeli defense firms are seen as an integral, amalgamated part of a particularly *Israeli* supplier network. Moreover, the Israeli government has created several state-supported institutions to support and promote innovation in general, and military innovation in particular.[46] Within the Ministry of Defense, the Administration for the Development of Weapons and

---

[44]Daphne Getz and Zehev Tadmor, *Israel: UNESCO Science Report, Toward 2030* (Paris: UNESCO), 409–229.
[45]Ori Swed and John Sibley Butler, 'Military Capital in the Israeli Hi-tech Industry', *Armed Forces & Society* 41/1 (2013), 123–141.
[46]Dyduch and Karolina Olszewska, 'Israeli Innovation Policy', 270; Getz and Segal, *The Israeli Innovation System*, 34–41.

Technological Infrastructure (Maf'at) coordinates R&D between the IDF and the various defense industries.

Networks and subsystems factors

As previously stated, Israeli society is remarkably non-hierarchical, casual, informal, and flexible.[47] At the same time, personal relationships frequently permeate and affect cooperation when it comes to military innovation activities. In this regard, the IDF serves as an agent of socialization and fraternization. Friendships born from serving together in the IDF often last for life, and this "old boys" network aids informal collaboration. At the same time, there is a "revolving door" of ex-IDF officers going to work for local defense firms, R&D institutions, and national security think-tanks, which further adds to the soft factors of institutional cooperation.[48]

Institutional factors

Military innovation is very much demand-pull in Israel, prompted by the threat environment, with an emphasis on practical problem-solving to meet immediate security needs (e.g., the development of drones for surveillance, intelligence-gathering, and as lures and decoys). In this regard, it is important to note Israel's distinct "culture of improvisation," born out of the hard-scrabble, "make-do" experiences of pioneering Jewish settlers in pre-independence Palestine and the early years of Israel's tenuous existence. To reiterate an earlier point, Israelis place a high value on being "doers, rather than talkers," and therefore approach innovation as a process of learning and adapting on-the-fly.[49]

Output factors

The IDF is "customer No. 1" for the Israeli defense industry. The primary function of the indigenous arms industry is to supply the IDF with the critical products it requires to carry out its functions. At the same time, Israel arms exports are intended to generate revenues that in turn underwrite R&D that will further aid the modernization of the IDF.

Overall, as Milana Israeli puts it, Israel possesses a well-established national innovation system:

> Israel has significant innovative potential due to a number of factors: highly qualified personnel, the availability of the latest technologies, the country is actively implementing the transfer from the military to the civilian sector, the availability of

---

[47] Katz and Bohbot, *The Weapons* Wizards, 9–12.
[48] Swed and Butler, 'Military Capital in the Israeli Hi-tech Industry.'
[49] Adamsky, *The Culture of Military* Innovation, 119.

financial opportunities, including the attraction of foreign specialists and know-how, as well as the implementation of a number of state programs and projects.[50]

Patterns of military-technological innovation: The case of Singapore

On the surface, Singapore resembles Israel in many ways. Singapore shares the same "small-state survival ideology" as Israel; in fact, in creating the Singapore Armed Forces (SAF), the Singapore looked to the IDF as both a model and for direct assistance.[51] In addition, Singapore sees technology as a critical force multiplier.[52] Both of these influences are evident in the country's ongoing "third-generation" (3 G) transformation of its military. The interests of the SAF in defense transformation stems from basically four factors:

- A perception of new unconventional threats – terrorism, piracy, insurrection, and destabilization in a neighboring state that could spill over into Singapore, hybrid warfare threats – resulting in new types of operational requirements, such as urban warfare and the protection of key installations, protection from cyber-attacks, and dealing with a host of hybrid attacks (i.e., a blend of conventional, irregular, and cyber warfare) that could undermine national resolve and resilience;
- Singapore's recognition of its traditional strategic weaknesses: a lack of strategic depth, a small and aging population, and relatively limited defense resources;
- Singapore's economic and technological advantages, particularly its highly educated workforce and its strengths in several categories of advanced technologies, e.g., aerospace, shipbuilding, computing and other information technologies, and the like.
- Since Singapore sees its relationship with the United States as "key to its defense position," a vital objective of the 3 G SAF is to be better able to interoperate with U.S. forces.[53]

This 3 G transformation was part of the SAF's adoption of a high-tech defensive posture and strategy dubbed the "smart dolphin" – an agile and maneuverable force, enabled by "intelligentization" and networking, able to move quickly away from danger but also able to protect itself with decisive

---

[50]Milana Israeli, 'National Innovation Systems of Israel: Features and Structure', *Scientific Journal of Economics, Social, and Engineering Science* 3/1–2 (2020), 157.
[51]Stephen McCarthy, *The Political Theory of Tyranny in Singapore and Burma* (New York: Routledge 2006), 115–116.
[52]Tim Huxley, *Singapore and Military Transformation*, paper delivered to the conference on 'The RMA For Small States: Theory and Application', Singapore, 25–26 February 2004, p. 2.
[53]Michael Urquhart, 'Singapore Faces Spending, Population Challenges', *Defense News*, 20 February 2006.

force and precision firepower. As such, the 3 G concept was transformational not only in terms of technology but also in terms of the SAF's conceptual, organizational, and operational reorganization.[54]

Singapore 3 G (and emerging 4 G) transformational efforts emphasize the acquisition, development, and integration of technologies – and particularly information technologies – for command and control with ISR systems and precision-guided weapons.[55] In particular, according to the authoritative consulting group, IHS Janes, "technologies considered force multipliers by Singapore are: stealth, stand-off precision weaponry, unmanned systems, C4ISTAR [command, control, communications, computing, intelligence, surveillance, targeting acquisition, and surveillance], training and protection technologies." Subsequently, all of these technologies are emphasized in Singapore's research and development (R&D) and procurement spending.[56]

Starting in the mid-1960s – and coinciding, not surprisingly, with the country's unexpected and unplanned-for independence – Singapore developed an arms industry primarily for strategic reasons. In particular, *the local defense industry plays an integral role in serving Singaporean strategic interests, particularly by providing the SAF with a "technological advantage over its regional rivals."*[57] The Singaporean arms industry is inexorably linked to the country's concept of "total defense," that is, the idea that the entire resources of the nation must, if necessary, be mobilizable for the sake of national defense. In this regard, therefore, the arms industry is an "integral part" of national security.[58] And while Singapore is hardly self-reliant when it comes to military equipment, the maintenance of at least some degree of indigenous armaments production is regarded as crucial to the physical and psychological defense of the nation.

Singaporean armaments production has therefore been focused first and foremost on meeting the immediate needs of the SAF. At the same time, arms procurement decisions have been generally measured against what the Singaporeans can affordably do by themselves and what makes more sense to buy from foreign sources.[59] Singapore has traditionally tended to take a more pragmatic and therefore more selective approach towards defense

---

[54]Evan Laksmana, 'Threats and Civil–Military Relations: Explaining Singapore's "Trickle-Down" Military Innovation', *Defense & Security Analysis* 33/4 (2017), 355.
[55]See Edward Chen, et.al., *Integrated Knowledge-based Command and Control for the ONE SAF Building the 3rd Spiral, 3rd Generation SAF* (Singapore: Pointer: Journal of the Singapore Armed Forces 2008).
[56]IHS Jane's, *Navigating the Emerging Markets: Republic of Singapore* (Coulsdon, Surrey: IHS Jane's 2011), 11.
[57]IHS Jane's, *Navigating the Emerging Markets: Republic of Singapore*, 18.
[58]Richard A. Deck, 'Singapore: Comprehensive Security – Total Defense', in Ken Booth and Russell Trood (eds.), *Strategic Cultures in the Asia-Pacific Region* (London: Palgrave Macmillan 1999), 247–269; Bilveer Singh, 'ASEAN's Arms Industries: Potential and Limits', *Comparative Strategy* 8 (1989), 251.
[59]Tim Huxley and Susan Willett, *Arming East Asia* (Oxford: Oxford University Press July 1999), 50; Tan Peng Yam, 'Harnessing Defense Technology: Singapore's Perspective', *DISAM Journal of International Security Assistance Management* 21/3 (1999).

industrialization. It has never sought nor even harbored the goal of autarky in armaments production. In particular, the country imports the bulk of its major weapons systems. Instead, the local defense industrial base is geared primarily towards guaranteeing the supply and maintenance of critical systems, and towards developing the capability to upgrade and modify imported weapons systems.[60]

Local arms production is centered mainly on the state-owned ST Engineering (STEngg),[61] formerly Singapore Technologies Engineering. ST Engineering dominates the domestic defense industry, and very few local small or medium-sized enterprises are involved in arms manufacturing, mostly as subcontractors to STEngg.[62] ST Engineering has its roots in Chartered Industries, established in the mid-1960s to produce small arms ammunition for the SAF. After going through several expansions and reorganizations, ST Engineering presently comprises four main subsidiaries: ST Aerospace (STAe; aircraft manufacturing and maintenance); ST Electronics (communications, sensors, software, and combat systems); ST Kinetics (land systems and ordnance); and ST Marine (shipbuilding). In 2019, ST Engineering employed around 23,000 workers worldwide and boasted revenues totalling US$5.73 billion.

Singapore has been the most successful in the domestic development and production of small arms, artillery systems, light armored vehicles, and certain classes of naval vessels. ST Kinetics has outfitted the SAF with the indigenously designed and manufactured SAR 21 (Singapore Assault Rifle – 21st Century) assault rifle, and it also produces machine guns, grenade-launchers, mortar systems, and both towed and self-propelled 155 mm howitzers. ST Kinetics' 120 mm Super Rapid Advanced Mortar System, for instance, is one of the most advanced mobile, rapid fire mortar systems in the world; it can be mounted on a wide range of light vehicles, enabling ground forces to achieve rapid and lethal firepower. The company's *Primus* 155 mm self-propelled howitzer is based on the US M109 but is significantly lighter, while its *Pegasus* 155 mm towed artillery piece is manufactured with titanium and aluminum alloys that make it light enough to be transported by helicopter and also able to withstand the recoil force of its gun system. The company also manufactures three light armored vehicles for the SAF and for export: the *Bionix* tracked infantry fighting vehicle, the *Terrex* 8 × 8 wheeled armored personnel carrier, and the Bronco all-terrain tracked carrier. In addition, during the 1990s and 2000s, ST Marine designed and constructed several *Fearless*-class patrols vessels (which are currently being replaced by the

---

[60]Ron Matthews, 'Singapore Buys Longbows and Grows its Defense Industry', *Asia-Pacific Defense Reporter*, December 1999, p. 20.
[61]Technically, ST Engineering is a 'government-linked company' (GLC); 50.15% of its stock is owned by Temasek Holdings, a state-owned holding company.
[62]IHS Jane's, *Navigating the Emerging Markets: Republic of Singapore*, 20.

Independence-class corvette, also indigenously built), along with five 8500-ton *Endurance*-class landing ships.[63]

Overall, Singapore appears to have adopted a core competencies/niche production approach to its defense industries. It has consciously decided to concentrate arms manufacturing in those areas where it believes it has particular key strengths – and also greater potential to either export its products or find foreign partners – and either abandoned or declined to enter into those areas where it believed that such armaments production would not be economically viable or technologically competitive.

The government-run Defense Science and Technology Agency (DSTA) and the DSO National Laboratories are largely responsible for coordinating defense R&D in Singapore. DSTA is responsible for implementing defense technology plans, acquiring defense materiel, and developing defense infrastructure for MINDEF.[64] DSTA manages the acquisition and lifecycle support of weapons systems and other military equipment and supports the building of the necessary infrastructure to further develop and sustain the SAF's operational capabilities.[65] Relevant fields where DSTA is currently focusing much of its efforts include advanced electronics and signal processing, information systems security, advanced guidance systems, communications, electronic warfare, sensors, and unmanned vehicles. DSO Labs engage in basic research on defense S&T, particularly in the areas of electronic warfare, battlespace situational awareness, unmanned systems, and cryptography.[66] DSO Labs also work closely with universities, defence firms, and research institutions within Singapore and overseas.

Overall, therefore, Singapore's defence ecosystem promotes a basically "evolutionary approach to innovation." According to Evan Laksmana, this helps to "sustain Singapore's procurement and modernisation plans, which have evolved around upgrading existing equipment while selectively introducing new-generation systems." The Singapore Armed Forces, he adds "has particularly maintained a consistent 'spiral' capability development in key technological areas central for its warfighting capability … .These policies have been central to SAF's evolutionary innovation and were spurred by a unified civil-military relation and rationalized in terms of the high level and diversity of threats Singapore has to continually confront."[67]

---

[63]Four vessels for the RSN and one for the Royal Thai Navy.
[64]http://www.dsta.gov.sg/index.php/About-Us.
[65]http://www.dsta.gov.sg/index.php/447-Core-Competencies.
[66]http://www.dso.org.sg/dso_story.aspx.
[67]Laksmana, 'Threats and Civil–Military Relations', 357–358; Michael Raska, 'A Nimble 4 G SAF Needs Space for Mavericks', *Straits Times*, 13 May 2017.

Again, if we apply Cheung's methodology of "hard" and "soft" innovation factors, we can make the following general observations about Singapore's national defense innovation system:

Catalytic and contextual factors

Singapore is often called the "accidental country," having been forced to become an independent state after its separation from Malaysia in 1965. At the same time, it sees itself as a small country surrounded by potentially hostile neighbors. Consequently, Singapore possesses, as previously argued, a "small-state survival ideology," compounded by a lack of strategic depth and a small and aging population.[68] These fears have manifested themselves in an "overt securitization of public and private life," what Alan Chong and Samuel Chan have described as a form of "calibrated nationalism."[69] Like Israel, therefore, Singapore sees a technologically advanced (and sizable) military as a crucial offset to its numerical and geographical disadvantages.

Input factors

The Singaporean government has long had a commitment to the modernization of the state along the lines of creating a high-tech society. As a result, considerable funding has been dedicated to furthering STEM education with an eye toward creating a pool of indigenous scientific, technological, and engineering talent, and encouraging domestic research and development in a variety of high-technological areas, such as microelectronics, artificial intelligence, biological, nanotechnologies, and the like.[70]

Organizational factors

Innovation in Singapore – and certainly most military-technological innovation – is almost entirely state-centric. In the first place, defense industrial base in Singapore is mostly concentrated in one "government-linked" company, Singapore Technologies Engineering (STEngg). In addition, most military R&D in Singapore is carried out under the auspices of the Defense Science and Technology Agency. DSTA coordinates with domestic military R&D institutes, such as the DSO Laboratories and the R&D offices within STEngg. The Singaporean government has also sponsored several high-tech incubators,

---

[68]McCarthy, *The Political Theory of Tyranny in Singapore and Burma*, 115–116.
[69]Alan Chong and Samuel Chan, 'Militarizing Civilians in Singapore: Preparing for "Crisis" within a Calibrated Nationalism', *The Pacific Review* 3/3 (2017), 365–366.
[70]Poh Kam Wong, 'From Using to Creating Technology: The Evolution of Singapore's National Innovations System and the Changing Role of Public Policy', in S. Lall and S. Urata (eds.), *Foreign Direct Investment, Technology Development, and Competitiveness in East Asia* (Elgar, 2002); Vivian Shao, 'Singapore Budget 2018: Innovation, R&D to Get Shot in the Arm', *Straits Times*, 20 February 2018.

including the Agency for Science, Technology, and Research (A*STAR) and Fusionopolis.

Institutional factors

Singapore's civilian leadership makes most of the critical decisions when it comes to R&D priorities. Singapore is noteworthy for possessing a tightly state-controlled and top-down innovation process, especially when it comes to military innovation, which has inhibited risk-taking and nongovernmental innovation.[71]

Networks and subsystems factors

Moreover, innovation in Singapore tends toward technology-push; military equipment is developed and indigenously procured as part of a conscious effort to raise the overall technological level of the defense industrial base. At the same time, the process of innovation in Singapore is very much a hierarchical system, tightly controlled and scripted by the government, picking winners and losers.[72] Considerable importance is given to government-supported R&D institutes and high-profile incubator projects and joint ventures. As in Israel, personal relationships resulting from shared service in the SAF extends into governance and civilian service. Most of the country's senior leadership (MPs, cabinet members, heads of state-owned enterprises, etc.) are ex-SAF officers and generally share a common commitment to the continual modernization of the military.

Output factors

Like Israel, the Singaporean defense industry – and especially the country's main arms producer, Singapore Technologies Engineering – exists mainly to serve the requirements of the SAF. In this regard, it has excellent manufacturing capacities in a few key areas, such as land systems and naval vessels. Its capabilities in other area are quite limited, however.

At this juncture, it is worth highlighting a key cultural difference between Israel and Singapore when it comes to approaching innovation. In the first place, Singapore's approach to governance is highly technocratic, in which policymaking is a purely "top-down process" that perceives "little need for external influences."[73] Singapore has been particularly criticized for

---

[71]Stephen Ortmann, 'Singapore: From Hegemonic to Competitive Authoritarianism', in William Case (ed.), *Routledge Handbook of Southeast Asian Democratisation* (Routledge 2015); Wong, 'From Using to Creating Technology.'
[72]Winston T.H. Koh, 'Singapore's Transition to Innovation-based Economic Growth: Infrastructure, Institutions, and Government's Role', R&D Management 36/2 (2006), 143–160.
[73]Ortmann, 'Singapore: From Hegemonic to Competitive Authoritarianism', 392.

possessing a "risk-averse" social and corporate culture, causing managers and employees to stay within their own "comfort zones."[74] This culture, in turn, supposedly retards innovation. According to Richard Carney and Loh Yi Zhang, however, the problem is *not* that Singaporeans are in and of themselves risk-averse. On the contrary, they find that Singaporeans are "extremely creative," but that they "stop short of applying their innovativeness outside their job specifications."[75] The reason for this lack of *applied* innovation, they argue, is due more to the nature of Singapore's corporate structures and institutions, which is heavily influenced by powerful families or the state (indeed, most of the countries' largest domestic industries or firms are state-owned, such as ST Engineering). Carney and Loh assert that "owners hold the decision of key managerial appointments, set the strategic directions of firms, and monitor performance as insiders ... managers are 'hired help,' subservient to the powerful family owners and the state." Consequently, "being accountable to the state or family blockholders ... managers will avoid very novel kinds of projects. Instead, together with the incentives provided by patient [i.e., long-term] capital, they will opt for lower-risk incremental improvements on established products."[76] Workers and employees, too, have little incentive to innovate, given that they are generally expected to just "fulfill their tasks as specified."[77]

In sum, Carney and Loh argue that while Singaporean "managers and employees may be exceptionally creative," the corporate institutions which within they toil "foster conflicting innovation styles [which] do not produce sustainable innovative activity."[78] For all these reasons, therefore, Singapore possesses a highly risk-averse corporate, institutional, and governance culture which permeates the actionable elements of societal culture. One effect of this state of affairs is that military-technological innovation is *at best* gradualist and evolutionary, i.e., sustaining innovation.

Determinants shaping national approaches to defense innovation: Comparing Israel and Singapore

In addition to these hard-soft function factors, Cheung, Mahnken, and Ross argue that there are five principal determinants involved in the shaping of national approaches to defense innovation. These are:

---

[74]Koh, 'Singapore's Transition to Innovation-based Economic Growth' 158.
[75]Richard W. Carney and Loh Yi Zhang, 'Institutional (Dis)Incentives to Innovate: An Explanation for Singapore's Innovation Gap', *Journal of East Asian Studies* 9 (2009), 299–300.
[76]Carney and Loh, 'Institutional (Dis)Incentives to Innovate', 301–302.
[77]Carney and Loh, 'Institutional (Dis)Incentives to Innovate', 305.
[78]Richard W. Carney and Loh Yi Zheng, 'An Explanation for Singapore's Innovation Gap', *RSIS Commentary* CO200849, 21 April 2008, p. 3.

- **The nature of the political system** (i.e., authoritarian vs. democratic; top-down vs. bottom-up; direct administrative vs. indirect regulatory)
- **The nature of the economic system** (i.e., central planning vs. market-oriented; competitive vs. monopolistic)
- **The level of science and technology development** (i.e., absorptive vs. original-innovative)
- **Type of international engagement** (i.e., open/cooperative vs. techno-nationalist/competitive; globalist vs. closed)
- **The role of the military** (i.e., dominant vs. subordinate, militarized vs. civilianized)[79]

Using these determinants as a guidepost, the differences between Israel and Singapore, when it comes to their national approaches to defense innovation (and particularly their approaches to military-technological innovation), can be gauged in a number of significant (and often significantly differing) ways (see Table 2).

Where Israel and Singapore are the most similar is in their economic systems, their approaches to international engagement, and civil-military relations. Both are essentially free-market and competitive economies, yet also possessing monopolistic (and usually state-owned) enterprises operating in key sectors, *particularly the defense-industrial sector*. Both are more or less globalized and open in terms of trade and the flow of ideas and technology – although both are also techno-nationalistic in terms of protecting and sustaining their arms industries. Finally, both Israel and Singapore are states where the military and civil are largely fused: both depend heavily on conscription (universal male national service exists in Singapore, while both men and women serve in the Israel Defense Forces) for self-defense and as a

Table 2. National determinants affecting innovation.

	Israel	Singapore
Nature of political system	Multi-party democracy, bottom-up political system	Semi-authoritarian, top-down, administrative
Nature of economic system	Mostly open, free-market	Mostly open, free-market
Science & Technology development	Original-innovative	Mostly adaptive
Type of international engagement	Open, global, technonationalist in some sectors (mostly defense-industrial)	Open, global, technonationalist in some sectors (mostly defense-industrial)
Role of the military	Close civil-military relations, military highly influential in civilian sector	Close civil-military relations, military highly influential but still subordinate in civilian sector

---

[79]Adapted from Tai Ming Cheung, Thomas G. Mahnken, and Andrew L. Ross, 'Analyzing the State of Understanding of Defense and Military Innovation in an Era of Profound Technological Change', Paper prepared for the 'Workshop on Comparing Defense Innovation in Advanced and Catch-up Countries', Washington DC, 3 May 2018, 5.

means of building national identity and cohesion; military leaders often rise to top political-bureaucratic-technocratic levels of government and society; and bonds formed in military service generally flow over into the civilian sector and determine social-civilian relationships.

There are important – perhaps even pivotal – differences as well. In terms of political systems, Israel is a freewheeling multiparty democracy, with a particular emphasis on bottom-up governing, due to its collectivist/socialist origins and anti-hierarchical social culture (epitomized in the kibbutz movement); in comparison, Singapore is the embodiment of the tightly controlled semi-authoritarian administrative-technocratic state, where all decision-making is done at the top (within the leadership cabal of a single governing party) and then handed down to the populace much like Moses delivering the Twelve Commandments to the Israelites.[80]

Most important of all – at least when it comes to military-technological innovation – Israel possesses a much more originally innovative science and technology (S&T) system than does Singapore. As Adamsky puts it, Israel's success in pursuing more original – that is, disruptive – innovation comes from a number of features found in Israeli society: "1) not playing by the rules; 2) high tolerance for risk-taking; 3) assertiveness; 4) flexibility towards planning and a strong ethos of improvisation; and 5) social informality and a cult for simplicity."[81]

When one examines the S&T environment in Singapore, a vastly different picture emerges. Particularly when it comes to R&D as it affects the military-technological sector, S&T in Singapore, as compared to Israel, is smaller, more concentrated, and more isolated from the civilian sector. Defense R&D is mostly carried out by a handful of state-run institutes, particularly DSTA, DSO, and Singapore Technologies. Most of their work revolves more around adapting or modifying existing weaponry or weapons concepts to Singaporean requirements – for example, license-producing foreign-designed military equipment, developing their own assault rifle and lightweight (helicopter-carried) artillery system, etc.

Based on this brief sketch of national determinants and capabilities, what are the Israeli and Singaporean capacities for military-technological innovation? Cheung lays out a useful ladder for illustrating rising levels of competencies and proficiencies:

- **Duplicative Imitation**: products, usually obtained from foreign sources, are closely copied with little or no technological improvements.

---

[80]See Seng Tan and Alvin Chew, 'Governing Singapore's Security Sector: Problems, Prospects, and Paradox', *Contemporary Southeast Asia* 30/2 (2008), 252–257.
[81]Cheung, Mahnken, and Ross, *Analyzing the State of Understanding of Defense and Military Innovation in an Era of Profound Technological Change*, 16.

- **Creative Imitation**: more sophisticated forms of imitation that generates imitative products with new performance features.
- **Creative Adaptation**: products "inspired" by existing foreign-derived technologies; also called advanced imitation.
- **Crossover Innovation**: products jointly developed by domestic and foreign partners but depending on technology and knowledge transfers.
- **Incremental Innovation**: limited updating and improvement of existing indigenously developed systems and processes, usually through the introduction of improved sub-systems.
- **Architectural Innovation**: the redesign of production systems in an integrated approach (involving management, engineers, and workers as well as input from end-users) that significantly improves processes but does not usually result in radical product innovation.
- **Component or Modular Innovation**: the development of new, indigenously derived component technology that can be installed into existing system architecture.
- **Radical Innovation**: major breakthroughs in both new component technology and architecture, requiring broad-based, world-class R&D capabilities and a willingness to take risks.[82]

Based on such a typology, it would appear from an empirical analysis of Israeli and Singaporean achievements in the realm of military-technological innovation that Israel is capable – not in all but in many critical areas – of radical, even significant, inventiveness and advances. Singapore, however, appears mostly stuck at the lower strata of innovation, capable of incremental innovation at best.

Conclusions

Both Israel and Singapore engage in military-technological innovation in areas deemed critical to strategic sovereignty. In both cases, top-level leadership support for a strong national defense is high, and, correspondingly, political elites in both countries have consistently championed high levels of funding for military R&D and for maintaining and nurturing indigenous defense industries. Both countries have also, to a varying degree, strongly supported the cultivation of local S&T, including the spin-on of commercial high-technology breakthroughs into the defense sector. And both nations have recognized the need to promote risk-taking in order to encourage

---

[82] Adapted from Tai Ming Cheung, 'Critical Factors in Enabling Defense Innovation: A Case Study of China's Defense Science and Technology System', Paper prepared for the 'Workshop on Comparing Defense Innovation in Advanced and Catch-up Countries', Washington DC, 3 May 2018, 6–8.

Table 3. Potential drivers of military-technological innovation.

	Israel	Singapore
Top-level leadership support	5	4
A severe threat environment	5	2
High-level scientific and technological talent	5	3
Securing access to external technology and knowledge transfers	5	4
High levels of funding for science and technology research and development	5	4
Ability to effectively mobilize a country's science and technology system	4	3
Adoption of governance norms that encourage innovation, such as high levels of risk taking	5	2

(key: 1 = lowest, 5 = highest)

innovation (especially military-technological innovation), although they have individually experienced contrasting success (see Table 3).

As a result, both countries have successfully carved out particular niches for themselves when it comes to armaments production. In Israel's case, these include unmanned systems, missile defenses, active armor defenses, precision-guided munitions, and C4ISTAR technologies. Singapore's core competencies are concentrated in such areas as small arms, light armored vehicles, naval ship construction, and the maintenance, repair, and overhaul (MRO) of weapons systems found in the SAF.

In a comparative sense, therefore, the Israeli military-industrial complex appears to be much more comprehensive than Singapore's, and more capable of state-of-the-art military-technological innovation. Singaporean efforts at innovation appear to be geared toward rather modest R&D efforts to retain the minimal means for supplying its armed forces with the basics of military requirements or else revole around adapting and modifying foreign innovations to national use. Therefore, while there is *military* innovation, there actually exists little actual *military-technological* innovation. In sum, while Israel's defense industry has engaged in a number of original, even disruptive types of innovation (*Iron Dome, Trophy*), Singapore – to use Cheung's ladder of typologies – is mostly engaged in "copy innovation," or, at best, "creative adaption."

Why is it that Israel seems to be out-performing Singapore when it comes to military-technological innovation? Much of it is motivation: Israel innovates because it *has* to, as its strategic situation is much more tenuous than Singapore's. Consequently, there exists a continuous need to innovate, to remain one step (or preferably several steps) ahead of its adversaries. In other words, necessity is the mother of invention, and as such, Israel devotes many more resources to its defense than Singapore and to underwriting military-technological innovation. Israel, therefore, has a large military R&D budget, it encourages strong links civilian high-tech/dual-use technology centers inside the country, and its defense industrial base is much more oriented toward creative innovation and adaptation.

Singapore, on the other hand, mostly innovates because it *wants* to. Singapore's leaders frequently describe the regional security calculus in "dark Hobbesian-like terms,"[83] and the country's "total defense" strategy is predicated on the idea of Singapore living on a razor's edge, requiring the securitization and mobilization of the entire populace.[84] In reality, however, Singapore faces much less of an existential threat than it professes – and certainly a much smaller threat than Israel. Singapore already possesses a huge technological (and numerical) advantage over its presumptive competitors or adversaries. That capabilities gap is not likely to narrow anytime soon. In the first place, most neighboring militaries in the region remain follower/adaptor types (even more so than Singapore), as opposed to true innovators. Most of these militaries could not even be called "fast followers" when it comes to military-technological developments. Sources of innovation and transformation come almost entirely from outside the region – indeed, most Southeast Asian militaries are still almost entirely dependent upon imports for key defense platforms, weapons systems, subsystems, and supporting technologies. In addition, while most fellow Southeast Asian nations possess some kind of indigenous defense industry, they generally lack the domestic S&T infrastructures to engage in almost any kind of innovation when it comes to leveraging offsetting or disruptive technologies. Local arms manufacturers are generally small, "metal-bending" companies – more often than not "job machines" – and self-sufficiency is mostly found in low-value final assembly work or low-tech systems (such as small arms). As a result, few transformational technologies (*à la* the information revolution or the fourth industrial revolution [4IR]) have so far found their way into regional militaries, and most of Singapore's neighboring armed forces remain decidedly platform-centric, outfitted with twentieth-century mechanized systems, and are barely networked, if at all.

At the same time, Singaporean and Israeli societies could not be more dissimilar. Israel's strategic culture is characterized by a casual, informal, assertive, and flexible style, and the dearth of hierarchy in social relations. Israelis are, by nature, much more risk-prone and improvisational, and more comfortable with on-the-fly decisionmaking and with making (and correcting for) errors. Hence, they are almost natural innovators.[85]

---

[83]Tan and Chew, 'Governing Singapore's Security Sector: Problems, Prospects, and Paradox', 249.
[84]Tan and Chew, 'Governing Singapore's Security Sector', 249, 251–252; Deck, 'Singapore: Comprehensive Security – Total Defense', 258–260.
[85]Bar-el, Schwartz, and Bentolila, 'Singular Factors Behind the Growth Of Innovation In Israel', 143–147; Getz and Segal, *The Israeli Innovation System*, 6–7.

Singapore is nearly the exact opposite: it is a stratified and stultified society, with a heavy emphasis on top-down governance and administration. The government (itself a single-party state) is involved in everything deemed worthwhile. Citizens are mainly asked to be patriotic, acquiescent, and hardworking.[86] In this regard, the Singapore Armed Forces plays a key role in promoting such a social culture, as soldiers are seen as "militarized civilians."[87] The SAF is a melting pot, designed to get the four main races (Chinese, Malay, Indian, and "other") to come together, interact, and learn to recognize that they all have a common identity (Singaporean) and a common goal (protecting and preserving the Singaporean state). It has been frequently pointed out that one of the largest challenges in promoting innovation in Singapore is the need to give "greater acceptance" to "non-conformity and [the] tolerance of failure."[88] This means going beyond conformism and simple loyalty.

Despite their superficial similarities, therefore, Israel and Singapore differ significantly when it comes to their approach to innovation, particularly military-technological innovation. Of course, technology is not the end all and be all of military innovation. As Cheung, Mahnken, and Ross put it: "Technology is the most visible dimension of military innovation, but military innovation is not to be equated with, or reduced to, technological innovation ... the organizational and doctrinal components of military innovation are no less significant than its technological component."[89] On other hand, Cheung, Mahnken, and Ross also agree that "technology, in the form of weapons and weapon systems, serves as the source of the hardware dimension of military innovation and its concrete products."[90] In the final analysis, technology is perhaps the most critical enabler for military innovation, since it is often the catalyst for all other change. In this regard, therefore, Israel has a distinct advantage over Singapore in possessing the capacities for military-technological innovation and adaptation.

Disclosure statement

No potential conflict of interest was reported by the authors.

---

[86]Ortmann, 'Singapore: From Hegemonic to Competitive Authoritarianism', 394–395.
[87]Chong and Chan, 'Militarizing civilians in Singapore', 366. See also Tan Tai Young, 'The Armed Forces and Politics in Singapore: The Persistence of Civil-Military Fusion', in Marcus Mietzner (ed.), *The Political Resurgence of the Military in Southeast Asia: Conflict and Leadership* (Routledge 2012); and Tan Tai Yong, 'Singapore: Civil-Military Fusion,' in *Coercion and Governance: The Declining Political Role of the Military in Asia*, edited by Muthiah Alagappa (Stanford University Press 2001).
[88]Koh, 'Singapore's Transition to Innovation-based Economic Growth', 158.
[89]Cheung, Mahnken, and Ross, *Analyzing the State of Understanding of Defense and Military Innovation in an Era of Profound Technological Change*, 4.
[90]Ibid.

Bibliography

Adamsky, Dima, *The Culture of Military Innovation: The Impact of Cultural Factors on the Revolution in Military Affairs in Russia, the US, and Israel* (Stanford, Calif.: Stanford University Press 2010).

Bar-el, Raphael, Dafna Schwartz, and David Bentolila, 'Singular Factors behind the Growth of Innovation in Israel', *Athens Journal of Mediterranean Studies* 5/3 (2019), 137–50. doi:10.30958/ajms.5-3-1.

Brun, Brig.-Gen, *Itai, "While You're Busy Making Other Plans": The "Other-RMA"* (Jerusalem: DADO Center for Interdisciplinary Military Studies, Israel Defense Forces 2010).

Carney, Richard W. and Loh Yi Zhang, 'Institutional (Dis)incentives to Innovate: An Explanation for Singapore's Innovation Gap', *Journal of East Asian Studies* 9 (2009), 291–319. doi:10.1017/S1598240800003015.

Carney, Richard W. and Loh Yi Zheng, "An Explanation for Singapore's Innovation Gap", *RSIS Commentary* CO200849, 21 April 2008.

Chen, Edward, et.al., *Integrated Knowledge-based Command and Control for the ONE SAF Building the 3rd Spiral, 3rd Generation SAF* (Singapore: Pointer: Journal of the Singapore Armed Forces 2008).

Cheung, Tai Ming, 'Critical Factors in Enabling Defense Innovation: A Systems Perspective', Research Brief 2018-2, May (UC Institute on Global Conflict and Cooperation, Study of Innovation and Technology in China 2018.

Cheung, Tai Ming, 'Critical Factors in Enabling Defense Innovation: A Case Study of China's Defense Science and Technology System', Paper prepared for the "Workshop on Comparing Defense Innovation in Advanced and Catch-up Countries", Washington DC, May 3 2018.

Cheung, Tai Ming, Thomas G. Mahnken, and Andrew L. Ross, 'Analyzing the State of Understanding of Defense and Military Innovation in an Era of Profound

Technological Change', Paper prepared for the "Workshop on Comparing Defense Innovation in Advanced and Catch-up Countries", Washington DC, 3 May 2018.

Chong, Alan and Samuel Chan, 'Militarizing Civilians in Singapore: Preparing for 'Crisis' within a Calibrated Nationalism', *The Pacific Review* 3/3 (2017), 365–84. doi:10.1080/09512748.2016.1249906.

Deck, Richard A., 'Singapore: Comprehensive Security – Total Defense', in Ken Booth and Russell Trood (eds.), *Strategic Cultures in the Asia-Pacific Region* (London: Palgrave Macmillan 1999), 247–272.

DeVore, Marc R., 'Commentary on the Value of Domestic Arms Industries: Security of Supply or Adaptive Innovation?', *Defense Studies* 17/3 (2017), 242–59. doi:10.1080/14702436.2017.1347781.

Dyduch, Joanna and Karolina Olszewska, 'Israeli Innovation Policy', *Polish Political Science Yearbook* 47/2 (2018), 265–83. doi:10.15804/ppsy2018208.

Evron, Yoram, '4IR Technologies in the Israel Defense Forces: Blurring Traditional Boundaries', *Journal of Strategic Studies* (December 7 2020), 1–22. online article, published. doi:10.1080/01402390.2020.1852936.

Getz, Daphne and Vered Segal, *The Israeli Innovation System: An Overview of National Policy and Cultural Aspects* (Haifa: The Samuel Neaman Institute for Advanced Studies in Science and Technology 2008).

Getz, Daphne and Zehev Tadmor, 'Israel', in Susan Schneegans, (ed.), *UNESCO Science Report: Toward 2030* (Paris: United Nations Educational, Scientific and Cultural Organization 2015), 408–429.

Hania, Nissim, *Transformations in the Israeli Defense Development and Production System, and the Contemporary Relevance*, DADO Center for Interdisciplinary Military Studies, Israel Defense Forces https://www.idf.il/en/minisites/dado-center/vol-6-force-design-a/transformations-in-the-israeli-defense-development-and-production-system(undated).

Huxley, Tim, 'Singapore and Military Transformation', Paper delivered to the conference on "The RMA For Small States: Theory and Application", Singapore, 25-26 Feb. 2004.

Huxley, Tim and Susan Willett, *Arming East Asia* (Oxford: Oxford University Press July 1999).

Israeli, Milana, 'National Innovation Systems of Israel: Features and Structure', *Scientific Journal of Economics, Social, and Engineering Science* 3/1–2 (2020), 155–63.

Jane's, IHS, *Navigating the Emerging Markets: Republic of Singapore* (Coulsdon, Surrey: IHS Jane's 2011).

Karniol, Robert, 'Singapore's Defense Industry: Eyes on Expansion', *Jane's Defense Weekly*, 30 April 2003.

Katz, Yaakov and Amir Bohbot, *The Weapons Wizards: How Israel Became a High-Tech Military Superpower* (New York: St. Martin's 2017).

Koh, Winston T.H., 'Singapore's Transition to Innovation-Based Economic Growth: Infrastructure, Institutions, and Government's Role', *R&D Management* 36/2 (2006), 143–60. doi:10.1111/j.1467-9310.2006.00422.x.

Laksmana, Evan, 'Threats and Civil–Military Relations: Explaining Singapore's 'Trickle-down' Military Innovation', *Defense & Security Analysis* 33/4 (2017), 347–65. doi:10.1080/14751798.2017.1377369.

Lewis, David A, 'Diversification and Niche Market Exporting: The Restructuring of Israel's Defense Industry in the Post-Cold War Era', in Ann Markusen, Sean DiGiovanna, and Michael C. Leary (eds.), *From Defense to Development:*

International Perspectives on Realizing the Peace Dividend (London: Routledge 2003), 121–150.

Lifshitz, Yaacov, 'Defense Industries in Israel', in Andrew T.H. Tan (ed.), *The Global Arms Trade: A Handbook* (New York: Routledge 2009), 266–278.

Matthews, Ron, 'Singapore Buys Longbows and Grows Its Defense Industry', *Asia-Pacific Defense Reporter*, December 1999.

McCarthy, Stephen, *The Political Theory of Tyranny in Singapore and Burma* (New York: Routledge 2006).

Orkand, Robert, 'Review: *The Weapon Wizards: How Israel Became a High-Tech Military Superpower*, by Yaakov Katz and Amir Bohbot', Reformjudaism.org (https://reformjudaism.org/jewish-life/arts-culture/literature/weapon-wizards-how-israel-became-high-tech-military-superpower, (accessed December 2, 2017).

Ortmann, Stephen, 'Singapore: From Hegemonic to Competitive Authoritarianism', in William Case (ed.), *Routledge Handbook of Southeast Asian Democratization* (Routledge 2015), 384–398.

Owen, William F., 'Punching above Its Weight; Israel's Defense Industry', *Defense Review Asia*, May 2010.

Raska, Michael, *Military Innovation in Small States: Creating a Reverse Asymmetry* (New York: Routledge 2016).

Rubin, Uzi, 'Israel's Defense Industries – An Overview', *Defense Studies* 17/3 (2017), 228–41. doi:10.1080/14702436.2017.1350823.

Saw, David, 'The Israeli Defense Industry', *Asian Defense & Diplomacy*, June/July 2011.

Shamah, David, "How Intel Came to Be Israel's Best Tech Friend," *Times of Israel*, April 23, 2015.

Shao, Vivian, 'Singapore Budget 2018: Innovation, R&D to Get Shot in the Arm', *Straits Times*, 20 February 2018.

Singh, Bilveer, 'ASEAN's Arms Industries: Potential and Limits', *Comparative Strategy* 8 (1989), 249–64. doi:10.1080/01495938908402779.

Swed, Ori and J S. Butler, 'Military Capital in the Israeli Hi-tech Industry', *Armed Forces & Society* 41/1 (2015), 123–41. doi:10.1177/0095327X13499562.

Tan, Peng Yam, 'Harnessing Defense Technology: Singapore's Perspective', *DISAM Journal of International Security Assistance Management* 21/3 (Spring 1999), 9–13.

Tan, See Seng and Alvin Chew, 'Governing Singapore's Security Sector: Problems, Prospects, and Paradox', *Contemporary Southeast Asia* 30/2 (2008), 241–63. doi:10.1355/CS30-2D.

Tan, Tai Yong, 'Singapore: Civil-Military Fusion', in Muthiah Alagappa (ed.), *Coercion and Governance: The Declining Political Role of the Military in Asia* (Stanford, CA: Stanford University Press 2001), 276–293.

Tan, Tai Young, 'The Armed Forces and Politics in Singapore: The Persistence of Civil-Military Fusion', in Marcus Mietzner (ed.), *The Political Resurgence of the Military in Southeast Asia: Conflict and Leadership* (New York: Routledge 2012), 148–167.

Urquhart, Michael, 'Singapore Faces Spending, Population Challenges', *Defense News*, 20 February 2006.

Wezeman, Pieter D., Alexandra Kuimova, and Siemon T. Wezeman, *SIPRI Fact Sheet: Trends in International Arms Transfers, 2020* (Stockholm: Stockholm International Peace Research Institute March 2021).

Index

Academy of National Defense Science 127–8, 139, 142
advanced developed regimes 10, 18, 97
American military operations 36
architectural innovation 14–15, 24, 102, 172
armaments 152, 155–6

catalytic factors 5, 8–10, 12, 16–17, 20–2, 24–5, 53–4, 101, 105, 160, 167
central military commands 84
China's quantum science 50
Chinese Academy of Sciences 63–4
Chinese defense innovation 74
Chinese scientists 54–5, 60, 66–7, 69, 71, 73
civil-military integration (CMI) 108
Cold War 19, 29, 31, 35–6, 43, 142
colored revolutions 85
communications 52, 55–6, 60, 63, 66, 69, 85, 152, 164–6
contextual factors 6, 8, 16, 20, 29, 115, 160, 167
creative adaptation 14, 102, 140, 172
creative imitation 14, 102, 140, 172
crossover innovation 14, 172
cybersecurity 52, 54, 56–7

Defence Acquisition Procedure (DAP) 111
defence budget 107–8
defence economy 100, 106, 109
defence procurement procedures 111
defense industry 30, 79–81, 86–8, 91, 93, 96–7, 160, 162, 166
defense innovation unit initiative 40
defense technology 50, 61, 97
disruptive technologies 49, 51–2, 85, 174
domestic capabilities 124, 137–40
domestic innovation 17, 123

DRDO 16, 103–4, 107–9, 112–15, 117–18, 120
dual-use research 61
duplicative imitation 13, 102, 140, 171

emerging technologies 2, 10, 22, 25, 47, 51, 54, 61, 75, 97

financial resources 15, 81, 90, 101
fissile material 131–2, 134–6, 138, 145
foreign absorption 123
foreign technologies 12, 14, 18, 48, 51, 101, 110–11, 124, 138, 140, 146–7; access to 12, 18, 29, 101, 110, 146
formal bilateral agreements 133
funding 29, 40, 49, 60–1, 64, 156, 167, 172

Guo Guangcan 69

hard innovation capabilities 12, 15
higher political leadership 105
Hindustan Aeronautics Ltd (HAL) 103, 109–11, 115, 117–19
human capital resources 61
hypersonic weapons 22, 80, 86, 97

incentives 10, 36–7, 43–4, 80, 104, 140, 169
incremental innovation 5, 14–15, 25, 102, 172
India 2, 9, 15, 17–18, 96, 99–108, 110–14, 116–17, 119–20, 124, 157
Indian DIS 16–17
Indian government 100, 110
India's ad hoc approach 101
India's defence innovation performance 99–100, 115, 119
India's innovation capabilities 105
information technologies 49, 57, 80, 94, 97, 158, 163–4

INDEX

innovation 2–6, 8, 14–17, 19–20, 25, 29–30, 38–41, 50–1, 100–2, 104–5, 112–13, 116–17, 140–1, 158–9, 166–9, 171–5; in Singapore 167–8
input factors 5, 10, 16, 19–20, 29, 57, 90, 120, 161, 167
input factors R&D expenditure 107
institutional factors 4–5, 9–10, 12, 16, 19–20, 30, 36, 111, 120, 162, 168
institutional structure 125
investments 31, 35, 48, 57, 60, 71, 156, 158, 161
Israel 2, 18, 20–1, 24–5, 38, 104, 110, 116, 151–63, 167–8, 170–5
Israel Defense Forces (IDF) 154–63, 170
Israeli Defense Industry 157, 161–2
Israel's defense strategy 154

Jiuzhang 70

Kim Il Sung 125, 130–1, 133–4, 139–41
Kim Jong Il 125, 127, 129
Kim Jong Un 17, 125–6, 128–9, 132, 144–6

leadership prioritization 56

mass communication technologies 79
Medvedev, Dmitry 83
Micius 56, 66–7
military: campaign 89; education 84; funding 61; innovation 2–3, 24–5, 75, 101, 161–2, 168, 173, 175; personnel 81, 83, 85; reforms 79, 96; technology 39
military-technological innovation 151–3, 158–60, 163, 167, 169–73, 175
missile: infrastructure 128, 137; programs 123, 125, 128, 130, 144–5; technologies 79, 141
modern technology 87
Mozi 56, 67–8
munitions 85, 138

national innovation systems 4, 22, 161–2
national security policy 154
navy 34, 37, 84, 92
networks 4, 6, 8, 40, 43, 50, 54, 67–9, 101, 105, 108, 125, 127
new component technology 15, 172
new institutions 64, 133
North Korea 17–18, 24, 82, 123–5, 132–42, 144–7
nuclear power 130, 132–3

nuclear programs 123–5, 128–31, 133, 138–40
nuclear technology 130–1, 133–4

organizational factors 124, 161, 167
output factor manufacturing base 116
output factors 6, 16, 21, 65, 120, 162, 168

Pan Jianwei 49, 52, 55, 62–3, 66, 68–71, 73
poor human resource management 109
prestige prioritization 56
professional military 36
provable security 52
Putin, Vladimir 81–2

quantum bit 52
quantum communications 50, 52, 55, 57, 63, 65–6, 68–9, 74–5
quantum computing 24, 50, 52–3, 55–7, 60, 62–5, 69, 71–2, 75, 99
quantum cryptography 52–3, 55–6, 63, 66, 75
Quantum CTek 68
quantum information age 75
quantum precision measurement 50, 52–3, 73–4
quantum radar 65, 73–4
quantum science 49–57, 60–4, 72, 74, 76
quantum supremacy 70–1
quantum technology 23, 48, 50–7, 60–2, 64–5, 71, 74–6

rearmament program 78
reforms 39, 79, 81–4, 86–8, 105
reservist training system 84
reverse engineering 14, 18, 102, 137–8, 140–1, 146
Russia, defense innovation 78, 80, 90, 95
Russian economy 87, 90, 95, 97
Russian government 79, 81–3, 86, 90, 95–7
Russian Information Security Doctrine 80
Russian military 78–9, 81, 84, 87, 89, 94–5, 97
Russian National Security Strategy 80
Russian strategy, defense innovation 84
Russian threat assessments 87

Second World War 34–5
Serdyukov, Anatoly 83
Singapore 2, 18, 20–1, 25, 151–3, 163–75
Singapore Armed Forces (SAF) 163–6, 168, 173, 175

INDEX

Singapore Technologies Engineering (STEngg) 165, 167
soft institutional factors 36
state-owned defense conglomerates 65
strategic missile defense systems 79, 85
strategic weapons innovation system 18, 124
subsystems 4, 6, 9–10, 16, 18, 21, 101, 105, 115, 120, 162, 168, 174
Syria 18, 78–9, 85, 89–90, 96, 124, 142, 146

talent training 62
technological capabilities 17, 21, 87, 98, 152
technological infrastructure 162
technology development 14, 39, 41, 170
technology transfers 5, 9, 105, 111, 113, 134, 140, 161
top leadership 8, 25, 86, 124, 128

weaponization 136–7
weapons of mass destruction 79

Xi Jinping 56–7
Xue Qikun 49, 62

Zeilinger, Anton 62–3
Zhang Xiaorong 72